The NANTUCKET Book

A Complete Guide

Rob Benchley

Great Point Lighthouse

THE NANTUCKET BOOK

A Complete Guide

SECOND EDITION

Betty Lowry

Berkshire House Publishers
Lee, Massachusetts

On the Cover and Frontispiece:
Front cover: *Nantucket's famed waterfront.* Photo © Paul Rezendes
Frontispiece: *Great Point Lighthouse.* Photo © Rob Benchley

The Nantucket Book: A Complete Guide
Copyright © 1998, 2001 by Berkshire House Publishers
Cover and interior photographs © 1998, 2001 by credited photographers and other sources

Library of Congress Cataloging-in-Publication Data

Lowry, Betty,
      The Nantucket book: a complete guide / Betty Lowry. — 2nd ed.
       p. cm – (the great destinations series, ISSN 1056-7968)
      Includes bibliographical references and index.
      ISBN 1-58157-022-8
      1. Nantucket Island (Mass.)—Guidebooks. I. Title. II. Series

      F72.N2 L69 2001
      917.44'970444—dc21

                                             00-058536

ISBN: 1-58157-022-8
ISSN: 1056-7968 (series)

Editor: Dale Evva Gelfand. Managing Editor: Philip Rich. Text design and typography: Dianne Pinkowitz. Cover design and typography: Jane McWhorter. Index: Diane Brenner. Maps: Matt Paul/Yankee Doodles

Berkshire House Publishers
480 Pleasant St., Suite 5; Lee, Massachusetts 01238
800-321-8526
E-mail: info@berkshirehouse.com
Website: www.berkshirehouse.com

Manufactured in the United States of America
First printing 2001
10 9 8 7 6 5 4 3 2 1

No complimentary meals or lodgings were accepted by the author and reviewers in gathering information for this work.

Berkshire House Publishers'
Great Destinations™ travel guidebook series

Recommended by NATIONAL GEOGRAPHIC TRAVELER and TRAVEL & LEISURE magazines.

Smart, literate, well-reported, and incredibly comprehensive.
— MID-ATLANTIC COUNTRY

. . . a crisp and critical approach, for travelers who want to live like locals.
— USA TODAY

Great Destinations™ guidebooks are known for their comprehensive, critical coverage of regions of extraordinary cultural interest and natural beauty. The authors in this series are professional travel writers who have lived for many years in the regions they describe. Every title in this series is continuously updated with each printing, in order to insure accurate and timely information. All of the books contain over 100 photographs and maps.

Neither the publisher, the authors, the reviewers, nor other contributors accept complimentary lodgings, meals, or any other consideration (such as advertising) while gathering information for any book in this series.

Current titles available:
The Adirondack Book
The Berkshire Book
The Charleston, Savannah & Coastal Islands Book
The Chesapeake Bay Book
The Coast of Maine Book
The Finger Lakes Book
The Hamptons Book
The Monterey Bay, Big Sur & Gold Coast Wine Country Book
The Nantucket Book
The Newport & Narragansett Bay Book
The Napa & Sonoma Book
The Santa Fe & Taos Book
The Sarasota, Sanibel Island & Naples Book
The Texas Hill Country Book
Wineries of the Eastern States

If you are traveling to, moving to, residing in, or just interested in any (or all!) of these enchanting regions, a **Great Destinations**™ guidebook is a superior companion. Honest and painstakingly critical, full of information only a local can provide, **Great Destinations**™ guidebooks give you all the practical knowledge you need to enjoy the best of each region. Why not own them all?

For Colleen, Greer, Megan, Nicholas, and Nori

Contents

CHAPTER ONE
"Blow Ye Winds High, O"
HISTORY
1

CHAPTER TWO
Getting On, Off, and Around Island
TRANSPORTATION
20

CHAPTER THREE
Forty Winks and a Nod
LODGING
37

CHAPTER FOUR
Mind, Matter, and Monuments
CULTURE
66

CHAPTER FIVE
Chowder to Fiddleheads
RESTAURANTS AND FOOD PURVEYORS
101

CHAPTER SIX
Beyond the "Nantucket Sleigh Ride"
RECREATION
139

CHAPTER SEVEN
The Fragile Island
NATURE AND THE ENVIRONMENT
174

CHAPTER EIGHT
A Tisket, a Tasket, More Than a Lightship Basket
SHOPPING
191

CHAPTER NINE
Needs to Know
INFORMATION
216

Acknowledgments

When I was browsing the new edition of Michelin's *New England* (the Green Guide) and turned to Nantucket, there was no surprise. The Island rated the top three stars, or in Michelin lingo, "Worth a special trip." My thanks are to all those who would nod wisely and say, "I knew that."

The fact is that most of the people who contributed to this book will never know it and can never be properly thanked. They are the ones on the shuttle to Madaket or Sconset who shared their discoveries from beaches to bargains; those who sat beside me on the plane going back to Boston or crowded the ferry deck approaching the Island; who chatted during intermission at a concert, lecture, or play; who buttered muffins with me in the morning or described their day on the moors over wine and cheese at my bed & breakfast inn.

What is it about this Island "away off shore" that so quickly breaks down the inbred distance of the native New Englander? Say Nantucket loud enough at a party on the mainland, and in a minute you will be surrounded by people who heard the magic word and want to know if such-and-such restaurant is as good as ever or tell you (in July) the problem they've had getting their favorite inn room for the Christmas Stroll.

On Island, a word of caring about the environment inevitably brings forth a flood of statistics and invitations to go hiking, boating, or birding. Every innkeeper and shopkeeper is an encyclopedia of Nantucket lore, and I especially appreciated those who took time to tell and send me more details than I requested.

Special thanks to special people as well: to Stephanie Barrett, my fact checker, and photographer Rob Benchley; to Tracy O'Reilly, Natasha Johnston, Kim Corkran, Mike Manville, Russ and Debbie Cleveland, Tracy Bakalar, Mimi Beman, and Walter Beinecke, who gave me insight as well as information.

I am truly grateful to my editor, Dale Evva Gelfand, and to the Berkshire House staff who have made writing this book a pleasure. Many thanks to Philip Rich, Mary Osak, Carol Bosco Baumann, Leslie Ceanga, and Jean Rousseau.

Then there are my friends and family off-Island (notably, my daughter, Robin, my son, Peter, and my working-writers group) who put up with months of hearing endless trivia about Nantucket. Most of all, my husband, Ritchie, who discovered Nantucket with me years ago and has toted my bag there ever since.

Introduction

They got it right the first time. In the language of the Wampanoags it was "The Land Far Out to Sea," concentrated in a single word that sounded like and was subsequently spelled NANTUCKET. Even today the thirty miles from the mainland of Massachusetts is a crossing: more than two hours by ferry from Hyannis on Cape Cod; nearly an hour from the time you board a plane in Boston until you land on the Island. Nantucket may be only fourteen miles long and three-and-a-half miles wide, but arriving there is the culmination of a journey.

You know at once why its familiars call it "The Gray Lady." The houses are the soft gray of homespun wool, their façades demure and without distracting trim. From the ferry or the air you have seen the neat collar of white beaches, the wharves that reach out like probing fingers. Only the spires of churches rise above the accepted rooflines.

Sailboats flit like summer insects across the Sound, remains of a day when the world's largest fleet of whaling ships called Nantucket home and the sea intimately affected every Nantucketer's life. When you get closer, when you walk the streets cobbled with stones brought here as ballast centuries ago, you see that the first impression was both true and false. The architecture is all of a period but of many minds: cozy colonial; imposing federal; foursquare brick; a few showy Victorian. The people, however homogenized their civility, are diverse. Even the revered past turns out to be less a closed book than a half-told tale, as once-accepted authorities are first questioned and then found alarmingly inaccurate.

What we do know for sure is that Nantucket is the only place in the United States where a town, county, and island all bear the same name. It is the smallest county in Massachusetts and has scarcely ten thousand year-round residents — though more than forty thousand are part-time owner-residents, and the Chamber of Commerce estimates 250,000 pass through the island during the hundred days of summer.

Having made a commitment to tourism 125 years ago when the whaling industry ceased does not mean Nantucket condescends to it. When funds are voted, they are allocated for projects — from bike paths to harbor revitalization — that benefit permanent residents, not "off-Islanders," however much they contribute to the economic base. Summer visitors and residents are not family, either. If you've ever lived in a small town, you will recognize the attitude.

The use of capital letters is revealing, too. It's Island, not island; Islander, not islander; Town, not town. That these can only be Nantucket is implied, and we have followed the custom throughout the book. We have also used *Sconset* and *Siasconset* interchangeably. This syllable dropping apparently began with the English settlers to whom variation in spelling and pronunciation of names and places showed intellectual refinement and sophistication.

Understatement and modesty were endemic to the New England character. The beauty of Nantucket, too, at first appears subtle rather than lush: silver and pewter, not chrome; the soft shimmer of beach grass, not the gaudy flame of hibiscus. Yet the houses, naturally weathered or painted to appear so, are dressed with pink roses in summer; the moors glow with the ruby-red leaves of high-bush blueberries in autumn; the bogs during cranberry harvest are a sea of crimson; the old seaport town turns into a Christmas card in December. The sunsets are downright extravagant.

I moved to Massachusetts with my husband and children years ago from the suburbs of Washington, D. C., and, before that, California. We had heard of Nantucket, but we didn't just rush out to the Island. It was, in fact, several years before we drove the two hours to Cape Cod and took the ferry for another two and a half. To our surprise, we met people who had crossed the continent just for a long weekend; Europeans who knew more about Nantucket than we did because Herman Melville's *Moby-Dick* was assigned reading in their schools. "The essence of America," their teachers called it. Was it? Our teachers had presented the tale as more the essence of mankind.

A copy of the book was in our room at the inn, and, skipping the dark side, I found Chapter Fourteen, a view of Nantucket so euphoric it might have been written by a 19th-century publicist yet so recognizable it was a shock. In a time when "historic" is applied to museum towns composed of assorted vintage structures transported from near and far then reassembled, Nantucket is original. In a day when a child's imagination is outguessed by adults and presented preformed on film or CD-ROM, Nantucket is its own place. Real people lived here and still do.

Since the first edition of this book came out, I have had the rare experience of having strangers ask me about Nantucket, not just about where they should stay and dine but whether it's true that the Island "doesn't like visitors." The Island does indeed like and welcome visitors — it's their cars they hate. Step off the ferry or the plane on your own two feet, and you've made friends instantly.

This book tells you how to go about getting, staying, and dining on Nantucket; what you can see and do without your own car. It gives an overview of the Island's history and a subjective view of its culture. It explains why the environment takes such a high priority. It offers clues on when to visit and tells you about annual events. Whether you are a single visitor, a couple, or a family traveling with children, you will find a niche — many niches. We also hope your experience will be richer for having had a good read.

Betty Lowry
Wayland, Massachusetts

THE WAY THIS BOOK WORKS

The nine chapters of this book cover the entire Island. Specific services and businesses are grouped by their location in Nantucket Town, Siasconset, or Everywhere Else. Listings are alphabetical and appear in the Index as well as in the appropriate chapter. Sidebars illuminate special facets of Nantucket and answer at least some of the questions that may occur to you.

Dining and lodging prices are indicated by range as shown below. Lodging prices are the per-room rate, double occupancy, and high season. (Generally, high season is mid-June to mid-September, plus Christmas Stroll weekend. Midseason is mid-May to mid-June, and mid-September through October. Low season or off season is early spring, late fall, and winter.) Off-season rates are much cheaper, and "packages" may include excursions, tickets, passes, and, in some cases, dining around, thus creating true bargains. Restaurant price ratings show the cost of a single meal including appetizer, entrée and dessert but not cocktails, wine, tax, or tip.

Price Ranges	*Lodging*	*Dining*
Very Inexpensive	Under $50	Up to $20
Inexpensive	$50–$75	$20–$30
Moderate	$75–$150	$30–$50
Expensive	$150–$250	$50–$60
Very Expensive	Over $250	Over $60

Credit Cards are abbreviated as follows:

AE	American Express
CB	Carte Blanche
D	Discover Card
DC	Diners Club
MC	MasterCard
V	Visa

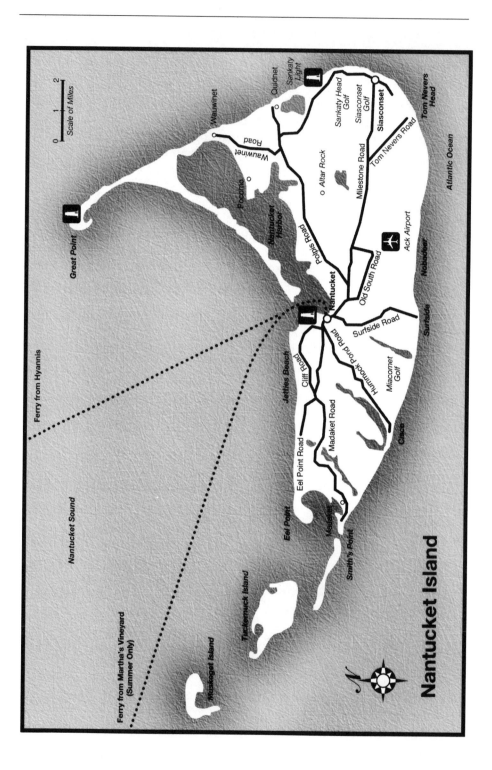

Nantucket Island

The
NANTUCKET
Book

A Complete Guide

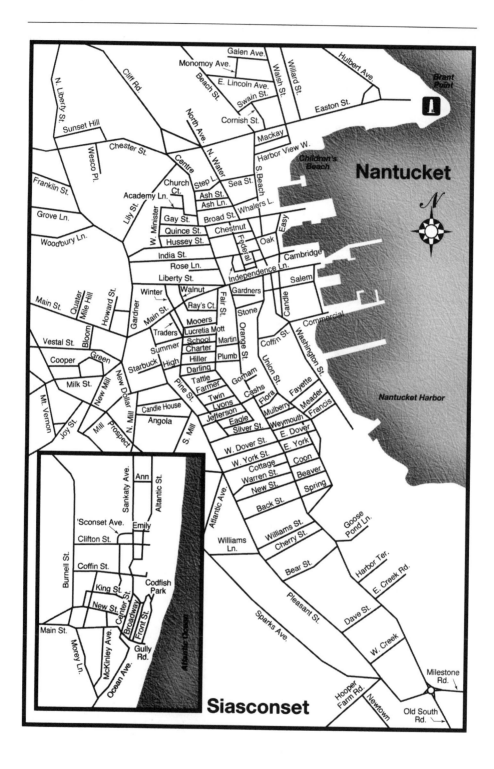

Siasconset

CHAPTER ONE
"Blow Ye Winds High, O"
HISTORY

Courtesy of the Nantucket Historical Association

Petticoat Row in 1870, where the wives of absent whalers once managed shops and businesses.

From the beginning it was destined to be an adventure story set on a faraway island. Its characters — major and minor — and plot seem to have been created with a miniseries in mind. Yet if history is, as Napoleon said, "a fable agreed upon," Nantucket's comes up short. "Agreed upon" is not the way it is. Despite copious original sources and two meticulous histories, what has been repeated as truth often turns out to be based on 18th- and 19th-century tabloid journalism plus a little 20th-century offhand conjecture and selective omission. Spurious chronicles of events appear to be the result of misremembering by naïve historians. Authors whose books have gone into numerous editions fail to get straight the orders of birth or to reconcile dates. The much-quoted *Letters From an American Farmer* (1782) by J. Hector St. John de Crèvecoeur painted such a euphoric picture of Nantucket that literally hundreds of Europeans came expecting a semitropical isle. Obed Macy's often-cited *History of Nantucket* (1835), now thought to have been ghostwritten by William Coffin Jr., brushes past crime and controversy, probably because the facts would not reflect well on the authors' forefathers.

Even the legends of the Native Americans are contradictory. Did Moshop the Giant create the Island in a fit of pique or merely arrive as an angry avenger in pursuit of the bird that stole his children? Does it matter? You choose.

As for the settlers, annotated family Bibles grew into genealogies, diaries into scrapbooks, and ship's logs into novels. First-person accounts may vary, but they can be reconciled. Fortunately, the truly dedicated Nantucket Historical Association has for more than a century preserved an extraordinary amount of original material for future scholars as well as holding in trust notable houses and other structures.

To the English settlers of 1659, Nantucket was an island in spirit as well as in fact. They had not come as persecuted or impoverished refugees but to get away from an encroaching authoritarianism. All were moderately affluent, educated, and, without rejecting king or country, believed wholeheartedly in independence and self-determination. Stung by the uncompromising self-righteousness of the Puritans in power in Massachusetts Bay Colony (Thomas Macy, an Anabaptist, had been heavily fined and threatened with jail for permitting four Quakers to stay in his barn while waiting out a rainstorm), the settlers regarded organized religion as a nonissue. While Bible reading was an established custom, building a house of worship had no priority at all. The Indians had two Christian churches long before the first dozen or so colonists who had become members of the Society of Friends raised a modest meetinghouse.

Living on an island in an age long before mass communication or easy transportation brought its own traumas. Physical isolation from the mainstream of colonial life narrowed options as well as points of view. The settlers were in effect one big family, however quarrelsome and, before long, woefully intermarried. Soon it would be "us" and "them," then "Islanders" and "off-Islanders." The time came when outsiders derisively called it "the Nation of Nantucket"— so foreign to the New England consensus that it was accused of seeing the Revolutionary War primarily as an inconvenience to shipping. The ships carrying English tea to Boston for what turned out to be the "Boston Tea Party" were Nantucket owned. The Continental Congress flatly labeled the Island "Tory," even as Quaker households were bitterly divided by loyalty to principles of nonviolence and a fighting anger toward British seizure of Nantucket ships and seamen. Nantucket men and boys served with Captain John Paul Jones, and the first man killed in the battle between the *Serapis* and the *Bon Homme Richard* September 23, 1779, was from Nantucket.

During the War of 1812, Nantucket suffered acute hardship when food and fuel from the mainland were stopped and whaling halted for nearly two years by a British blockade. They received little sympathy and no rescue from Boston or Washington, though running the blockade meant the loss of more craft and still more Americans incarcerated aboard prison ships or impressed into the Royal Navy. When it was over, Nantucket resumed its hard-won place in international commerce without a backward glance.

On July 13, 1846, a fire started on the docks, spread rapidly, and burned for two days. Trinity Church, the Atheneum Library, the wharves, and about 400 buildings were gone, though miraculously no lives were lost. Afterward the main business district was slightly relocated, but rebuilding began immediately.

During the Civil War, Nantucketers rallied to the Union cause, sending many more men than their quota and putting devastating pressure on the dual Quaker fundamentals of ending slavery and practicing nonviolence. Coming from a place known throughout the Confederacy for its early and ardent abolitionists, Nantucket ships received no quarter from the South. Unarmed, they were captured and sunk. In both world wars, Nantucket was a training station

Civil War monument on upper Main Street.

Betty Lowry

and base for the United States Navy. The Nantucket Municipal Airport was built by navy Seabees during World War II, and the old navy base at Tom Nevers Head is now the site of the county fair and various sporting events of the demolition-derby stripe considered too raucous for anyplace else on Nantucket.

From the beginning the sea always set Nantucket apart, not only physically but economically, as well. In a single generation Nantucket rose from an unknown sheepherding sandspit to the recognized provider of one of the necessities for civilized life — whale oil. The demand then was endless: lamps, candles, lubricating clockworks, with new uses being developed constantly not only for oil but also bone and ivory. The Island became a prosperous if one-industry place, and by the mid-19th century Nantucket Town was the third largest city in Massachusetts, surpassed only by Boston and Salem. It is claimed that the Town had a greater percentage of millionaires (per total population) than anywhere else on earth.

The oldest house in Sconset, built about 1676

Betty Lowry

As its whaling ships roamed the world, the Island grew increasingly cosmopolitan. The bell of South Church had been cast and purchased in Portugal. Women and girls received Parisian trinkets for Christmas. At least one home is reported to have used Fijian tapa cloth for wallpaper. Ship captains had their portraits painted in Canton and Hong Kong.

In Europe, Nantucketers were seen as a different kind of Yankee, and in the South Seas they were for some years the only kind known. For half a century they dominated the world's whaling business, and when that ended, they endured a brief but intense economic depression before setting their sights on a new target: tourism.

NATURAL HISTORY

The Native Americans said Nantucket was formed when Moshop the Giant, resting on Cape Cod, shook the sand from his moccasins into the Sound. Still uncomfortable, he irritably threw the moccasins in, too. The left shoe became Nantucket; the right, Martha's Vineyard; while the sand made the Elizabeth Islands, Tuckernuck, and all the rest.

A concept nearly as fanciful is the great ice sheet advancing from the north, then dumping its accumulation of earth, rock, and rubble, creating a moraine

Betty Lowry

The moors.

Making Love, Not War on Nantucket

Today Nantucket is an undisputed romantic getaway; in fact, the Island is considered such an ideal spot for a wedding that it is almost impossible to make arrangements on short notice. Nantucket's reputation as a setting for affairs of the heart goes way back — as the following two stories illustrate.

The Story of Wonona and Autopscot

Before the settlers came, the two tribes of Nantucket were in an almost constant state of war. The Kauds of the eastern end and the Tomkauds of the west raided each other's villages, burning and killing. Wauwinet, the eastern sachem, had a daughter, Wonona, who was a skilled medicine woman as well as being beautiful, intelligent, etc. The sachem of the Tomkauds was a handsome young man named Autopscot.

When a mysterious disease broke out in Miacomet, Autopscot sent a desperate plea for help. Wonona and her women assistants responded secretly, cured the sick with their herbs, and returned to their home village — but not before Wonona and Autopscot had fallen in love.

A short time later Tomkaud braves were found hunting on Kaud territory, and a council of war planned a retaliatory attack. Wonona overheard them and slipped away to warn her lover, running only on the beaches so that she would leave no incriminating footprints. When the Kauds attacked, they found the Tomkauds expecting them. The battle ended in a draw, and the Kauds retreated.

Now it was Autopscot's turn, but instead of attacking he came alone to the enemy camp. He greeted Wauwinet and presented an unusual idea: He would personally punish the offenders and forbid their crossing the boundary again. Wauwinet was astonished, but more was yet to come. Autopscot said he and Wonona loved each other and wanted to be husband and wife. The two tribes would live in peace forever, he said, and Wonona would be chief medicine woman of the island.

Wauwinet agreed, and the island was not only at peace but also enjoyed good health. (Wonona and Autopscot were really named Askammapoo and Spotso — but never mind. Apparently the medicine woman neglected to pass on her secret remedies, and epidemics wiped out both tribes in the next century.)

The Story of Mary and Jethro

John Gardner and Tristram Coffin clashed bitterly over shareholder rights and everything else. Presumably they were not even speaking when, in 1686, their wives told them that John's daughter, Mary, and Tristram's grandson, Jethro, had fallen in love. Forbidding the match was useless, the mother and grandmother assured their feuding spouses, but perhaps there was another solution. Each man was persuaded he could one-up the other with a magnanimous wedding gift. The young couple would need a house, wouldn't they?

John Gardner offered a prime piece of land on top of Sunset Hill. Tristram Coffin countered with a promise to provide the building materials. (He could get the lumber wholesale from his son in Massachusetts.)

Though slightly delayed because Grandfather Coffin demanded that the deed for the land be filed first, the wedding finally took place. So the house now known as "the Oldest House" (1686) was built. At this point the chronicle of the young couple fades away in a romantic mist, but history does at least record that they lived in the house for twenty years, then moved to the mainland. We are left to imagine their relief at getting away from their kinfolk. The feud never really ended, but the house is owned by the Nantucket Historical Association and is open for tours.

before it expired. Nantucket was not always an island, and now, constantly etched by the sea, it is in the terminal stages of geological life — probably only two millennia away from extinction. Nantucketers worry about this.

THE SEA ALSO RISES

When the Atlantic Ocean was six hundred feet lower, Nantucket was part of a low range of hills as much as forty miles inland from the eastern edge of North America. When the glaciers melted and the sea rose, it became an island, a strip of sand, rock, and swamp peaking at 109 feet above sea level and blessed with freshwater ponds.

Change is forever the norm. Sandbars created saltwater ponds out of inlets. Natural harbors silted until eventually no vessels of appreciable draft could use them. Shifting shoals, impenetrable fogs, and sudden violent storms would make navigation a nightmare. (It was the sight of the sea churning over the shoals in 1620 that caused the captain of the *Mayflower* to change course after he left Provincetown and head for Plymouth instead of the Island.) The sea around Nantucket is a graveyard full of the skeletons of lost vessels, from fishing skiffs and whalers to warships, yachts, and even an Italian luxury liner, the *Andrea Doria*.

In the near future scientists hope to explore the deep ocean trenches bordering the continental shelf. The site for the proposed deep-sea laboratory to be called Ocean Base One (OB1) is the Veatch Trench, eighty miles south of Nantucket. From the 540-foot-deep sea-floor lab and a second observation habitat 200 feet below the surface, a total of forty-five researchers will investigate sea-floor and deep-sea marine life. The OB1 station off Nantucket would be the deepest in the world. The project's main sponsor is the University of Connecticut's Marine Science and Technology Center.

WHERE THE WILD THINGS ARE/WERE

Nantucket has one-third of all the moors found in the hemisphere and a greater variety of vegetation than any space of similar size in America. It is the only place on the continent where true Scottish heather grows wild, and it has what was until recently the world's largest contiguous cranberry bog. In what appears to be inhospitable soil, rare plants thrive, and endangered species hang on. These days they get help from people who care.

Much of the flora and fauna on Nantucket has been imported. Broom was lovingly transplanted from Scotland and ivy from English gardens. Deer, foxes, rabbits, sparrows, and grouse were brought in and liberated a few at a time, perhaps to give this improbable place the ambiance of an English heath. Many of the wildflowers that fill the marshes and enliven the roadsides, including the signature wild roses, were not scattered accidentally by birds or winds but carried here deliberately by people actively engaged in beautification.

First Purchasers

Name-dropping on Nantucket is history as well as status. The nine men and their friends who invested "the sum of thirty pounds current pay . . . and also two beaver hats, one for my self and one for my wife" in the 1659 purchase from Thomas Mayhew have not lacked descendants. By one count Tristram Coffin is said to have more than 25,000.

The nine (plus Thomas Mayhew who retained a full share) were each allowed to choose a partner, so there were twenty in all. You will see and hear these names frequently, and Islanders will glibly trace their ancestors back to several.

Thomas Mayhew and partner John Smith
Tristram Coffin and partner Nathanial Starbuck
Peter Coffin and partner James Coffin
Thomas Macy and partner Edward Starbuck
Christopher Hussey and partner Robert Pike
Richard Swayne (Swain) and partner Thomas Look
Thomas Barnard and partner Robert Barnard
Stephen Greenleafe (Greenleaf) and partner Tristram Coffin Jr.
John Swayne (Swain) and partner Thomas Coleman
William Pike and partner John Bishop

You will notice a certain similarity of names. Since each share was worth a vote it made political sense to create a like-minded block, and Tristram Coffin, for one, didn't leave much to chance. He had aristocratic connections back home in England and could foresee a manorial system developing here, too. Naturally, he wanted to be the lord of the manor. Since no one outside the Coffin clan found this an appealing idea, and Tristram had no retinue of mounted knights to back it up, things on the Island continued to be resolved in a more haphazard way.

The purchasers discovered almost immediately that they needed craftsmen with essential skills to do the everyday work of building houses, catching fish, grinding grain, and generally making the community run properly. They sent out word that each of those who qualified would receive land for a home and a half share in the proprietorship. Among the fourteen who responded were Peter Foulger (Folger) of Martha's Vineyard, a surveyor and miller among other talents and the only man around who spoke Algonquin; Captain John Gardner, a master mariner who became the leader of the half-share men; Richard Gardner, his brother; the Worths; and the Mitchells. Unfortunately, no knowledgeable farmers were in the group, so agricultural endeavors continued to be pretty much a failure. Foulger, the Island intellectual, became the Town record keeper with colorful results, but he is most famous as being the grandfather of the multitalented Benjamin Franklin.

The names of purchaser descendants still appear in the Nantucket phone book, of course, and novelists find these surnames convenient for book characters who need to be defined as Islanders. Keeping them straight, however, is not absolutely necessary for enjoying the Nantucket life.

Today, with overdevelopment threatening the Island, organizations have been created solely to purchase and hold land in its natural state, and more than 40 percent of the Island (80 percent of what is not already developed) is permanently protected. Property owners have voted to tax themselves to the same end and businesses to set aside a portion of their profits to support environmental ideals. (See Chapter Seven, *Nature and the Environment*.)

Whether there were ever groves of tall trees on Nantucket is a point of debate. Given the shallow soil and the winds, it seems unlikely, and we know the settlers needed to bring lumber and even firewood from the mainland. Yet the Wampanoag called the barrier strip *Coatue* ("at the pine woods"), and there still exists the Hidden Forest, a small but enchanting stand of old ash and beech in a sheltered spot near the bogs off Polpis Road. The earliest inhabitants may have cleared land by burning too often for natural reforestation to take place, or perhaps some unrecorded hurricane wrought irreparable havoc. Even the experts can only guess.

SOCIAL HISTORY

NATIVES AND NEWCOMERS

Although Nantucket has been inhabited for at least 8,000 years, the first English settlers to arrive were lucky. In 1659 the Island was occupied by the Wampanoag, a friendly Algonquin tribe whose experience with white missionaries had been positive. Thomas Mayhew Jr. had overseen the building of Christian churches (Presbyterian) and established a school attended by thirty children. Several adults spoke a little English. How many Wampanoag resided on Nantucket then is not clear, but 2,500 is frequently given as a reasonable estimate. Certainly they vastly outnumbered the handful of mainland colonists. Inevitably there would be certain breakdowns in communication. The concept of private property, for instance, was unknown to the natives. Fortunately, the desire for peaceful coexistence was strong on both sides. Unfortunately, "the Great Sickness" of 1763–1764 and subsequent illnesses to which the settlers were immune decimated the tribe, and by the mid-19th century none was left.

GIVEAWAYS AND PURCHASES

Bartholomew Gosnold, on his way from England to Virginia, officially discovered the Island of Nantucket in 1602. He didn't bother to stop but assigned the Island and everything else he saw to Charles I as a matter of policy. In 1635 the king, in turn, gave the package to William Alexander, Earl of Sterling, who, in 1641, sold the rights unseen through his agent to Thomas Mayhew of Massachusetts and his son Thomas Mayhew Jr. for £40.

Mayhew's package included Martha's Vineyard and sixteen other islands south of Cape Cod, but by 1659, after his missionary only son was lost at sea,

The Old Mill, a Nantucket Historical Association property, is the oldest American windmill still in operation.

Rob Benchley

he was willing to pass Nantucket on to nine disgruntled colonists from Salisbury, Massachusetts. The price agreed upon was £30 and, as an afterthought, two beaver hats — one for himself and one for his wife. He also retained a share of the Island.

These purchasers had an equal number of designated purchase partners, and most of them packed up their goods and sailed for their new home as soon as they could. By 1660, the first ten families had moved to the Island. While they owned the English rights, they still had to purchase the Island a piece at a time from the Wampanoag, but they understood that in advance and were prepared to do so.

The shareholders, though intending to make their livelihood from raising sheep, found themselves in dire need of skilled craftsmen. To entice a weaver, carpenter, joiner, cooper, miller, and other artisans plus a mariner to explore the idea of a codfish harvest, they offered half shares. The problems of a two-tier society surfaced immediately when the half-share men led by John Gardner demanded an equal voice in Island affairs. This was particularly galling to Tristram Coffin, who had craftily hoped to corner voting power by purchasing shares in the names of his nonresident sons. Not to be totally thwarted, he purchased Tuckernuck Island for a few pounds as a Coffin preserve, but no one really wanted to live there.

For all their apparent homogeneity and family ties, the settlers were a cantankerous bunch. Disagreements erupted into feuds and personality differences into clashes. When Gardner persuaded the governor of New York Colony not only to change the rules of future land acquisition but also to rename the village the Indians called *Wesko* (after a white rock in the harbor) for his own English hometown of Sherburne, tempers flared. It was decided that the Wampanoag place names would prevail — with the exception of Wesko, which no one liked very much. Henceforth the village was to be called Nantucket Town, after its own Island.

A Sailor's Wife

When Eliza Brock accompanied her husband, Capt. Peter C. Brock, on a whaling voyage aboard the ship *Lexington* from May 1853 to June 1856, she kept a highly literary journal full of her own poems and essays. However, on one of the back pages she had also written down this poem:

The Nantucket Girl's Song

I have made up my mind now to be a sailor's wife,
To have a purse full of money and a very easy life.
For a clever sailor husband is so seldom at his home,
That his wife can spend the dollars with a will that's all her own.
Then I'll haste to wed a sailor and send him off to sea,
For a life of independence is the pleasant life for me.
But every now and then I shall like to see his face,
For it always seems to me to beam with manly grace,
With his brow so nobly open and his dark and kindly eye,
Oh my heart beats fondly towards him whenever he is nigh.
But when he says "Good bye my love, I'm off across the Sea"
First I cry for his departure, then laugh because I'm free.
Yet I'll welcome him most gladly whenever he returns
And share with him so cheerfully the money that he earns.
For he's a loving husband, though he leads a roving life
And well I know how good it is to be a sailor's wife.

Martha Ford
Bay of Islands, New Zealand
February 1855

Martha Ford was the wife of a physician on one of the islands Eliza visited; she may have given the poem to Eliza without knowing the name of the poet. Eliza probably thought it was hilarious and brought it home to share with her friends. Whoever wrote it, the frank message is not the norm for mid-19th-century verse on the sacred topic of marriage. To be sure, Nantucket women themselves were not the norm, either.

QUAKERS AND WHALERS

Although the purchasers were straining under the Puritan yoke of Massachusetts Bay Colony and, in part, were attracted to Nantucket because it was then part of New York Colony, they did not constitute a single religious minority. However, led by the charismatic Mary Coffin Starbuck, a convert to Quakerism at age fifty-nine, many joined the Society of Friends. By the end of the 18th century, two-thirds of the population declared themselves Quaker, and half regularly attended meetings. With the Quaker faith came a special set of values: nonviolence, hard work, strict morality, equality for women, prohibition of slavery, and a ban on frivolous spending. Nantucket abolished slavery nearly a century before the Civil War and welcomed

Ship captains' houses on Orange Street.

Betty Lowry

escapees and freed alike. Thanks to Capt. Absalom Boston, the son and grandson of slaves, schools were integrated before the first gun was fired at Fort Sumter. As for morality, Nantucket may have been the only sailors' town anywhere on earth without a whorehouse district, but licentiousness and wholesale debauchery by Nantucket seamen appalled the missionaries in the Pacific.

Principles of nonviolence did not extend to whales. In fact, the years that Nantucket was dominated by Quakerism were also the years of its whaling supremacy. The Wampanoag taught the colonists how to harvest the whales that swam in close to shore, though a taste for whale meat never really took hold among the settlers. In 1672 the first whale was caught and killed (as opposed to finding a carcass on the beach), and the following year whaling began in earnest in boats from the shore. It wasn't until 1712 that the first sperm whale was taken far out at sea by a sloop blown in a gale. The sperm's enormous head held a reservoir of fine oil, vastly more valuable than the boiled-down blubber of the ordinary whale, and Nantucket's seagoing entrepreneurs took note.

By 1774 some 150 Nantucket whalers sailed in the Atlantic, and despite the destruction or capture of most of the fleet during the Revolutionary War, the first whalers entered the Pacific in 1791. The world of the Pacific began to look like a Nantucket world. More than three hundred Islands were discovered by Nantucket whalemen, and thirty were promptly named for Nantucket captains and families. Voyages into the Antarctic Ocean not only predated official explorers but resulted in Nantucket names attached to land masses as well as islands from Antarctica to Canada. On that most southerly continent are Mitchell Peak, Gardner Inlet, Nantucket Inlet, and Folger Cape. As a matter of fact, it is claimed that the continent of Antarctica was first discovered by Capt. Christopher Burdick of Nantucket on a sealing voyage to the South Shetland Islands in 1821.

The first whale killed in the Pacific was by a Nantucket man (though he was impressed on an English ship at the time). The first cargo of sperm oil brought home from the Pacific was by a Nantucket captain sailing a Nantucket-owned ship (though it was officially out of Dunkirk, France). In fact, the first time the American flag was displayed in a South American Pacific port was from the mast of a Nantucket whaler.

From 1800 to 1849, Nantucket was the undisputed whaling capital of the world, and the decade between 1820 and 1830 saw 237 ships in service. The whale ships were self-contained factories that processed the oil, bone, teeth, baleen, and ambergris of the whales right on board. Ships' coopers built the barrels, and both officers and crew scratched and whittled the ivory into works of art.

Whaling voyages lasting four years were the norm, and families more often separated than together developed independent ways. Eventually some captains' wives and children went along, too, and babies were born on islands thick with palm trees and fragrant with frangipani. The whaling capital of the world had some curious outposts.

WINDS OF CHANGE

Prosperity reigned. The population of the Island doubled, and shipowners' mansions went up on Main Street. Ship captains' houses, neatly constructed by ship carpenters and furnished in the spare fashion of shipboard efficiency, grew side by side on Orange Street. Even the great fire of 1846 that destroyed one third of the Town and all of the wharves with their warehoused cargoes could not slow the rush. Rebuilding meant more-than-before and better-than-ever. Whaling money paid for a Golden Age of culture, a time when being invited to speak in the Nantucket Atheneum (Greek for "temple of arts and literature" as well as "library") was a plum sought by the New England literary elite.

Then it all came down. First a sandbar blocked the harbor, and despite ingenious attempts to get ships across the bar, the larger and heavier whalers were diverted to New Bedford. Then crews in the Pacific began to jump ship for the California gold fields, and the like-minded emigration from Nantucket reduced the population by half. As if that hadn't been enough, the production of kerosene and the discovery of petroleum wiped out the market for whale oil. By the time the Civil War literally destroyed the whaling fleet, it scarcely mattered.

The end of whaling created an economic slump on the Island that extended psychologically to a common sulk among men who had tilted with leviathans of the deep. Nantucket women, accustomed to running the show while the men were away for years at a time, are credited with holding it all together. Without money to follow mainland fads, the Nantucketers made do with their old-fashioned houses and furniture, unknowingly saving pearls of architecture and handcraft for future generations.

Even as the grimier aspects of the Industrial Revolution also passed the Island by, small manufacture was rejected as impractical if not unworthy. Commercial fishing was unprofitable. The winds of postwar prosperity inflating America were not blowing on Nantucket.

Nevertheless, the emergence of a national leisure class had major consequences for the Island and most immediately for a small fishing village at the easternmost point named Siasconset (though always abbreviated to "Sconset"). Wealthy off-Islanders, fleeing the heat of summer in Manhattan and embracing the latest fad of saltwater bathing, discovered Nantucket's cool breezes and more than eighty miles of beaches. They first filled the half-empty boardinghouses in Town, then moved on to the sleepy hamlet seven miles away. Two summer hotels went up. The visitors built vacation houses of considerable size where there had been only shacks made of driftwood and scrap lumber. By the 1880s the Broadway theater crowd had declared Sconset no longer Land's End (3000 Miles to Spain the sign read) but the only place to be in July and August.

Delirious with the prospect of attracting more of the same big spenders exemplified in the actors' colony, the Island power elite laid out a railroad to connect Steamboat Wharf in Nantucket Town first to Surfside, which was experiencing an ill-fated land boom (summer resort hotels were being built quickly and badly), and then to Sconset. Next, in 1899–1900, the Casino was built, the Smart Set's symbol for the resort that had arrived. Incidentally, the Casino was — and still is — a theater, not a gambling establishment, and had — and still has — a bevy of tennis courts.

Sconset made history in 1901 when it was the site of the first wireless station in America to transmit and receive messages from Atlantic ships. The *New York Herald* financed the operation in order to beat its rivals by announcing ship arrivals a day early. Guglielmo Marconi, inventor of the wireless, came in person to see his project in action and won the Nobel Prize in 1909.

The Twenties roared in, and on law-abiding Nantucket bootlegging flourished. Then the worldwide Great Depression closed everything down.

A SPECIAL PLACE

It remained for Island planners to recognize the value of their heritage and to preserve the past and protect Nantucket from blatant commercialism while developing tourism. Here the dual obsessions of honoring family and never throwing anything away served the Island well. Nantucket has more buildings on the National Register of Historic Places qualifying as totally preserved than anywhere else in New England, including more than eight hundred antebellum houses in pristine condition. The Jethro and Mary Coffin dwelling, or the Oldest House, is a National Historic Landmark. The Town's museums and libraries overflow with priceless historical memorabilia, and in 1955 both Nantucket Town and Siasconset became registered Old and Historic Districts.

The Notable Nantucket Woman

From the beginning, Nantucket women appear to have been ahead of their time. They received the same education as their brothers and had equal rights in the Society of Friends, where they were encouraged to speak out in meeting. As early as 1750, wives' names appeared on land records along with their husbands'.

During the years when Nantucket was the whaling capital of the world, the Island was a matriarchal society, with women sometimes outnumbering the men and boys by a ratio of four to one. They were notoriously self-sufficient. While the men went whaling for three to five years at a time, the women literally ran the stores. What is now Centre Street was once called Petticoat Row for the number of female merchants.

After 1850 they apparently weren't even content to stay at home. So many captain's wives and families went along on the expeditions, there were little communities all over the Pacific where wives met to stay over for a few months at a time, perhaps to recover from an illness or bear a child, perhaps just to visit their friends.

It may be apocryphal that a girl was expected to refuse a boy until he had taken his first whale, but those rooftop platforms seen on 18th- and 19th-century homes were called "roof walks" on Nantucket, not sentimental "widows' walks" as in other coastal communities. Nantucket women said they found the roof walks invaluable when it was necessary to dump sand down on chimney fires, catch a fresh breeze after an afternoon spent baking bread, or keep an eye on what was happening in their neighbors' yards. Chances are they could spot a returning whaleship, too.

Nantucket women have been leaders on their Island and in world history:

Mary Coffin Starbuck (1644–1717) was Nantucket's first English bride (aged eighteen) and first mother (aged nineteen), bearing ten children. She became the community's charismatic spiritual leader as well as its first storekeeper. Converted to Quakerism in her late fifties, she held meetings in her home and by her example led many Islanders to membership in the Society of Friends.

Less appealing a protagonist was **Kezia Folger Coffin** (1723–1798), cousin to Ben Franklin and the ill-disguised leading character of Joseph C. Hart's best-selling 19th-century novel *Miriam Coffin*. Kezia was a successful shipping entrepreneur, probably a smuggler, and certainly a devout Tory who was tried and acquitted of treason in 1779. It wasn't her free spirit that did her in but the fact that she overcharged her neighbors and then ordered her lawyer son-in-law to foreclose on every mortgage on the Island. She was involved in litigation of one sort or another until the day she died.

Lucretia Coffin Mott (1793–1880), leading abolitionist and advocate of women's rights, was born on Nantucket. She and Elizabeth Cady Stanton called the first women's rights convention at Seneca Falls in 1848; before that, in 1840, Lucretia went to London as a delegate to the World Anti-Slavery Convention. The organizer of the Anti-Slavery Convention in 1841 and secretary of the Nantucket Abolitionist Society was **Anna Gardner**, the white teacher in a segregated black school.

Maria Mitchell (1818–1889), Atheneum librarian and amateur astronomer, discovered a comet (official in the books as "Miss Mitchell's Comet") on October 1, 1847. For this she received a gold medal from the King of Denmark and international fame. She became the first woman member of the American Academy of Arts and Sciences, the Association for the Advancement of Science, and the American Philosophical Society. In 1865 she was named the first professor of astronomy and director of the observatory at Vassar College in Poughkeepsie, New York, and in 1873 she founded the American Association for the Advancement of Women. On Nantucket you'll find her well remembered by the Maria Mitchell Association (508-228-9198; 2 Vestal St., Nantucket, MA 02554), which oversees her birthplace as well as a science library and two observatories

The first American-born woman doctor was **Lydia Folger Fowler** of Nantucket. The first woman voter at any public election in the United States was **Louisa A. Swain**, a resident of Wyoming but born on Nantucket. In 1934 the first female presiding justice in Massachusetts was **Ethel Mackiernan** of Nantucket; her successor was **Caroline Leveen**, also of Nantucket.

Built in 1770, the Thomas Macy house at 99 Main Street is a Nantucket Historical Association property.

Rob Benchley

In the 1990s the sites of Nantucket's black community were at last recognized, and the 1820 African Meeting House has been restored.

So Nantucket is not some place-that-never-was, with houses, barns, and country stores moved from other locations for the education of schoolchildren and the attraction of tourists. No theme park offers cute interpreters or cozy fairytales under the guise of serious history. Nor does one find the old literally attached to the new in the manner of façades on a movie lot. Sensible updating has gone on, of course, as in adding modern bathrooms, central heat, and handicap access. Structures have changed their original purpose: A mansion is now an inn; a captain's house has become a bed & breakfast; a fisherman's shanty is renewed as an art gallery. A beloved but derelict summer-only restaurant once known for its 50¢ lobster dinners is now a posh and pricey resort. Scalloping became commercially important in the 1880s, but a century later the Nantucket variety was recognized as a gourmet delicacy, and gather-

Moby-Dick or The Whale

At one time on Nantucket a copy of Herman Melville's masterpiece was likely to be next to your pillow, but now you are lucky to find one anywhere in the inn. "Guests found it too long to finish on vacation so just took the copy home," I was told.

So here, in brief, is the narrative: The whaling ship *Pequod* sails from Nantucket on Christmas Day under command of Captain Ahab and with a crew drawn from every part of the globe. Ishmael, the young outcast who represents Melville himself, tells the story. On a previous voyage Ahab lost a leg and is so obsessed with finding and killing the sperm whale responsible that he offers a gold ducat to the first man who spots the creature. The whale, he says, has a white head, wrinkled brow, crooked jaw, and three holes punched in his starboard fluke. His name is Moby Dick, and he is known to other whalers, too, for he has killed and maimed sailors as well as destroyed boats.

Finally Moby Dick is sighted and, on encounter, bites the captain's boat in two. The next day Moby Dick appears again and upsets three boats. On the third and final day the whale rams the *Pequod*, then attacks the boats. Captain Ahab is caught around the neck by a fouled line and pulled into the vortex of the diving whale.

This is the symbolic story of mankind trapped by fate and with leadership gone amok. Only the human spirit survives and has the last word. The crew representing the entire world includes Asian, African, American Indian (a Wampanoag from Gay Head, Martha's Vineyard), Polynesian, and Caucasian. Everyone is lost except Ishmael, the observer, who must live to tell the tale.

The whale voyage setting is meticulously and accurately drawn from Melville's own experience of eighteen months in 1841–1842 on the whaler *Acushnet*. In fact, the book is a compendium of information about the science, nature, art, and economy of 19th-century whaling.

Herman Melville (1819–1891) spent five years at sea, but it was reading *Narrative of the Most Extraordinary and Distressing Shipwreck of the Whaleship Essex* by Owen Chase of Nantucket that gave him the slant he needed for *Moby-Dick*. In 1820 Chase, who as first mate kept the ship's log of the *Essex*, was there when it was rammed and sunk by a whale. He spent ninety-three days in an open boat along with a handful of other survivors, including Captain George Pollard, eventually resorting to cannibalism to stay alive. Pollard, who had lost two ships, was reduced to working as the Town night watchman when Melville finally met him on a visit to Nantucket a year after the publication of *Moby-Dick* in 1851. Pollard died in poverty, a disgraced old man, and Owen Chase was so haunted by fears of starvation that he was even known to hoard scraps of food in his attic.

Another book Melville probably read was *A Narrative of the Mutiny, On Board the Ship Globe of Nantucket in the Pacific Ocean, Jan. 1824*. One of the two young survivor-authors was Cyrus M. Hussey of Nantucket.

Moby-Dick was no bestseller — it sold fewer than fifty copies the second year after publication — disappointing readers who thought Melville had written another one of his high-adventure yarns like *Typee*. With its hidden meanings and near-occult observations, the book was so out of the mainstream, it vanished from view until rediscovered by critics long after the author's death.

According to an article in *Knickerbocker Magazine* published twelve years before Melville's book, there really was a fierce white whale reported to have destroyed three whalers, fourteen whaleboats, an Australian trader, and a French merchant-man. The beast survived nineteen harpoons and killed thirty men. His name was "Mocha-Dick."

ing scallops is now a viable off-season occupation for Islanders as well as a potential attraction for tourists.

When statistics showed Nantucket to be the fastest-growing county in Massachusetts, the Island did not rejoice but instead mobilized as if to repel invaders. Historic houses and conservation land had for many years been passed on by bequest to the appropriate organizations, but now the nation's first Land Bank was established specifically to hold property in trust for the community. More recently still, the business community and chamber of commerce have set up the country's first fund to divert a percentage of profits solely to purchase environmentally important acres and keep them free of development forever. (See Chapter Seven, *Nature and the Environment*.)

The winds of change are not always welcome. Automobiles were first rejected, then permitted by narrow margin of popular vote. (Automobiles from the mainland would probably be forbidden today if it were possible to do so.) Nantucket Memorial Airport is second only to Boston's Logan International in air traffic for Massachusetts, and the number of airplanes flying in and out is predicted to double again within five years. More families whose professions allow them to commute by computer are leaving the stress of urban life behind and finding their way to Nantucket. Every summer the Island population goes from seven to forty thousand in a blink. "Whose Island is it, anyway?" year-round residents mutter. The answer is still blowing in the wind.

Nantucket is, and will continue to be in the foreseeable future, an upscale getaway. There are good values, even bargains, especially in the off-season, but they are not widely advertised off-Island. Nor is it just the high end of the lodging and dining spectrum that is, after all, predictable in a place where nearly everything must be imported but a general consensus of what Islanders want in their visitors. The very idea of the huge national business and fraternal conventions that other tourist destinations cry for appalls Nantucketers. Boisterous vacationers, however free spending, may find themselves lectured on good manners. High-rise hotels? Budget motels? Wild dogs would be preferable. Nantucket is, in the words of its people, "A Special Place" — and aims to stay that way.

NEIGHBORS ALL AROUND

As long as you're in the southeast Massachusetts neighborhood, consider dropping in on Nantucket's nearest and dearest. They share history as well as location, and all are prime tourist destinations in their own right, with sights, shops, and a variety of good places to stay and dine. For more information, contact: Massachusetts Office of Travel and Tourism (800-227-MASS; www.massvacation.com; State Transportation Bldg., 10 Park Plaza, Suite 4510, Boston, MA 02116).

Cape Cod

The great curved arm of Cape Cod is only thirty miles from Nantucket and worth more of a visit than a pass-through before or after your trip to the Island. You'll find historic villages and towns, beaches, bike paths, twenty-three public and private golf courses, and 365 lakes and ponds — one for every day of the year. Once a peninsula, the Cape was severed from mainland Massachusetts by the world's longest sea-level canal, then reconnected by two bridges, both subject to traffic tie-ups on summer and holiday weekends. Its greatest treasure is the twenty-seven-thousand-acre Cape Cod National Seashore, a wealth of dunes with plant and animal life intact that always seems remote from civilization, even when under siege by hundreds of people bearing picnic baskets.

Two state roads extend the length of the Cape: Route 6, the freeway, and Route 6A, the bayshore country road that is properly — though not often — called Old King's Highway. It helps to know that "up-Cape" is toward the mainland and "down-Cape" towards Provincetown, a holdover from the Pilgrims landing on the tip and proceeding to explore "up the Cape." While many visitors on the Cape take the ferry to Nantucket for a day trip, to many Nantucketers, going "off-Island" means a day or two on Cape Cod.

For more information, contact: Cape Cod Chamber of Commerce (508-362-3225; www.capecodchamber.org; 307 Main St., Suite 2, PO Box 790, Hyannis MA 02601).

Martha's Vineyard

The friendly rivalry between Nantucket and Martha's Vineyard may have begun when Moshop the Giant dropped the other shoe, but it has progressed to the annual high school Big Game. The islands are different, remarkably so considering they lie only twenty miles apart and share the same waterways and the same economic base of tourism. The Vineyard is about twice the size of Nantucket and was settled first, though it was part of the package Thomas Mayhew purchased from Lord Sterling. Early settlers often traveled to Nantucket via the Vineyard, which lies nearer the mainland, and people moved back and forth between them. When the first purchasers arrived, cattle from the Vineyard were grazing on the west end of Nantucket; later, many of the half-share holders moved over from the larger island.

As time passed, the Vineyard's road took different turns. It, too, had a whaling period centered in Edgartown, but this was never a solitary commitment. It also has late colonial architecture, but of its six towns, the most singular today is Oak Bluffs, a relic of Victorian times with lollipop-colored Carpenter Gothic cottages and a history as a Methodist campground. The Island's main viewpoint is Gay Head cliffs, striated walls of red clay at the western end now reclaimed by the Wampanoag, who have changed the name to Aquinnah. Despite the proximity, there is no appreciable traffic between Nantucket and Martha's Vineyard either by tourists or residents. The possible exception is the weekend of the Big Game between the rival high schools' football teams.

For more information, contact: Martha's Vineyard Chamber of Commerce (508-693-0085; Box 1698 Beach Rd., Vineyard Haven MA 02568).

New Bedford

When the big whalers could no longer make it across the sandbar that blocked Nantucket Harbor, they went on to New Bedford, an important whaling town on the southern mainland of Massachusetts. This is where *Moby-Dick* opens, where Ishmael decides to go on the hellish voyage, and the town is making the most of that connection. In its Historic District on Johnnycake Hill, there's a fine Whaling Museum with a permanent Moby Dick exhibit. Also in New Bedford's Whaling National Historic Park, you can board a fully rigged eighty-nine-foot-long, half-scale replica of the whaling bark *Lagoda* as well as take a self-guided "Dock Walk" tour. The Seamen's Bethel of *Moby-Dick* still stands. As a fishing industry center, New Bedford celebrates with a Whaling City Festival the second weekend in July. If you are driving from New York or Connecticut, you can miss the bottleneck traffic of Cape Cod by leaving your car at New Bedford Regional Airport (508-991-6161) and flying directly to Nantucket in twenty-two minutes.

For more information contact: Bristol County Convention and Visitors Bureau (508-997-1250, 800-288-6263;www.bristol-county.org; 70 N. Second St., PO Box 976, New Bedford 02740) or New Bedford Whaling National Historical Park (508-996-4095; www.nps.gov/nebe; 33 William St., New Bedford, MA 02740).

CHAPTER TWO
Getting On, Off, and Around Island
TRANSPORTATION

O ld-time Nantucket-ers reduce trans-portation to "getting on-Island" (coming), "going off-Island" (leaving), and — in between — "getting around-Island." Keeping it all as simple and straightforward as possi-ble is the "Island way."

For the first pur-chasers natural harbors were essential, and Nan-tucket had several plus inlets that served small boats well. Nantucket-ers could sail point to point around the periph-ery of the Island, trans-

Rob Benchley

The Steamship Authority ferry Eagle *rounds Brant Point lighthouse on its approach to Nantucket Harbor.*

porting goods or making calls on other Islanders. The first commercial ferry between Cape Cod and the Island began when post-Civil War summer visitors demanded something more reliable than a boat hired on the spot. A family with servants and wardrobe trunks preferred a prearranged schedule, and soon the crossing became a seagoing party for those on holiday, a chance to see old friends or make new ones.

The new tourism was truly launched when the Old Colony Railroad was extended from Boston to Hyannis and Woods Hole, then connected with steamboats to the islands. Nantucket's entrepreneurs stopped mourning the death of the whaling industry and looked ahead. Surfside could have a future with hotels on its beach, they opined, and Siasconset was obviously perfect for an upscale summer colony. Visions of enormous Nantucket family reunions if not corporate meetings danced in their heads. If only the roads weren't so bad that they knocked the wheels off the coaches one week, then sucked them into yards of mud the next.

Promoters with off-Island money worked fast. In 1881, before anyone really knew what was going on, Nantucket had a railroad. Well, maybe not exactly a railroad but a steam locomotive, named *Dionis* in honor of the first matriarch of the Coffin clan, and a pair of open-air passenger cars. Each seated fifteen, their riders more or less protected from foreseeable hazards by a cowcatcher and a "spark-arrester." Though the original plans were more grandiose, eventually three-foot-gauge track was laid from Steamboat Wharf to Sconset and Surfside.

The Surfside land scheme languished (in 1899 one summer hotel literally fell down), but never mind. Café society had discovered Sconset, and the train was *the* fashionable way to go there.

The train leaving for Sconset, 1915.

Courtesy of the Nantucket Historical Association

Yet at best it ran irregularly, confounded both by storm and sabotage, until 1917. In 1918 the tracks were ripped up and the rolling stock shipped to France — except for the surviving car that has become the bar of the Club Car restaurant. Various oversize horse-drawn vehicles were tried and found uneconomical. The day of the automobile was then at hand, whether Nantucketers liked it or not.

In 1894 a steam-powered horseless carriage was built on Island, and in 1900 a Stanley Steamer was imported. This was getting serious, and so Nantucket sent a delegation to Boston to do something official about the threat to the Island Way of Life. In 1907 automobiles on Nantucket were banned by act of the Massachusetts State Legislature, a statute that was not repealed until the spring of 1918, when it squeaked through in a popular election by a mere 40 votes out of 632 cast.

Regular passenger airplane service between Boston and Nantucket began in 1927, though the mail didn't get the same privilege until the late 1930s. Nantucket's airport is now the second busiest in Massachusetts after Boston's Logan International, but the commercial planes are small, and the private and corporate planes are many. This year an ad for an aircraft manufacturer enticed with: "Work in Manhattan — live on Nantucket!"

In the last several years ferry service has perked up with the addition of the "Fast Ferry" of the Steamship Authority and the catamaran of Hy-Line Cruises.

Both take about one hour and carry only passengers, bikes, and pets. Secured parking is available for a fee in Hyannis, and while reservations are recommended in the summer, the off-season ferry always seems to have room for a few more.

Some inns provide pickup for their guests at the airport or the pier (make these arrangements in advance). Otherwise, taxis meet all flights and go by fixed rates to any point on the Island. If you travel light and don't mind a short hike, you can catch a bus. At the dock it gets a little more complicated, since the number of passengers on a ferry is much greater — but somehow it all gets sorted out. You probably can walk to your inn. Ask for directions, and they will be cheerfully given, along with a smile and a "Welcome to Nantucket."

GETTING TO NANTUCKET ACCESS

BY CAR TO HYANNIS

If you take a ferry or the fifteen-minute flight from Cape Cod, you must get to the port first. On summer weekends this can be a slow and frustrating procedure, though it has been improving with new traffic controls and approaches. Just to be sure you don't miss the boat or plane, allow plenty of time. **SmarTraveler** now services the Steamship Authority. You can get up-to-the-minute traffic information on the easiest and quickest way to get to the ferry: 617-374-1234 from a touch-tone phone or #1 from a cellular phone.

From New York: Follow Route 95 to Providence, RI; Route 195 to Wareham, MA; Route 25 over Bourne Bridge; Route 6 to Exit #6; Route 132 into Hyannis. Follow signs to airport or docks. Approximately five hours, depending on traffic, and 265 miles.

From Boston: Follow Route 3 (Southeast expressway); Route 6 over the Sagamore Bridge; Route 132 into Hyannis; follow signs to airport or docks. Approximately one and one-half hours, depending on traffic, and 72 miles.

Automobiles must have a reservation; for passengers, pets, and bikes, no reservation is necessary. Approximately two-hour-and-fifteen-minute cruise. Secured fee parking at Hyannis terminal.

For more information: 508-477-8600, TDD 508-540-1394.

BY BUS TO HYANNIS

These bus lines connect with lines from other parts of Massachusetts and the rest of the country:

Bonanza Bus Line will take you from New York City or Providence. For more information: 212-947-1766, 800-556-3815; www.bonanzabus.com.

Plymouth & Brockton Bus Line offers service between Boston and Hyannis, including direct transfer from Logan International Airport. For more information: 508-771-6191; www.p-b.com.

Peter Pan Bus Line from western Massachusetts does not go to Hyannis. You must change to Bonanza in Providence or Plymouth and Brockton in Boston. For more information: 800-343-9999; www.peterpanbus.com.

GETTING TO NANTUCKET

BY AIR

Nantucket's ACK airport is the second busiest in Massachusetts thanks to private and fun-size commercial airplanes.

Rob Benchley

Getting on-Island by air is literally a hop, and the low-flying little planes are great fun. It's not cheap, but you can have an extra day on Island with the time you save over other means of transportation. Nantucket Memorial Airport is a small, friendly place (it was the setting for the TV show *Wings*), with cash machine, rental cars, and taxis readily available. Except for times of dense fog (go back to your inn and put your feet up) it's open year-round. Another surprise: Hutch's, the very good and reasonable airport restaurant, is open from 6am, serves breakfast, lunch, and dinner, and has take-out. (Would that the big-city airports could say as much.)

    Nantucket Memorial Airport: 508-325-5300, fax 508-325-5306; www.nantucketairport.com.

MAJOR AND LOCAL AIRLINES

From Boston: Approximately fifty-minute flight, nonstop.

    Cape Air: 800-352-0714; www.flycapeair.com

    US Airways Express (operated by Colgan Air): 800-428-4322; www.usairways.com

    American Eagle (seasonal): 800-433-7300; www.aa.com

From Hyannis: Approximately fifteen-minute flight.

    Island Airlines: 508-228-7575, 800-248-7779 (every half hour) islandair@nantucket.net

NANTUCKET ACCESS

G etting to Nantucket really means getting to the ferry or the airport, so this is approximately how long a drive will take to **Hyannis,** Cape Cod, the point of departure nearest the Island. The following figures are according to the American Automobile Association.

City	Miles	Approximate time
Boston	72	1 1/2 hours
Hartford	161	3 hours
Providence	76	1 1/2 hours
New York City	265	5 hours
Montreal	379	6 3/4 hours
Philadelphia	349	6 3/4 hours
Washington D.C.	483	9 hours

Nantucket Airlines: 508-228-6234, 800-635-8787 (every hour) www.nantuck etairlines.com

From Martha's Vineyard: Approximately fifteen-minute flight.
  Cape Air: 800-352-0714; www.flycapeair.com
  Continental Express (seasonal): 800-525-0280; www.continental.com
  US Airways Express (seasonal): 800-428-4322; www.usairways.com
From New Bedford: Approximately twenty-two-minute flight.
  Cape Air: 800-352-0714; www.flycapeair.com
From La Guardia, NY: Approximately one-hour-and-ten-minute flight.
  US Airways Express: 800-428-4322; www.usairways.com
  From Newark, NJ: Approximately one-hour-and-fifteen-minute flight.
  Continental Express: (seasonal and special events) 800-525-0280; www.conti nental.com
  From T.F. Green, Providence, RI: Approximately forty-five-minute flight.
  Note: Providence is an uncongested alternative to Boston and other East Coast points. Most major airlines can connect with Cape Air.
  Cape Air: 800-352-0714; www.flycapeair.com

Why ACK?

You've seen it in crossword puzzles; now on-Island you'll see those three letters on T-shirts, sweats, caps, and bumper stickers. What does it all mean? *ACK* is merely the Nantucket Memorial Airport's international identification letters — the ones you see on your checked baggage tag. Boston may have *BOS;* Kennedy may shorthand *JFK;* little Hyannis spells out *HYA.* But *ACK* for Nantucket?

Give up? Seems the United States Navy keeps the letter "N" out of the pool. *ACK* is short for Ackerly Field, which was, ironically, the name of a *navy* airfield on Nantucket. Predictably, *ACK* has come to be an insider mark, especially among college students, the cool way to let the less fortunate know that you spend your holidays on Nantucket.

Private air charter services

Air Service, Inc.: 508-945-7458, 800-872-1704; airser@gis.net
Chatham Air Charter: 508-945-9000
Desert & Island Air Charter: 800-835-9135; www.desertislandair.com
eBiz Jets, Inc.: 888-393-2853; fly@ebizjets.com
Nantucket Express: 508-228-626-8825, 800-626-8825, ext. 247
NY Air Charter: 800-692-4724
Ocean Wings Air Charter: 508-325-5488, 800-253-5039; wings@nantucket.net
Primac Air Charter Services: 201-871-1800, 800-232-6245; primac@idt.net
Westchester Air: 914-761-3000, 800-759-2929

Private plane

Nantucket Memorial Airport is tower controlled between 0600 and 2100 (summer). Runway 6-24 (6303') has an instrument-landing system. Fuel available twenty-four hours a day (1100LL, Jet "A"); overnight parking and tie-downs are available. Aircraft repair and servicing facilities on premises provided by Grey Lady Aviation, 508-228-5888. For private plane landing information, 508-325-3000.

Airport operations: 508-325-5307, fax 508-325-7092
Airport Mgrs. Office: 508-325-5300, fax 508-325-5306
Airlines: Contact airlines directly.

BY SEA

Hyline Cruises offers regular and high-speed ferry service to and from Hyannis.

Rob Benchley

The two-hour-and-fifteen-minute ferry ride from Hyannis, Cape Cod, to Nantucket is touted as a necessary winding-down from stress to stress-free, but obviously many find decompression can be accomplished in a shorter time. You can, for example, take the year-round Fast Ferry of the **Woods Hole, Martha's Vineyard & Nantucket Steamship Authority** from South Street Dock, Hyannis (one hour), the high-speed catamaran service on **Hy-Line Cruises** from Ocean Street Dock, Hyannis (one hour), or seasonal **Freedom Cruise Line** from Harwich Port (ninety minutes).

You can take your bike on any ferry for an extra fee. Snack-bar food is available on board, or you can bring a picnic lunch. Pets must be leashed at all times. When you arrive, you'll find public telephones along the wharves and taxis at the Steamship Authority. Your hotel may offer transfer service, or if you're staying downtown, you can probably walk. If you make the trip by private boat, you will find marinas and mooring facilities as well as a community of boat owners waiting for you on Nantucket.

Ferry

The approach by ferry is, for many residents and visitors alike, the only way to arrive at the "Grey Lady." More likely than not and especially off-season, seals will be sighted. An old departure custom is to toss a penny (some pessimists use two) into the water as the boat rounds Brant Point to assure your return to Nantucket.

Hy-Line Cruises (508-228-3949 or 778-2600, 888-778-1132; www.hy-line cruises.com; 36 Ocean Street, Hyannis MA 02601; Ocean Street Dock) High-speed and regular boat service year-round; catamarans take one hour; high-speed ferry regular service, one and one-half hours; carries passengers, pets, bicycles, no reservations required (no automobiles). (Note that travel time is shorter than that of the Steamship Authority service below, but only the Steamship Authority vessels carry automobiles.) Seasonal ferry May–October has a first-class section and 1.9-hour cruise time. Fee parking, Hyannis. Also goes between Nantucket and Martha's Vineyard May–October.

Freedom Cruise Line (508-432-8999; www.capecod.net/freedom; 702 Rte. 28, Harwich Port, MA 02646; Saquatucket Harbor) once a day, May–October, carrying passengers, bicycles, most pets. Parking available in private lot.

Woods Hole, Martha's Vineyard & Nantucket Steamship Authority (508-477-8600, 508-228-0262; www.islandferry.com; 1 Railroad Ave., PO Box 284, Woods Hole, MA 02601) Year-round; carries vehicles by reservation only. Trip is two and one-quarter hours. **Fast Ferry** (508-495-3278) One hour; passengers, bikes, and pets only. No reservations necessary. Additional service is offered mid-May to mid-November and Christmas Stroll Weekend. The Steamship Authority also offers transport (including automobile) between Martha's Vineyard and Nantucket year-round.

Private boat

Call the harbormaster at the Marine Department for boat mooring information (508-228-7260) or the Nantucket Boat Basin (508-228-1333).

Seagoing Nantucket prides itself on its facilities, including the following:
Nantucket Boat Basin: 508-325-1350, 800-626-2628; New Whale St., PO Box 1139, Nantucket, MA 02554.
Nantucket Moorings: 508-228-4472; 62 Bartlett Rd., Nantucket, MA 02554.
Town Pier: 508-228-7260; 38 Washington St., Nantucket, MA 02554.

Boating supplies and services are available at
Brant Point Marine: 508-228-6244, fax 508-325-4693; www.brantpointmarine. com; 32 Washington St., Nantucket, MA 02554.
Grey Lady Marine Service: 508-228-9095; 96 Washington St. Ext., Nantucket, MA 02554.
Madaket Marine: 508-228-9086, fax 508-228-4527; madmar@nantucket.net; 20 N. Cambridge St., Nantucket, MA 02554.

Nantucket Ship Chandlery: 508-228-2300; www.nantucket.net/boating/chandlery; 1 Old South Wharf, PO Box 417, Nantucket, MA 02554.

GETTING AROUND-ISLAND

Nantucket on Two Wheels: Courtesies of the Path

Wide, paved bicycle paths parallel every main road on Nantucket, and route signs illustrated with a bike direct you to them. Bikes belong on the paths — mopeds belong on the road — but you will also find runners, walkers, and strollers making use of them. *Slow down, watch out, and give a clear warning (bell, horn, or voice) both before and while passing.*

Rules for bicyclists in Town:
- Keep to the right; ride single file except when passing.
- Obey all one-way street signs.
- Walk bicycles on sidewalks.
- Use a light at night and proper pedal and side reflectors.
- Signal (bell, horn, or voice) when passing.
- Park bicycles so as not to obstruct pedestrian or vehicle traffic — this includes when you stop to consult your map.
- One person per bike except with child carrier or trailer.
- Always wear a helmet (required by law for children twelve and under).

Rules for mountain bikes:
- Stay on established trails.
- Respect Nantucket's fragile environment.
- Avoid soft sand.
- Be aware of other users. Share the trail safely.
- Leave no trace of your passage.

Violations of these rules are subject to a fine and/or bicycle impoundment.

Rules for mopeds:
- A valid driver's license or learner's permit is required.
- Mopeds and scooters are subject to all motorized vehicle laws.
- Island speed limit for mopeds and scooters is 25 MPH.
- Avoid soft sand and dirt roads, and use caution on wet roads.
- No motorized vehicles are allowed on bike paths or sidewalks. Keep to the main roads.
- State law requires use of an approved helmet.

Violations of these rules incur the same penalties as for any motor vehicle.

Nantucket's size is part of its charm. It's manageable. You really can escape the pressure of long commutes and bumper-to-bumper traffic. You can go the length and breadth of the Island without ever seeing a traffic light (indeed, there are none on the Island), much less a traffic jam. A seasonal ten-fold increase in the number of automobiles can slow things considerably, however. The problem is especially acute entering and exiting Nantucket Town on streets laid out in the 18th and 19th century. There are no parking meters — but no parking lots, either. Islanders are quick to point out alternatives. Going by bike, moped, or just walking are all recognized and approved ways of getting around. The seasonal shuttle bus service begun only a few years ago has been so successful, the routes have already been expanded to include Jetties and Surfside Beaches and will be expanded again. Taxis are available when you need them, even if it's raining, though in summer taxi drivers complain that they are delayed by tourist vehicles.

BY BIKE AND MOPED

Whether you bring your own two wheels on the ferry or rent when you get there, bikes are the ideal transportation for the Island. The first bike path was laid out in 1896, connecting Nantucket Town with Sconset, then another in 1898 between Madaket and Water Works Roads. Today you'll find great bike trails to Surfside, Sconset, and Madaket, all easy riding on mostly flat terrain. In summer it's prudent to call ahead and reserve your wheels from the bike shops located only steps from the ferry dock. Helmets are available free of charge when you rent your bike. Wearing a helmet is compulsory up to the age of twelve and an excellent idea for everyone.

Bike riders must observe all rules of the road, including one-way streets, and walk their bikes on the sidewalks. Where there are official bike paths, you can't ride in the road.

Young's Bicycle Shop is one of several bike rentals right on Steamboat Wharf.

Rob Benchley

Mopeds are available at the bicycle shops. Helmets are compulsory. Moped riders must stay on the roads and follow the same rules as automobiles. They are not allowed on bike paths or in the Old Historic District between 10pm and 7am.

Affordable Rentals of Nantucket: 508-228-3501, 877-235-3500; 6 S. Beach St., Nantucket, MA 02554.
Bikes-to-Go:. 508-228-0076; 8 West Creek Rd., Nantucket, MA 02554.
Cook's Cycles: 508-228-0800; 6 S. Beach St., PO Box 1206, Nantucket, MA 02554.
Holiday Cycle: 508-228-3644; 4 Chester St., Nantucket, MA 02554.
Island Bike Co.: 508-228-4070, 877-228-4070, fax 508-325-6071; www.bikenan tucket.com; 25 Old South Rd., PO Box 1153, Nantucket, MA 02554.
Nantucket Bike Shop: 508-228-1999; www.nantucket.net/trans/nantucket bike; 4Broad St, Nantucket, MA 02554; Steamboat and Straight Wharves.
Young's Bicycle Shop: 508-228-1151, fax 508-228-3038; www.youngsbicy cleshop.com; 6 Broad St., PO Box 1229, Nantucket, MA 02554.

BY BUS

Public bus

The neat gray-and-maroon shuttle buses of the **Nantucket Regional Transit Authority** (NRTA) are handicap accessible, comfortable, and reasonable alternatives to the automobile. You can even take along your bike. The shuttles run as often as every ten minutes and cost 50¢ or $1 each way, depending on the route, but, alas, at present only from Memorial weekend to October 1. Demand may change that. Riders six and under or sixty-five and older go free. The shuttles also run from parking lots out of Town free to special events such as the county fair in late September. This convenience is noted in the newspaper.

For more information: 508-228-7025; nrta@nantucket.net; www.nantucket.net/ trans/nrta.

Hotel jitney

Several out-Island resorts have regular jitney (van) services for guests from their properties to the centrally located Visitor Services building on Federal Street. They also convey diners with advance reservations to their restaurants. The Nantucket Inn at the airport will take you to town. Point Breeze will take you to the ferry or the airport (NRTA bus stops outside the door). The Summer House has regular runs between its Sconset and Town properties. The Wauwinet has a twice-daily boat transfer as well as hourly buses. Ask what is available when you book a room or meal out of Town. Pickups at dock or airport are often complementary. The White Elephant not only supplies these but takes guests to the beaches, as well.

Carriage Rides

For brides and grooms or just the romantically inclined, nothing beats a horse and buggy in a 19th-century town.

Rosewood Carriage Co.: 508-228-9252; rosewood@gis.net; 8 Winn Ln., Nantucket, MA 02554.

BY CAR

Nantucket doesn't have a whole lot of roads outside the villages, and all are two lane. (At least road repairs are taken care of off-season, which is more than can be said for other country roads of Massachusetts.) Summer traffic and parking in Nantucket Town are horrendous, leading to periodic talk of turning the warren of shopping streets into a pedestrian-only district.

Bringing your own car

The friendly Islander turns into a grump at the sight of off-Island license plates. Bringing your own car is expensive ($316 round-trip in summer, not including driver or passengers) and requires reservations made far in advance. Permits to drive on conservation and beach land are by the year, not the day or week, and cost $85.

Consider the Cape Cod ferry terminals, where you can leave your car safely in adjacent parking lots for about $7.50 per day.

The only off-street parking in Nantucket Town is a public lot opposite the Town Pier. (Note: The A&P supermarket lot is *not* a public lot. Islanders reasonably think this should be left free for them to do their grocery shopping.)

If you positively must bring your own car, take a midweek ferry, not a weekend one.

Renting a car

Cars, vans, and four-wheel drives are available at the airport and in Town. Four-wheel drive vehicles come with beach permits. From mid-June until after Labor Day you will need a reservation.

Affordable Rentals: 508-228-3501, 877-235-3500; 6 S. Beach St., Nantucket, MA 02554 (next to Cook's Cycles)

Around Nantucket Car Rentals: 508-228-5666, 888-2289-5666, fax 508-228-5111 (Nantucket Memorial Airport)

Budget Rent-A-Car: 508-228-5666 (airport), 888-228-5666 (Mass. only), 800-527-0700 (national); budget@radix.net (cars, vans, four-wheel drives)

Don Allen Auto Service: 508-228-0134, 800-698-4666 (Mass. only), 800-258-4970 (national), fax 508-228-0297; 24 Polpis Rd., Nantucket, MA 02554.

NRTA Routes and Rates

The Nantucket Regional Transit Authority (NRTA) shuttle makes getting around Nantucket easy. The buses operate Memorial weekend through October 1, seven days a week, from approximately 7am to 11:30pm. Times may vary, so check, especially for the less-frequent runs. All are wheelchair-accessible and equipped with bicycle racks. Paratransit service is available with forty-eight-hour notice. Stops are identified by gray posts with red and maroon stripes. Maps of the routes showing all street names are available from the bus drivers, at the Visitor Services Center (25 Federal St., Nantucket, MA 02554), the Nantucket Chamber of Commerce office (48 Main St., Nantucket, MA 02554), or from the NRTA Office (508-228-7025, TDD 508-325-0788; NRTA@nantucket. net; www.nantucket.net/trans/NRTA; 22 Federal St., Nantucket, MA 02554). There are "Park and Ride" areas along the routes. You pay when you board, and exact change is required.

Routes and times are subject to change.

Routes

Mid-Island Loop (formerly South Loop): From Salem and Main Streets to Surfside Beach and return. 7am to 11:30pm every fifteen minutes.

Miacomet Loop: Washington Street (corner of Salem Street) to Fairground and Bartlett Roads and return, 7am to 11:20pm every twenty minutes.

Madaket Route: Broad Street (in front of the Peter Foulger Museum) to Madaket every thirty minutes. From Town, 7am to 10:30pm; from Madaket to Town, 7:30am to 11:15pm. Buses stop corner of Lower Main and Easy Streets at 10am, 11am, 5pm, 6pm.

Sconset via Polpis Road: From Washington and Main Streets every hour and twenty minutes, 7:30am to 10:30pm. From Sconset (in front of the Casino) on the hour, 8am to 11pm.

Sconset via Old South Road/Nobadeer Farm Road: From Washington and Main Streets every hour and twenty minutes, 7am to 11pm. From Sconset, 7:30am to 11:15pm. (Note: This bus does not service Nantucket Memorial Airport, but if you travel light, the airport is only three-tenths of a mile to the nearest stop on Old South Road, and there's a bench at the stop.)

Beaches: To Jetties and Surfside Beaches, call for schedule: 508-228-7025; nrta@nantucket.net

Rates

Mid-Island Loop	50¢ each way
Miacomet Loop	50¢ each way
Madaket Route	$1 each way

(50¢ between Crooked Lane and Town)
Sconset Routes $1 each way
(50¢ between the Rotary and Town)

Free: sixty-five and older, six and under.

Passes: $10 (three day), $15 (seven day), $30 (one month). Purchase at the Visitor Services Center, 25 Federal St., or the NRTA office, 22 Federal St., 508-228-7025,

TDD 508-325-0788. (Some businesses offer "Shuttle Special" shopping discounts to pass holders; ask for a list of current participants when you buy your pass.)

Riding the shuttle has proved so popular, routes will be expanded. They are also likely to run on slightly limited schedules in early June and late September if demand falls way off.

Hertz Rent-A-Car: 508-228-9421, 800-654-3131; PO Box 2476, Nantucket, MA 02584 (Nantucket Memorial Airport)

Nantucket Car Rental: 508-228-7474; 4 Broad St., Nantucket, MA 02554 (Steamboat Wharf)

Nantucket Jeep Rental: 508-228-1618; PO Box 117, Nantucket, MA 02554

Nantucket Windmill Auto Rental: (Specializes in four-wheel drive vehicles) 508-228-1227 (airport), 800-228-1227; 35 Macy's Ln., PO Box 1057, Nantucket, MA 02554

Thrifty Car Rental: 508-325-4616 (airport), 800-367-2277; www.thrifty.com; PO Box 225, Nantucket, MA 02554 (Nantucket Memorial Airport)

Young's Bicycle Shop & Car Rental: 508-228-1151; bicycles@nantucket.net; www.youngsbicycles.com; 6 Broad St., PO Box 1229, Nantucket, MA 02554

BY TAXI

Taxis can be found at the airport, in Town at the foot of Main Street beside the Pacific Club (the large brick building), and at the Steamship Authority, as well as being available on call and by appointment. Fares to all destinations are set, so taxis are not metered. Most companies have vans available. There are a number of taxis (often driver-owned), and here are a few to try:

Nantucket Town

A-1 Taxi: 508-228-3330; 15 Trotters Ln., Nantucket, MA 02554

Aardvark Taxi: 508-228-2223; 64 S. Shore Rd., Nantucket, MA 02554

All Point Taxi & Tours: 508-228-5779; 9 Solros Rd., Nantucket, MA 02554

Anne's Taxi (also Dave's, John's and Sally's): 508-228-8936; 15 Helen's Dr., Nantucket, MA 02554

Atlantic Cab: 508-228-1112 (vans only); 30 Macy's Ln., Nantucket, MA 02554

Around Nantucket: 508-325-5508; 57 Cato Ln., Nantucket, MA 02554

Betty's Tours & Taxi Service: 508-228-5786; betty@nantucket.net; PO Box 2755, Nantucket, MA 02584

Cranberry Transportation Service: 508-825-9793; benc@nantucket.net (limo)

Judy's Taxi: 508-228-7722, 5 Somerset Rd., Nantucket, MA 02554

Siasconset

Tippy's Taxi: 508-325-5555; 4 S. Pasture Ln., Nantucket, MA 02554

Is This Car Really Necessary?

Whenever an Islander was asked what they most of all wanted a visitor to know before coming to Nantucket, the reply was always, "Tell 'em to leave the car at home." Consider yourself told.

It's not such a bad idea, either. First, taking a car on the ferry is extremely expensive and in high season requires a reservation made months in advance. Once on-Island you find parking in Town is next to impossible, and, with possibly two exceptions, Nantucket lodgings do not come with parking lots attached nor will you get a reserved space on the street. (Recently overheard at one Nantucket B&B was the innkeeper on the phone, saying "Well, don't count on staying here!" to a potential guest who had the temerity to mention bringing an automobile.) Plus you don't even want to think about what driving on cobblestones can do to your car.

You can bring a bike on the ferry for $5, and there are bike and moped rental shops next to the wharf. Wide bike paths parallel every major road on the Island. The first bike trail went in more than a century ago to connect Nantucket Town and Sconset. Today the seven-mile ride on a perfectly maintained path takes no more than an hour.

Public transportation is excellent. The Nantucket Regional Transit Authority (NRTA) shuttle buses are sparkling new and run frequently on routes that cover the Island. The buses have bike racks on the front and are wheelchair-accessible. Rates are reasonable, especially for those six and under or sixty-five and over — in which case rides are free.

You will find taxi stands at all points of entry and at the Pacific Club Building on Lower Main Street. You can also telephone for pick-up. Rates are based on mileage, with flat fees for destinations like the airport.

If you absolutely, positively do need a car, rentals are available, including four-wheel drive vehicles for the beach with the necessary permit attached. (This must be purchased from the police department for your own private car.) The Nantucket Conservation Foundation issues its own permits for its properties from late May to mid-October at the Wauwinet Gate House, Wauwinet (508-228-0006; off-season, contact the foundation at 508-228-2884. Vehicles on the beach without valid permits are fined.

Out-of-Town resorts have their own free shuttles to the central Visitor Services Center at 25 Federal Street and to the docks. The Nantucket Inn is across from the airport but will take you to town whenever you like as well as to Surfside Beach. The Summer House runs guests back and forth between its Sconset and Town properties. The Wauwinet has an hourly jitney to town. Reserve for lunch or dinner at Topper's, the Wauwinet's award-winning restaurant, and you can get there and back to Town on the inn's own boat.

Don't overlook the convenience of using your own feet on this almost flat Island. Walk the bike paths. The exercise is tops, distances are reasonable, and there's a lot worth seeing up close.

The Pacific Club, surely the most historic taxi stand in the country. Built in 1765 as a marine counting house for the man who owned two of the three ships involved in the Boston Tea Party, it later became a private club for whaling captains who had sailed the Pacific Ocean.

Betty Lowry

BY FOOT

Whether you stroll, walk briskly, power walk, or jog, the bicycle paths are made for your exercise and enjoyment. Walk from Nantucket Town seven miles to Sconset, five miles to Madaket, or two and one-half miles to Surfside. The free biker's map available at any bike shop or tourist office will show you the way, and there are signs to the bike paths. If you're a tad out of shape, you can always try walking for a mile or so, then let the NRTA shuttle bus pick you up to continue or return. You can also take the shuttle to the end of the line, and do your further exploring by foot. Whether you stow a picnic in your backpack or find lunch at your destination, you'll agree this Island was made for walking.

BY TOUR

A guided tour of Nantucket, whether on foot or by van or bus, is a great way to get acquainted with the Island, either for a general survey or for a closer look at a specific interest.

You can get a good overview of Nantucket in just an hour and a half and spot places you'll want to visit at greater length. The tours are fun, and the guides are knowledgeable and witty. They answer questions and stop so you can take pictures. The vans are comfortable, air-conditioned, and pick you up at either your in-Town hotel, their designated parking area at the foot of Main Street, or the Visitor Services Center at 25 Federal Street. The price is right, too: generally $10 per person for the minimum tour, more for the half day. The walking tour of Nantucket Town is also recommended. Chances are you'll remember the gossip long after the architecture has been forgotten.

For more tours on specific topics, including self-conducted walking tours, see Chapter Four, *Culture,* Chapter Six, *Recreation,* and Chapter Seven, *Nature and the Environment.*

Adventure Tours of Nantucket (508-228-1686; www.nantucket.net/tours/
adventure; 37 Milk St., Nantucket, MA 02554) Pickup at all in-Town hotels;
one-and-one-half-hour tours from 8am to 5pm daily. A general survey of
Town and Island (not active adventure travel, despite the name).

All Point Tours & Taxi (508-325-6550; 9 Salros Rd., PO Box 3122, Nantucket, MA
02584) Excursions to Great Point by four-wheel drive and various tours to order.

Barrett's Tours (508-228-0174, 800-773-0174 [Eastern Mass.]; 20 Federal St.,
Nantucket, MA 02554) Air-conditioned buses with large windows. A family
company for more than 75 years, Barrett's has frequent tour departures
daily from their office at 20 Federal Street. Charter bus service for group
tours, clambakes, weddings, and the like are also available.

Betty's Tour & Taxi Service (508-228-5786; betty@nantucket.net; PO Box 2755,
Nantucket, MA 02584) Betty and her drivers give a good survey of the Island in
one-and-one-half-hour tours departing from Town at 10am, noon, and 2pm.

Gail's Tours (508-257-6557; www.nantucket.net/tours/gails; PO Box 3276,
Nantucket, MA 02584) Gail is a seventh-generation Islander who has her
thumb on the pulse of the Island. She drives a cranberry-red van that accom-
modates twelve and generally does three tours a day, at 10am, 1pm, and
3pm. Every year Gail is voted the Islanders' own favorite.

Great Point Natural History Tours (508-228-6799; PO Box 581, Nantucket, MA
02554) June to October, this three-hour guided tour by the Trustees of Reservations covers ten miles of barrier beach and a climb to the top of Great
Point lighthouse.

Robert Pitman Grimes Historic Nantucket Tours (508-228-9382; 22 Pleasant
St., Nantucket, MA 02554) Pit Grimes is a descendent of the original purchasers. His van takes up to eight, and his one-hour-and-forty-five-minute
tours start at 10am, 1pm, and 3pm. Private tours arranged, too.

The Maria Mitchell Association (508-228-9198; 3 Vestal St., Nantucket, MA
02554) Nature walks and bird walks led by naturalists on alternate days in
the summer, nature walks in the mid or low seasons. Special rates for children and seniors.

Nantucket Island Tours (508-228-0334; PO Box 581, Nantucket, MA 02554)
Guided tours departing from Straight Wharf are by a twenty-three-passenger
minibus and so can handle a group in comfort. Daily times are 10:45am,
12:15pm, 1:45pm, 3:30pm, 5pm. These are good backups if the small van tours
are already booked, and you can usually get on just by showing up. It's always
a good idea to call ahead in July and August. Tours operate May to October.

Nantucket Walking Tours with Dick Gardiner Roggeveen (508-221-0075; PO
Box 1827, Nantucket, MA 02554) Story-telling historian and twelfth-genera-
tion Nantucketer gives one-and-one-half-hour walking and talking tours
through Town. Call for times.

CHAPTER THREE

Forty Winks and a Nod

LODGING

T he term "charming" is much overused for describing the lodgings of Nantucket, but it is true you won't find impersonal hotel or motel rooms on the Island. Instead you will find inns, resorts, guesthouses, and bed & breakfasts where no two rooms are alike and where everyone will know your name after you've been there a day. You will sleep in four-poster and canopy-topped beds, probably under handmade quilts. You will step on rag rugs and stenciled floors, and wake to find yourself in another century.

Rob Benchley

Wide, sunny porches are a feature at the Nesbitt Inn in the heart of downtown.

Even in the bargain winter season or on a foggy day possible any time of year, Nantucket lodgings are cozy — many of the bedrooms have working fireplaces. So when the beach scene doesn't beckon, either by your choice or the weather's, your inn or B&B is the perfect base for a variety of other pleasures. Bring books. Go out to great dinners. Walk the dunes. Shop. Amble over to down-home events one night; take in a movie the next. The weekly auctions are entertaining as well as bargain productive.

Nantucket has no chain or high-rise hotels, and most of the inns are owner-run or at least owner-overseen. You never quite lose that sense of being a guest in someone's home. And you will find your hosts infinitely helpful, whether it's a matter of finding the perfect spot to dine or getting to the ferry on time. Inevitably, return visitors have been known to develop such profound loyalties to a particular lodging house that they are devastated when they find it fully occupied. Yet it is also fun to try a different place on every visit or even to divide a week between two.

Staying in a restored and converted 18th- or 19th-century house has aspects you may not anticipate. For example, the unexpectedly low rate quoted can mean a shared rather than a private bath. (The innkeeper will tell you this, but in your price-induced euphoria, it may go right past you.) You should also ask where the bathroom is — it could be on a different floor. Another caution: Narrow, steep stairs may be difficult to negotiate by anyone with an arthritic knee as well as impossible for a wheelchair. While most of the restaurants on Nantucket have ramps, most of the lodgings do not. At the end of this chapter we have listed the inns with handicap access, although these are more often than not in garden cottages rather than in the main building. (More about general handicap services is in Chapter Nine, *Information*.) Cottages available through renting agencies offer even greater selection.

Families coming for a few weeks or a full summer often find a fully equipped house the best answer to their needs. Seasonal rentals include beach houses that are generally heated only by fireplace or woodstove, but there are also winterized cottages of all sizes available in or near Town and in Sconset. Although they are not cheap, many off-season rentals fall into the category of reasonable when the cost is figured per night and per person. Unless otherwise noted, the larger inns have air-conditioning in summer.

Nantucket's reputation as a pricey destination is deserved, though the Island has far more available in the high-to-middle range than in the extremely expensive. There is a youth hostel but no campground. No overnight camping (including not spending the night in a tent, in your car, or on the beach in your sleeping bag) is permitted anywhere on the Island. Beaches and vehicles are monitored, and violators are fined $200.

In Nantucket, generally high season is mid-June to mid-September, plus Christmas Stroll Weekend. Midseason is mid-May to mid-June and mid-September through October. Low season or off-season is early spring, late fall, and winter. It's a good idea, though, to ask your potential innkeeper for his or her specific interpretation of these sometimes loosely applied terms.

Off-season rates drop by 50 percent and much more. Midseason and off-season packages are loaded with extras, from ferry and air tickets to dinners out and passes to events. Furthermore, off-season and particularly midseason includes the vibrant spring and the color-intensive autumn as well as winter. Wine and film festivals and other events occur outside those overcrowded months of July and August, and while Christmas Stroll Weekend is high season, the days before and after are low season (see Chapter Four, "Special Events"). The lights twinkle as brightly; the shop windows are as full of temptations; the holiday-decorated historic houses are open to the public for free nearly every other day for the month. There are even sales in the shops before Christmas to clear out the last bits of summer merchandise (but who's to know when the gift is unwrapped?), and after Christmas prices drop again. And there you are, smugly paying $65 a night for a room that is listed at $215.

Be aware that the summer crowds can seem to fill every available room, and the Stroll certainly requires bookings far in advance. Also, since lodgings are small on Nantucket (only two establishments have one hundred rooms), you may not find space in your first choice or even your second.

However, it was worse — much worse — in the 1870s when tourism first came to Nantucket, primarily because the last thing the Island was expecting was a sudden influx of visitors. The Island was then in a post-war, post-whaling major economic slump, mourning its loss of men to the gold fields of California and Alaska. Meanwhile, the Industrial Revolution and general Northeast mainland prosperity had created both new attitudes and a new kind of traveler. Not many Islanders knew or cared about this, or that seawater bathing was approaching the status of fad with the rich and restless of New York and Boston. Nor did they put this into any perspective with their own miles of clean and empty beaches.

The first portent was the whistle of a train beginning to run between Boston and Cape Cod. Once those passengers settled in on the Cape, wasn't it logical to make a day's sail "way off-shore" for an Island outing? In less than a decade, the Island that had lost two-thirds of its population to forces beyond its control was scrambling to respond to a demand no one had remotely foreseen.

In some cases Islanders overreacted. Land speculation deals built summer resort hotels too fast and none too well. However, in the long run, the influx of visitors also meant the fixing up of old and historic structures that might conceivably become restaurants or provide shelter to off-Island guests, plus the reopening of boardinghouses. Homeowners with empty bedrooms gladly and uncharacteristically offered them to total strangers. As Nantucketers began paying attention to demand, hospitality — the industry that was to replace whaling as the Island's chief source of revenue — fell into place, and the Island's lodgings, from quaint to posh, opened their doors.

NANTUCKET LODGING NOTES

Not every lodging establishment on the Island is listed here. You can also contact the Visitor Services & Information Bureau (508-228-0925; 25 Federal St., Nantucket, MA 02554) and tell them your needs. This helpful office keeps track of vacancies as reported by innkeepers, including those occurring at the last minute. After hours (6pm in summer; 5:30pm the rest of the year) a list of rooms still possibly available for the night is posted on the door. To help your advance planning, you can also find prices and pictures on the Internet: www.nantucketlodging.org and www.nantucket.net/lodging.

RATES

The price range given for each lodging in this chapter is based on a two-person, one-night stay during the high season, generally Memorial Day through Labor Day; sometimes the season extends to mid-October plus Christmas Stroll Weekend. (Cottages and houses may rent only by the week or longer.)

Nearly all rates drop dramatically in the winter, and even beach resorts that close for half the year will adjust their rates down in spring and fall, as well. At these times there may even be a further unadvertised discount on the second or third night, midweek, or weekend. Your automobile club membership may also give you 10 percent off the top. Always ask whether any special prices or packages are in effect during or near the dates of your planned visit. By adjusting your schedule, you may receive tantalizing extras such as museum passes, theater tickets, dining-around meals, and even free travel on the ferries and airlines.

It's true that rates here are higher overall than at many resort areas; however, you will find some pleasant surprises at checkout time when you see what is *not* added to your bill. For example, local telephone calls are often free and so is tennis-court time. Where it is available, off-street parking is free. Afternoon tea and cookies, wine and cheese, or hors d'oeuvres are complimentary. Gratuities are generally left to your discretion.

Nearly always, breakfasts are included. Incidentally, we have used the term "continental" to describe the juice-and-muffin breakfast with coffee or tea, "expanded continental" if cereal and fresh fruit are offered, too. These light breakfasts can get quite elaborate, as owners strive to please while staying within the bounds of health-department regulations, which permit only licensed commercial kitchens to prepare eggs or grilled foods. Full hot breakfasts include eggs, ham or bacon, pancakes, and all the trimmings.

All establishments renting more than three rooms are licensed by the Town of Nantucket and must collect 9.7 percent state and local room occupancy taxes. Even this is lower than many comparable resort regions.

While prices quoted here are for high-season double occupancy and per room, there may also be single rates for double rooms and single rooms, as well. Additional charges may be levied for the addition of another adult or for a rollaway bed in the room. Suites are significantly more expensive.

Lodging Price Ranges

Very Inexpensive	Under $50
Inexpensive	$50–$75
Moderate	$75–$150
Expensive	$150–$250
Very Expensive	Over $250

Credit cards are abbreviated as follows:
AE   American Express
CB   Carte Blanche
D   Discover Card
DC   Diners Club
MC   MasterCard
V   Visa

MINIMUM STAY

Minimum-stay requirements of two to four nights in summer, over holidays, and on weekends throughout the year are commonplace, but even so, finding a place for a single night is not impossible. Last-minute cancellations do occur, and in the low seasons single nights may be reserved in advance. For a list of single-night availability, call the Visitor Services Information Bureau, 508-228-0925.

DEPOSIT CANCELLATION AND REFUNDS

Since there is no single rule on the Island, you should ask about cancellation and refund policies when you reserve. General policies are as follows:

For three nights or fewer, full prepayment is expected when booking or within seven days. For four or more consecutive nights, a 50 percent deposit within seven days and balance on arrival.

Deposit (less service fee, usually 10 percent) will usually be refunded if notice of cancellation is received at least fifteen days before expected arrival.

On shorter notice, deposits (less 10 percent service fee) may be refunded if the room is rebooked for the entire cancellation period.

PRIVATE RENTALS AND RESERVATION SERVICES

Private Rentals

Cottages and houses are rented privately through advertisements in newspapers and from nearly all Island real estate agents as well as by rental services. Guesthouses may also have separate cottages on (and off) the main property (see listings of individual lodgings). Rents are high during the summer but often reasonable to low in winter. Privately rented cottages are not subject to state and local taxes. A number of year-round homeowners who use their houses only in summer leave them managed by realtors for the balance of the year and are happy to have them occupied by responsible renters. Note that the demand for house-sitting jobs often exceeds the supply, so you should get your request and deposit down as far in advance as possible. You might also ask to be put on a waiting list.

Here are some rentals and rental services that cover the Island:

Corkish Cottages (508-228-5686; www.nantucket.net/lodging/corkishcottages; 320 Polpis Rd., Nantucket, MA 02554) "The family pet is welcome if he doesn't chase deer" tells a lot about the three-bedroom country cottages each on ten private acres. Driving time is given as fifteen minutes from Town and five from the beach. Open Memorial Day–Oct. 10. Expensive.

Country Village Rentals (508-228-8840, 800-599-7368; info@cvandr.com; www. cvandr.com; 4 Cherry St., Nantucket, MA 02554) Very expensive properties with gourmet cooks, masseuse, drivers, and maid service available. Specializes in pre-1890 and contemporary country homes both as rentals and for weddings and special events in places such as Nantucket, St. Barths, and Stowe, Vermont.

Deb Mar Cottages (203-255-3192; 16 Meadow Court, Fairfield CT 06430) Four two- and three- bedroom cottages in different locations on the Island but all with cable TV, outdoor showers, and grills. Expensive.

Lowell Cottage (508-228-1182; Main St. at New Lane; PO Box 1054, Nantucket, MA 02584) Ida Lowell rents her one-bedroom (queen-size bed) completely equipped cottage only by the week (Saturday–Saturday, June–Sept.) or for holiday weekends off-season. Honeymooners get flowers and champagne. The cottage was completely renovated in 1995 and is at the quiet top of Main Street, one-half mile from the center of Town. Lawns, trees, and shrubs give it privacy. Ida once worked with Margaret Harwood at the Maria Mitchell observatory and can discuss variable stars and other fascinating topics as well as answering less cosmic questions about the Island. No smoking or pets. No credit cards. Moderate.

The Maury People (508-228-1881, 508-2257-4050;info@maurypeople.com; www.maurypeople.com; 35 Main St., Nantucket, MA 02554) Nantucket and Sconset. This is the Island's Sotheby's International affiliate. Various properties and prices, expensive to very expensive.

Nantucket Whaler (508-228-6597, 800-462-6882; 8 N. Water St; PO Box 1337, Nantucket MA 02554) This 19th-century guesthouse offers ten one- and two-bedroom air-conditioned suites and studios with kitchens, maid service, and private baths and entrances. Some also have private decks, fireplaces, and harbor views. Rates are very expensive (breakfast not included) and are by the night or by the week. No smoking; no pets; children over 12.

Old North Wharf Company (508-228-6071; PO Box 187, Nantucket MA 02554) These are seven gray-shingle cottages on the water that will look so fabulous in your Christmas card photo. Expensive.

Tristram's Landing (508-228-0359, 800-442-NANT; 5 S. Cambridge St., Nantucket MA 02554; in Madaket) The Tristram's Group Inc. has fully equipped all-season condo units and homes, some with private beach and fresh pond waterfront with biking, fishing, canoeing, and tennis courts. One- or two-week rentals are preferred. Expensive.

Westbrook Associates (508-257-4669; www.westbrookrealestate.com; PO Box

262, Siasconset MA 02564) Check with them early for rental possibilities, primarily in Sconset. This is a high-demand village, and rates are generally expensive to very expensive.

Wharf Cottages (508-228-4620, 800-ISLANDS; www.nantucketislandresorts.com; New Whale St., PO Box 1139, Nantucket, MA 02554) These fully equipped cottages on the docks in the Nantucket Boat Basin are managed by Nantucket Island Resorts, which also manages **The White Elephant** on Easton Street and **Harbor House.** They have daily maid service and come as studios or with one, two, or three bedrooms. Expensive to very expensive.

Reservation Services

All Seasons Vacation Network (info@weneedavacation.com)

Faraway Island Vacations (508-228-3828; vacation@nantucket.net; www.nantucket.net/lodging/faraway; PO Box 478, Nantucket, MA 02554)

Heaven Can Wait (508-257-4000; fax 413-473-5295; PO Box 622, Siasconset MA 02564) Honeymoon planning by expert Dorothy Vollans.

Nantucket Accommodations (508-228-9559; nanacc@nantucket.net; www.nantucketaccommodations.com; 4 Dennis Dr., Nantucket, MA 02554)

Nantucket & Martha's Vineyard Reservations (508-693-7200, 800-649-5671 [Mass. only]; www.mvreservations.com; PO Box 1322, Vineyard Haven, MA 02568) Year-round service.

Nantucket Concierge (508-228-8400, fax 508-228-8422, concierg@nantucket.net; www.nantucketconcierge.com; PO Box 1257, Nantucket, MA 02554) Carolyn Leigh Hills has a full range of services as well as lodging reservations. She will book your boat, carriage ride, charter fishing, golf, health and fitness programs, walking tours, bus tours, massages, whale watching, weddings, and more.

Nantucket Vacation Rentals (508-228-3131, 800-228-4070, fax 508-228-9476; www.nantucketrealestate.com; 17 N. Beach St., PO Box 426, Nantucket, MA 02554)

Real Estate Rentals

Compass Rose Real Estate (508-325-5500; compass@nantucket.net; 25 Dulces Rd., PO Box 935, Nantucket, MA 02554)

Country Village Rentals & Real Estate (508-228-8840, 800-599-7368; info@cvrandr.com; www.cvrandr.com; 4 Cherry St., Nantucket, MA 02554)

Jordan Real Estate (508-228-4449; www.jordanre.com; 8 Federal St., Nantucket, MA 02554)

Lee Real Estate (508-325-5800, 800-495-4198; leerealestate.com; 58 Main St., Nantucket, MA 02554)

Nantucket Real Estate Co. (508-228-2530, 800-228-4070, fax 508-228-9476; 17 N. Beach St., PO Box 426, Nantucket, MA 02554)

Sconset Real Estate (508-257-6335, 800-662-8260, winter: 508-228-1815, fax 508-

228-8110; www.coffinrealestate.com; PO Box 122, Siasconset, MA 02564; at Post Office Square)

Tamzin Realty (508-228-3155; tamzin@nantucket.net; 8 Bayberry Ln., Nantucket, MA 02554)

LODGING IN NANTUCKET TOWN

The Roberts House Inn, in the middle of the historic district along Centre Street, is one of the "Accommodations Et Al" properties.

Betty Lowry

ACCOMMODATIONS ET AL
Owners: Sara and Michael O'Reilly.
508-228-0600,
fax 508-325-4046,
800-588-0086;
RHInn@aol.com.
www.robertshouseinn.com.
11 India St. (PO Box 1436, Nantucket, MA 02554)
Corner Centre St.
Open: Year-round.
Price: Moderate to Very Expensive.
Credit Card: AE, D, MC, V.
Special Features: Restaurant; smoking and nonsmoking buildings; fireplaces; off-season packages; continental breakfast.

This trio of restored B&B inns plus a cottage (**The Roberts House Inn, The Manor House Inn, The Meeting House Inn, Linden House Cottage**) are all right in the middle of the historic district along Centre Street, with Roberts House Inn the pivot and the café/restaurant in the Meeting House Inn. Although the furnishings and ambiance are strictly 19th century, even to the fireplaces in the Manor House Inn, you will still have cable TV, air-conditioning, hairdryers, coffee makers, refrigerators, irons, ironing boards, and room telephones. No two rooms are alike, so you should be specific: king, queen, or twin beds? View? Ultraquiet? Suite? You will find the occasional Jacuzzi as well as a few shared baths. The O'Reillys take pride in their family-owned-and-operated enterprise — six children are, have been, or will be actively involved in the hospitality business. Change is the norm, and a new cottage or inn can be added at any time. Their packages, such as the

"Romantic Getaway" in mid- and off-seasons, are good bargains. See also the Periwinkle Guest House & Cottage.

The eleven guest rooms at the Anchor Inn are all named for Nantucket whaleships.

Rob Benchley

ANCHOR INN
Owners: Charles and Ann
 Balas.
508-228-0072; anchorin@
 nantucket.net.
www.anchor-inn.net.
66 Centre St., PO Box 387,
 Nantucket, MA 02554
Next to the Old North
 Church.
Open: Apr.–Dec.
Price: Moderate to
 Expensive.
Credit Cards: AE, MC, V.
Special Features:
 Nonsmoking; garden
 patio; continental
 breakfast; no pets; no
 children.

You may have read about the Anchor Inn in the 1950s book *Innside Nantucket* by the Gilbreths (the *Cheaper by the Dozen* folks), who wrote about the agonies of running a B&B. Ann and Charles Balas are a different sort and obviously enjoy their innkeeping life to the fullest. The white clapboard house with black trim next to the Old North Church was built in 1806 for Archaelus Hammond, captain of the whaleship *Cyrus* and the first man to kill a whale in the Pacific Ocean. Each of the eleven guest rooms is named for a Nantucket whaleship. Further expression of the inn's comfort and congeniality are the fireplace burning in the common room, and the shelves of books and games. Queen-size beds for double or single occupancy. All have private baths (most with shower only), phones (with voice mail), TV, air-conditioning, and hair dryers.. There are window boxes full of flowers, and a neat pocket garden is tucked behind a white picket fence. Breakfast (Charles is a whiz of a muffin baker) is served on the sunny enclosed porch accompanied by classical music, and, suitably fortified, you can walk to everything in Town from here.

THE BEACHSIDE AT NANTUCKET

Manager: Mary Malavase.
508-228-2241, 800-322-4433,
  fax 508-228-2241;
  info@thebeachside.com.
www.thebeachside.com.
30 N. Beach St., Nantucket,
  MA 02554.
Open: Apr.–Dec.
Price: Expensive to Very
  Expensive.
Credit Cards: AE, D, DC,
  MC, V.
Special Features: Parking;
  restaurant; meeting
  rooms; pool; packages.

With ninety rooms, Beachside is one of the Island's larger lodging establishments. It is also as close as it comes here to a motel — if only because there is ample parking on the property — though it is definitely more complete resort than motel, and a friendly staff provides a country inn atmosphere. A short walk to Town, the inn is also near beaches and harbor. It has its own outdoor heated swimming pool (rare on Nantucket) and is next to public tennis courts. If a traditional B&B is too cozy for you, the Beachside will probably be perfect.

BRANT POINT INN AND ATLANTIC MAINSTAY

Owners: Peter and Thea
  Kaizer.
508-228-5442/5451;
  bpi@nantucket.net.
6 N. Beach St. (Brant Point),
  8 N. Beach St. (Atlantic
  Mainstay), Nantucket,
  MA 02554.
Open: Apr.–Dec.
Price: Moderate.
Credit Cards: AE, MC, V.
Special Features:
  Nonsmoking; working
  fireplaces; off-street
  parking; continental
  breakfast; children over 6.

Captain Peter Kaizer, an enthusiastic fisherman, will be happy to arrange for any kind of modern boating expedition. However, if your idea of seafaring is to walk down to Brant Point lighthouse to watch the yacht races, then look for shells on the beach or to climb up to the Brant Point Inn's own roof walk and enjoy the harbor view, that's ok too. These two side-by-side guesthouses are traditional post-and-beam with wide-plank floors, and all rooms are queen or twin bedded. There's also a suite with its own kitchen, an especially nice arrangement for families.

THE CARRIAGE HOUSE

Owners: Jeanne McHugh
  and H. B. Jackson.
508-228-0326.
5 Rays Court, Nantucket,
  MA 02554.
Open: Year-round.
Price: Moderate.
Credit Cards: None.
Special Features:
  Nonsmoking; expanded
  continental breakfast.

Jeanne and her son Haziel jointly operate this seven room Victorian B&B in the historic district. The inn has been in the family for twenty-five years, and the owners live on the premises. In 1865 it truly was a carriage house and so sits on a quiet lane paved with crushed clamshells that winds behind Main Street. There's a "Nantucket Loving Steps" entrance (those double staircases are also known as "Friendship Steps," depending, perhaps, on your attitude as you meet at the top); sheltered patio; and a common room with cable TV and books. Each of the queen, double, and twin bedrooms has a private bath or shower. Incidentally,

Courtesy of the Carriage House

The Carriage House Bed & Breakfast, built in 1865, is on a lane paved with crushed clamshells.

small children are welcome here, and there's space for a rollaway in one of the queen bedrooms.

CENTRE STREET INN
Owners: Sheila and Fred
 Heap.
508-228-0199, 800-298-0199;
 inn@nantucket.net.
www.centrestreetinn.com.
78 Centre St., Nantucket,
 MA 02554.
Open: Year-round.
Price: Moderate to
 Expensive.
Credit Cards: AE, MC, V.
Special Features:
 Nonsmoking; expanded
 continental breakfast;
 garden patio.

Among the many nice things about this 18th-century house turned comfortable B&B inn are the on-the-wall paintings in many of the rooms. No two of the thirteen rooms are alike, by the way, and they range from grand master bedrooms with four-posters and fireplaces to cute little garret singles tucked up under the eaves and sharing the baths. The house was built as a home by Peter Folger — "One of many Peter Folgers," Sheila says. This one was a whale-oil trader and undoubtedly another cousin to Benjamin Franklin. When hospitality replaced whaling in the Nantucket economy, it became one of the Island's early boardinghouses. A previous owner called it Holiday Inn and named each room for a holiday. The Heaps kept the room names but changed the inn's when they bought and renovated it in 1994. There's a welcoming garden to one side and a welcoming Austrian terrier named Murphy Brown waiting just inside the door.

CHESTNUT HOUSE
Owners: Jeannette and Jerry Carl.
508-228-0049.
www.chestnuthouse.com.
3 Chestnut St., Nantucket, MA 02554.
Open: Year-round.
Price: Moderate; Expensive for cottage.
Credit Cards: AE, MC, V.
Special Features: Nonsmoking; no pets; refrigerators; breakfast at nearby restaurant in season; cottage.

Two artists own this 1850 home-cum-inn, and it shows. The hooked rugs are Jerry's work, and the paintings are Jeannette's. They both get credit for the subtle use of color inside and the orchestrated flower garden outside. There are four suites, one double bedroom, and a two-bedroom cottage with a Murphy bed in the sitting room. You can choose from king, queen, or twin beds, and all rooms have refrigerators. The location in the Historic District couldn't be better. The Carls own (or, rather, are owned by) two cats, who naturally do not deign to accept other pets.

CLIFFSIDE BEACH CLUB
General Manager: Robert Currie.
508-228-0618, 800-932-9645, fax 508-325-4735.
www.cliffsidebeach.com.
46 Jefferson Ave., PO Box 449, Nantucket, MA 02554.
West of Jetties Beach at end of N. Beach St.
Open: Memorial Day–Oct. 15.
Price: Very Expensive.
Credit Cards: AE.
Special Features: No pets; private beachfront; health club and spa; smoking; refrigerators; expanded continental breakfast.

It comes as no surprise to learn that this luxury hotel was a beach club named Conrad's Beach in 1924, a private club in 1949, and a hotel in 1970. It was completely renovated in 1988 and crisply redecorated in 1999, yet the original aura of pre-Depression opulence lingers. The lobby is large and airy, with white antique wicker furniture and collectible quilts shown to advantage on the slopes of the cathedral ceiling. A fireplace takes the chill off when necessary. The walls throughout are white to match the sand, while deep blue-greens pick up the color of the sea. In fact, most of the twenty-eight units have ocean views. Some of the nice old woods used by the Nantucket craftsmen who worked on the inn and its furnishings were reclaimed from vintage Beach Club changing rooms and others from the Old South Station in Boston. The newest suites, in an area bordered by large dunes, are two-story. There are also studios, one three-bedroom apartment, and a cottage. The Galley Restaurant is next door to the Beach Club. A full health club and spa is located in a new building. No additional charge for use by guests.

COBBLESTONE INN
Owners: Robin and Keith Yankow
508-228-1987, fax 508-228-6698;
cobble@nantucket.net.

The word "cozy" wasn't invented to describe the Cobblestone Inn just as "delicious" didn't come into being just for Robin's homemade granola, but both pinpoint the essence of the Cobblestone Inn. Built in 1725 and in the heart of the Historic District,

www.nantucket.net/lodging
/cobblestoneinn.
5 Ash St., Nantucket, MA
02554.
Open: Year-round.
Price: Moderate to
Expensive.
Credit Cards: MC, V
Special Features:
nonsmoking; no pets;
some room refrigerators;
expanded continental
breakfast; complimentary
drinks and snacks all
day.

**CORNER HOUSE CIRCA
1790**
Owners: John and Sandy
Knox-Johnston.
508-228-1530; info@corner
housenantucket.com.
www.cornerhousenan
tucket.com.
49 Centre St., PO Box 1828,
Nantucket, MA 02554.
Open: Apr. 1–Dec. 15.
Price: Moderate.
Credit Cards: AE, MC, V.
Special Features:
Nonsmoking; no pets;
expanded continental
breakfast; afternoon tea;
two-room suite with
kitchenette

EASTON HOUSE
Owners: Cyril and Judith
Ross.
508-228-2759;eastonhse
@aol.com.
www.eastonhouse.com.
17 N. Water St., PO Box
1033, Nantucket, MA
02554.
Open: Mid-June–mid-Oct.
Price: Moderate to
Expensive.
Credit Cards: None.
Special Features:
Nonsmoking; garden
cottage.

it's tucked away on a quiet street you might not even know is there. Never mind. It's only five minutes from the ferry and all the shops and restaurants of Town. This is a good choice for a home away from home.

Seventeen rooms are available in three different 18th- and 19th-century lodges that, as Sandy explains, have been "brought very gently into the 20th century." Rooms still have the original wide-board pine floors, paneling, and fireplaces to set off the English and American antique furnishings. Most rooms have television and some refrigerators, too, but you'll sleep under down comforters in canopy and tall post beds. A screened porch overlooks the garden and garden terrace. Sandy's interest in historic preservation (she's on the Island's architectural review board) and John's British-colonial background (he grew up in northern Rhodesia and Kenya) are clues to the authentic colonial touches and the downright necessity for a complete afternoon tea.

This ten-room B&B dates from 1812, though the Oriental rugs, canopied beds, down comforters and line-dried sheets you'll find here today are much more elegant and comfortable than anything dreamed of by its earlier residents. Easton House is a scant three minutes from Main Street, but dropping into a lawn chair in the private backyard can transport you far from the bustle of summer in Town. There's also a garden cottage that sleeps two and is handicap accessible.

EIGHTEEN GARDNER ST. INN

Manager: Beth Dupont.
508-228-1155, 800-435-1450;
b&b@nantucket.net.
www.18Gardner.com.
18 Gardner St., Nantucket,
MA 02554.
Open: Year-round.
Price: Moderate to Very
Expensive.
Credit Cards: AE, MC, V.
Special Features:
Nonsmoking; working
fireplaces; room
refrigerators;
complimentary use of
bicycles; parking;
packages; expanded
continental breakfast;
afternoon tea; garden.

The inn's main building was built in 1835, and the antique and reproduction furnishings including four-poster and canopied beds are right to the period. There's a roof walk, friendship steps, and a garden. It was built for a whaler with the inspiring name of Captain Robert Joy (honeymooners love this). Some of the seventeen rooms have refrigerators; some, working fireplaces. King, queen, and twin beds are available, and rooms have private baths, air-conditioning, and TVs. The suites are especially good for families, and you won't be surprised to learn the inn has been named "Best B&B" more than once by Island and off-Island publications. Bicycles are provided for you — a nice touch.

GREY LADY AND THE BOATHOUSE

Owner: Seamus Lafferty.
508-228-9552, 800-245-9552;
greylady@nantucket.net.
www.nantucket.net/lodging
/greylady.
34 Center St., PO Box 1292,
Nantucket, MA 02554.
Corner of Hussey St.
Open: Apr.–Dec.
Price: Moderate.
Credit Cards: AE, D, MC, V.
Special Features: Pets and
children welcome; room
refrigerators; on-street
parking permits,
cottages.

Only eight units are in this 1850 guesthouse, some of them bright sunny suites with kitchenettes and decks. No breakfast is served, but even if you don't have a kitchenette, you are near some of Nantucket's best breakfast restaurants. Family reunions have rented the whole house.

The same owner also offers several cottages including The Boat House Cottage, a two-story gray-shingle cottage with a Franklin stove on Old North Wharf, the residential wharf between Steamboat Wharf and Straight Wharf. The Boat House is open year-round and falls into the Very Expensive category.

HARBOR HOUSE

Owner: Stephen and Jill
Karp.
508-228-1500, 800-
ISLANDS;
resinfo@nantucket.net.
S. Beach St., PO Box 1048,
Nantucket, MA 02554.
Open: Apr.–Dec.
Price: Very Expensive.
Credit Cards: AE, MC, V.

This is a full-service resort right in the historic downtown and very near the ferry dock. The heated outdoor swimming pool, boutiques, meeting facilities, dining room, and lounge with nightly entertainment keep things lively. It's so family-friendly, it has a "Happy Harbor Club" for five- to thirteen-year-olds in the summer and provides baby-sitting in the evening. The inn has been welcoming guests for a century, beginning with those who shipped in and out of the harbor during

Rob Benchley

Convenient to the ferry docks, Harbor House has been welcoming guests for a century.

Special Features:
  Restaurant; swimming pool; full children's program; pickup at Steamship Authority Terminal; packages.

Nantucket's great whaling days. Now with 109 rooms and townhouse accommodations, the Harbor House can arrange any activity from whale watching to an afternoon of tennis or golf. If you must stay in touch, everything the business traveler needs is at hand. If you're planning a corporate meeting, they'll fit that in, too.

HAWTHORN HOUSE
Owners: Diane and Mitchell Carl.
508-228-1468 (phone and fax);
  hhguests@nantucket.net.
www.hawthornhouse.com.
2 Chestnut St., Nantucket, MA 02554.
Between Federal and Centre Sts.
Open: Year-round.
Price: Moderate.
Credit Cards: MC, V.
Special Features:
  Nonsmoking; no pets; most with room refrigerators; breakfast vouchers for nearby restaurants; studio apartment next door.

This nice Nantucket home was built in 1849, just as gold was being discovered in California and the exodus of the Island was about to begin. It's been an inn for some sixty years. There are nine guest rooms — seven with private bath — and "Cubbyhole," a cottage that sleeps two. You can have king, queen, full, or twin beds. Single rates are available in the mid- and low seasons. The house is furnished with antiques and handmade quilts. Paintings by local artists hang on the walls.

HOUSE OF THE SEVEN GABLES
Owner: Sue Walton.

Unlike most Island lodgings, this was never a private home. It was, in fact, built in the 1880s as an annex for the posh Sea Cliff Inn and so is a lit-

508-228-4706.
32 Cliff Rd., Nantucket, MA
02554.
Open: Year-round.
Price: Moderate to
Expensive.
Credit Cards: AE, MC, V.
Special Features:
Nonsmoking; no pets;
continental breakfast.

tle beyond the center of Town, overlooking the mouth of the harbor and facing north across Nantucket Sound. The architecture is unabashedly Victorian, not at all what you would expect on Nantucket. The illusion of an earlier day continues: breakfast served in your room (flowers on the tray, of course) by a chambermaid; late-19th-century antiques; an authentic parlor. Eight of the ten rooms have private baths, and the beds are king, queen, or full-size as you prefer. Be sure and say hello to the cats.

HUSSEY HOUSE – 1795
Owner: Mrs. H. Johnson.
508-228-0747.
15 N. Water St., PO Box
552, Nantucket, MA
02554.
Open: May–Oct.
Price: Moderate to
Expensive.
Credit Cards: None.
Special Features:
Nonsmoking; off-street
parking; room
refrigerators; garden;
continental breakfast;
weekly rates available

A fireplace is in every room, just as Uriel Hussey probably ordered when he built the house in 1795 (though the bedroom hearths are no longer in use). The rooms are named for early Nantucketers, and Mrs. Johnson, a former teacher who has owned and operated the inn for more than twenty-five years, can tell you all about them. Though the inn is only three minutes' walk from the steamer landing, it has an atmosphere of country tranquillity. There's a pleasant garden, bike racks, off-street parking, and a choice of queen or double beds. Families are welcome here.

THE INDIA HOUSE
Owner: Charles W. Kesser
III.
508-228-9043; india@
nantucket.net.
37 India St., Nantucket, MA
02554.
One block north of Main St.
Open: Apr.–Dec.
Price: Moderate.
Credit Cards: AE, D, MC,
V.
Special Features:
Restaurant; garden café;
nonsmoking; gourmet
breakfast.

The eleven very different guest rooms of India House always seem to be occupied, a tribute to the friendly ambiance of the place and its good value as well as historic authenticity. The innkeeper, who has gone from a life of corporate finance to running an inn and playing piano and bass, sets the flexible style. The inn itself was built as a home in 1803 by a man who made his money in the East India trade and is the second-oldest operating inn on Nantucket. All rooms have private baths, and some have working fireplaces, double-canopy beds, early-19th-century pine antiques, and ceiling fans.

The gourmet breakfast is served in the outdoor garden café and includes freshly squeezed orange juice, homemade breads and muffins, plus entrées such as blueberry-stuffed French toast, pumpkin pancakes, tenderloin tips with herbed scrambled eggs, and poached eggs with smoked salmon and caviar.

THE BREAKERS

Owners: Stephen and Jill
  Karp.
508-325-1142,
  800-ISLANDS;
  resinfo@nantucket.net.
www.nantucketislandresor
  ts.com.
42 Easton, PO Box 1139,
  Nantucket, MA 02554.
Open: May-Oct.
Price: Very Expensive.
Credit Cards: AE, MC, V.
Special Features:
  Nonsmoking; no pets;
  room service; full
  breakfast served in room.

When the Karps take over a property, they have luxury in mind. These twenty-six rooms on the waterfront are no exception. Some terraces, some balconies, wine and cheese in the common room every afternoon, room service—it's all there.

In 1845 Jared Coffin built a mansion for his fussy wife. In 1963 it became the Jared Coffin House in 1963. Now it's the Town's most famous hostelry.

Rob Benchley

JARED COFFIN HOUSE

Manager: John Cowden.
508-228-2400,
  800-248-2405; jchouse@
  nantucket.net.
www.jaredcoffinhouse.com.
29 Broad St., PO Box 1580,
  Nantucket, MA 02554.
Open: Year-round.
Price: Moderate to Very
  Expensive.
Credit Cards: AE, CB, D,
  DC, MC, V.
Special Features: Two
  restaurants; winter
  packages.

The Jared Coffin House is such a part of Nantucket history that visitors are sometimes surprised to find that it's a real place. It is actually six places: sixty guest rooms spread through a collection of six historic buildings, having expanded from the original brick mansion built in 1845 for the fussy wife of wealthy shipowner Jared Coffin. When she flounced off to Boston two years later, the elegant home became Ocean House, a hotel owned by the Nantucket Steamship Company. The hotel changed hands many times, with subsequent owners adding to the original structure. Finally it was purchased and restored by the preservation-minded Nantucket Historical Trust, reopening in 1963 as the Jared Coffin House.

Owners Phil and Peg Read brought it to its present status as such a symbol of Island hospitality that its façade is reproduced on souvenirs from tea tins to T-shirts. Each room is distinctive, and queen, full, and twin beds (most of them canopied) are available. Be warned: Reservations for holiday weekends are often made a year in advance, and wedding receptions and corporate meetings need to be scheduled months ahead. On the other hand, winter packages offer great bargains.

MARTIN HOUSE INN
Owner/Innkeeper: Debbie
  Wasil.
508-228-0678; martinn@
  nantucket.net.
www.nantucketnet/lodging
  /martinn.
61 Centre St., PO Box 743,
  Nantucket, MA 02554.
Open: Year-round.
Price: Moderate to
  Expensive.
Credit Cards: AE, MC, V.
Special Features:
  Nonsmoking; expanded
  continental breakfast.

This is a beautiful old house, the sort of place any ship's captain would have dreamed about as he stood on some faraway atoll. It was built in 1803 and became an inn during the great need for visitor housing in the 1920s. On a foggy morning, when the fire burns cheerfully on the hearth and there is the scent of muffins just out of the oven, it's tempting to forego even the pleasures of the Historic District.

Martin House has thirteen bedrooms, nine with private baths, and you have your choice of queen, double, or twin beds. Two doubles or two twins sharing a bathroom is a nice arrangement for families. There's even a veranda for idle summer afternoons. Debbie also owns the seven-bedroom Centerboard Guest House next door (centerbo@nantucket. net), an 1886 Victorian facing on Chestnut Street.

THE NESBITT INN
Innkeepers: Dolly & Nobby
  Noblit.
508-228-0156, 508-228-2446.
21 Broad St., Nantucket,
  MA 02554.
Open: Mar. 1–Jan. 2.
Price: Inexpensive.
Credit Cards: MC, V.
Special Features:
  Nonsmoking; children
  welcome; working
  fireplaces; continental
  breakfast in high season.

Nantucket's oldest inn built as such has operated continuously for more than 125 years and has been run by the same family for four generations. It's a delightful, authentically preserved Victorian two blocks from, and on the same street as, the Steamship Authority. There are twelve rooms with either king, full, or twin beds, and the baths are down the hall. Each room has a sink and a ceiling fan. There's a front porch, a back deck, and a fenced yard with bike racks and swings for the children. Some of the furnishings and much of the atmosphere are original to the house. At Christmas Stroll, when the porch is swathed in pine and red ribbon bows, you'll want to line up the kids for a picture worth enlarging to poster size.

PERIWINKLE GUEST HOUSE & COTTAGE

Innkeeper: Sara Shlosser-O'Reilly.
508-228-9267, 800-837-2921, fax 508-325-4046, rhinn@aol.com.
www.theperiwinkle.com.
7 and 9 N. Water St., PO Box 1436, Nantucket, MA 02554
Open: Year-round.
Price: Moderate to Expensive.
Credit Cards: AE, D, MC, V.
Special Features: Nonsmoking; no pets; young children welcome; packages; continental breakfast.

The sunny yellow exterior of this 1846 guesthouse and the cottage next door shelters a variety of rooms: large; small; doubles; singles; a full-floor family suite; harbor views; neighborhood views; some refrigerators; king, queen, or twin beds; private and shared baths; plus TV and a phone in the air-conditioned rooms. Breakfast with its oversized goodies is served in the double backyard garden or a sunny breakfast room. Everything is bright, friendly, and cheerful — it's another O'Reilly family operation (see "Accommodations Et Al") only a few blocks away from the rest of the collection.

The pineapple on the door once told friends that a sailing man was home and ready to greet them. Now it's the theme and the name of one of the Island's most elegant B&Bs.

Betty Lowry

THE PINEAPPLE INN

Owners: Caroline and Bob Taylor.
508-228-9992, fax 508-325-6051; info@pineappleinn.com.
www.pineappleinn.com.
10 Hussey St., Nantucket, MA 02554.
Open: Apr.–Dec.
Price: Expensive to Very Expensive.
Credit Cards: AE, MC, V.

Built in 1838 for Captain Uriah Russell, this historic house on a quiet side street was reconstructed and refurbished with great taste in 1997. The twelve-room inn has king- or queen-size handmade four-poster canopy beds, Ralph Lauren bedding, goose-down comforters, Oriental carpets, white-marble baths, fine reproduction furniture, and authentic 19th-century antiques and art. This version of the romantic past, however, also features cable TV and telephones with voice mail and computer access in each of the air-conditioned

Special Features: No
smoking; no pets; voice
mail and computer
access all rooms; patio;
expanded continental
breakfast.

rooms. The location is ideal — just off Centre Street in the historic district. On sunny days you breakfast on the brick garden patio smelling the roses while a fountain splashes. This is no buffet breakfast, either, but a sit-down affair where you are served fresh-squeezed orange juice; a fresh-fruit plate; a selection of pastries, breads, and cereals; and tea or coffee anyway you want it, including espresso or cappuccino. Carolyn and Bob formerly owned and operated the Quaker House Inn and Restaurant, and they brought their expertise (along with their espresso machine) to this dream B&B.

The pineapple is the long-time New England symbol for hospitality. The story is that when a seafaring man came home after years away, his return from faraway lands was announced by the presence of the exotic pineapple on the door.

Old-fashioned porches surround the Point Breeze Hotel, which has been an Island mainstay since 1892.

Rob Benchley

POINT BREEZE HOTEL
General Manager: Paul
Gonnella.
508-228-0313, 800-365-4371,
fax 508-325-6044;
Ptbreeze@nantucket.net.
www.pointbreeze.com.
71 Easton St., Nantucket,
MA 02554.
Open: Apr.–Dec.
Price: Moderate to
Expensive.

For years this was the Folger Hotel, but before that it was Point Breeze, and the new owner decided to restore the original historic name. The old-fashioned front porch is a wonderful place to sit with the morning paper and a cup of coffee or before dinner with an aperitif. The guest rooms are being upgraded from "nothing special" to "special," and the place has a nice family-friendly atmosphere. And Point Breeze is large enough to be the meeting place for a number of community

Credit Cards: AE, MC, V.
Special Features:
 Restaurant; nonsmoking;
 no pets; children
 welcome; full breakfast
 in season; cottages;
 packages; courtesy van to
 airport and ferry.

QUAKER HOUSE INN
Owners: Stephanie Silva.
508-228-0400, 508-228-9156;
 quaker@nantucket.net.
www.thequakerhouse.com.
5 Chestnut St., Nantucket,
 MA 02554.
Open: Apr.–Jan.
Price: Moderate.
Credit Cards: AE, D, MC, V
Special Features:
 Restaurant; nonsmoking;
 no pets; full breakfast.

**SAFE HARBOR GUEST
 HOUSE**
Owners: Sylvia and
 Lawrence Griggs.
508-228-3222 (also fax);
 sharbor@nantucket.net.
www.beesknees.net/safe
 harbor.
2 Harbor View Way,
 Nantucket, MA 02554.
At Children's Beach.
Open: Year-round.
Price: Moderate to
 expensive.
Credit Cards: AE, MC, V.
Special Features: Smoking
 and pets permitted;
 expanded continental
 breakfast.

SEVEN SEA STREET INN
Owners: Matt and Mary
 Parker.
508-228-3577,
 fax 508-228-3578;
 seas7@nantucket.net.
www.sevenseastreetinn.com.
7 Sea St., Nantucket, MA
 02554.
Open: Year-round.

activities. The NRTA shuttle stops at the door, a great convenience.

There was a time when the sleeping rooms in Nantucket Town were over the stores, and at the Quaker House, built in 1847, the eight very different rooms are over Kendrick's. Quaker austerity has long been banished in favor of flowers and cheerful colors. The beds are queen size, and many have canopies; the rooms vary in size but not in charm. Another charmer on the premises is son Malcolm.

"You can see us from the ferry," Sylvia said. "You mean the big gray house with the white trim?" was the innocent reply. And Sylvia laughed. "That's the one. Nantucket liked our color scheme so much, everyone else has copied it." The friendly five-room guesthouse is right on Children's Beach and minutes from the ferry and Town. Some rooms have private decks, and all have private baths. Naturally there are harbor views — "Wave to your friends," Sylvia invites — and you can walk to Jetties Beach and its public tennis courts. The house is furnished with Oriental, English, and American antiques and reproductions, and there's a lawn and gardens

If you've ever wondered what it would be like to stay in a new Nantucket-style house, Seven Sea Street Inn can satisfy your curiosity. This red oak post-and-beam guesthouse was built in 1986 to the owners' own plans. Early-American furnishings are combined with such contemporary comforts as a Jacuzzi spa. The eleven double rooms and suites each have a queen-size fishnet-canopy bed, TV,

Price: Moderate to
  expensive.
Credit Cards: AE, D, MC, V.
Special Features:
  Nonsmoking; no pets;
  Jacuzzi spa; limited off-
  street parking; classic
  library; expanded
  continental breakfast;
  packages.

THE 1739 HOUSE

Owner: Lenore V. Martin.
508-228-0120, 800-672-0908.
www.newengland.com.
43 Centre St., Nantucket,
  MA 02554.
Open: June–Oct.
Price: Inexpensive to
  Moderate.
Credit Cards: None.
Special Features:
  Nonsmoking; no pets;
  continental breakfast.

SHERBURNE INN

Owners: Dale Hamilton
  and Susan Gasparich.
508-228-4425, 888-577-4425,
  fax 508-228-8114;
  sherinn@nantucket.net.
www.sherburneinn.com
10 Gay St, Nantucket, MA
  02554.
Open: Year-round.
Price: Moderate.
Credit Cards: AE, D, MC,
  V.
Special Features:
  Nonsmoking; no pets;
  garden; expanded
  continental breakfast.

phone, refrigerator, hair dryer, and private bath. You can even have breakfast in bed if you like. The deck — built in the style of a 19th-century roof walk — has a view of Nantucket Harbor. The inn is on a side street minutes from the beaches and Main Street. Conveniences such as beach towels, bike rack, and limited off-street parking are available, too. The suites are especially nice for families with children over the age of five, since Children's Beach is just at the end of the block. Note that the friendly orange cat answers to the name Puddy.

This historic colonial homestead on what was once Petticoat Row has been featured in a major architecture book — ask to see it if it isn't out and open on the table. You'll recognize at once how much of the original look of 1739 remains. Many fireplaces, wide floorboards, and antiques maintain the ambiance. You can choose from single, double, or triple rooms with private or shared baths, and there's also a two-room family suite with bath. The continental breakfast is served in the garden patio, a pleasant way of starting the day that probably never occurred to folks in 1739.

The Sherburne Inn was originally the Atlantic Silk Factory, a short-lived enterprise of the early 19th century. The present inn, with its two parlors and eight bedrooms, is an elegant place with imported wall coverings, Oriental rugs, and original art — a long way from factory days — and the centrally air-conditioned rooms all have private baths and either king- or queen-size beds, phones, and cable TV. While relaxing by the fire on a foggy morning you can read all about the one-time dream of mulberry trees on Nantucket and never-to-be-realized competition for the silk works of China and France in the inn booklet, *Tales of Sherburne*. The inn also has that oxymoron, "a real ghost," described as "a soft vaporous image." Alas, it doesn't linger long enough to answer such questions as, "Why don't more people discover this lovely Island in the winter?"

SHIPS INN

Owners: Mark and Ellie
    Gottwald.
508-228-0040; shipsinn@
    nantucket.net.
www.nantucket.net/lodging
    /shipsinn.
13 Fair St., Nantucket, MA
    02554.
1-1/2 blocks off Main St.
Open: May–Dec.
Price: Moderate to
    Expensive.
Credit Cards: AE, D, MC, V.
Special Features:
    Restaurant; nonsmoking;
    no pets; expanded
    continental breakfast;
    afternoon tea; children 12
    and up.

The twelve guest rooms are named for the ships commanded by Obed Starbuck, a whaler captain whose success enabled him to retire at age thirty-three and who built the inn as his home in 1831. Lucretia Mott, Nantucket native, abolitionist, and early leader in women's suffrage, was born in a house on this site but not in the Ships Inn. Today's inn has ten guest rooms with private baths and choice of queen or full beds plus two twin-bed single rooms that share a bath. In addition to staying in a truly historic place, there's much to be said for being literally right on top of one of Nantucket's finest restaurants.

STUMBLE INNE

Owners: Jeanne and George
    Todor.
508-228-4482,
    fax 508-228-4752;
    romance@nantucket.net.
www.stumbleinne.com.
109 Orange St., Nantucket,
    MA 02554.
Open: Year-round.
Price: Moderate to
    Expensive.
Credit Cards: AE, MC, V.
Special Features:
    Nonsmoking; no pets;
    room refrigerators;
    garden cottage; packages.

The Stumble Inne offers seven mostly air-conditioned rooms with queen- or full-size beds in the main house plus a two-bedroom cottage with a king-size and twin beds. Nice colonial antiques and reproductions embellish the house, and you'll find sample menus from all the local restaurants waiting to be browsed in the old-fashioned parlor. Readers of *Cape Cod Life* magazine have repeatedly voted the Stumble Inne the Island's best B&B.

TUCKERNUCK INN

Owners: Ken and Phyllis
    Parker.
508-228-4886, 800-228-4886;
    tuckinn@nantucket.net.
60 Union St., Nantucket,
    MA 02554.
Four blocks east of Main St.
Open: Year-round.
Price: Moderate to
    Expensive.
Credit Cards: AE, MC, V.
Special Features:
    Restaurant (seasonal);

The Tuckernuck is on the south end of Town beyond the Town pier and one block from the beach. Phyllis and Ken created this homey inn out of a century-old structure in 1985 and have operated it ever since. They've put in croquet and badminton on the back lawn and are constantly upgrading the property.

Children are welcomed in the suites during high season or anywhere in the house during low season. There's also a two-bedroom family unit. Queen and twin beds are available in the rooms, while the luxury or honeymoon suite has a nonsmoking; no pets; parking; packages; room refrigerators; voice mail and data ports; expanded continental breakfast included Nov.–Apr. only.

UNION STREET INN
Owners: Ken and Deborah Withrow.
508-228-9222, 800-225-5116, fax 508-325-0848; unioninn@nantucket.net. www.union-street-inn.com. 7 Union St., Nantucket, MA 02554.
Between Main St. and Stone Alley.
Open: Year-round.
Price: Expensive.
Credit Cards: AE, MC, V.
Special Features: Nonsmoking; off-season and midseason packages; room refrigerators; many working fireplaces; full breakfast.

THE WHITE ELEPHANT INN
Owners: Stephen and Jill Karp.
508-228-2500, 800-ISLANDS; resinfo@nantucket.net. 50 Easton St., PO Box 1139, Nantucket, MA 02554.
At the harbor front.
Open: Apr.–Dec.
Price: Very Expensive.
Credit Cards: AE, CB, D, DC, MC, V.
Special Features: Restaurant; boat slips; working fireplaces; in-room Internet access; business lounge; library; jitney service to beaches; ferry transfers; exercise room; concierge; no pets.

canopied king-size bed. The popular American Bounty Restaurant is part of the inn, in season.

Some of the twelve handsome guest rooms in this elegant 18th-century inn have working fireplaces and canopied or high-post beds. All have private baths, air conditioning, and cable TV. There are suites and connecting rooms, too, as well as a brick garden patio where you can enjoy the full country breakfast on sunny mornings. The inn has the original wide-plank pine floors, raised-wood-panel walls, colonial antiques, and furniture of the late 1700s. After many incarnations, it was completely restored between 1990 to 1995, just in time for Deb and Ken to leave major hotel management and retail display positions and move to Nantucket. They enjoy sharing their knowledge of special places around the Island, beginning with the view from the garden of the golden tower of historic South Church, with its famous Town clock and Portuguese bell.

Even if you're a longtime fan of the White Elephant, you'll scarcely recognize it. The inn was totally redone in 2000 and now has fifty-four guestrooms and suites and twelve garden cottages. Some cottages have working fireplaces, water views, and are in an adjacent new location: The Captain's Court. This luxurious contemporary resort has not, however, lost Nantucket style. The atmosphere is sumptuous harbor front, and even if your yacht isn't parked outside your door, you may feel it should be just in case you want to run an errand on the Cape. If you need anything, just ask. Rooms have free movies, and most have harbor views. The Brant Point Grill will whip up a nifty picnic lunch as well as a premier lobster or steak dinner.

THE WOODBOX INN

Owner: Dexter Tutein.
508-228-0587;
woodbox@nantucket.net.
www.woodboxinn.com.
29 Fair St., Nantucket, MA
02554.
1-1/2 blocks from Main St.
Open: Memorial Day–Jan. 1.
Price: Moderate to
Expensive.
Credit Cards: None.
Special Features:
Restaurant; nonsmoking;
no pets; working
fireplaces in suites.

Built in 1709, this is Nantucket's oldest restaurant-inn — it's not just colonial "style" here, it *is* colonial. The private baths for the nine rooms and suites are reluctant concessions to the 20th century, when the house became an operating inn. Much is original, including the wide-board floors and the pine-paneled, low-ceilinged dining room.

The one- and two-bedroom suites have working fireplaces. All rooms have queen-size beds, some canopied, and one of the two-room suite's bedrooms has twin beds, as well. Resident owner Dexter Tutein, a CPA and tax consultant, has operated the Woodbox for nearly half a century and is a rare observer of the Town and Island. Note that no credit cards are accepted and that breakfast is available but not included. A 10 percent service charge is automatically added to your bill. The Woodbox Inn Restaurant is as well known for its innovative cuisine as for its 18th-century ambiance.

LODGING IN SIASCONSET

Sconset is still essentially a summertime village as far as visitors are concerned, and even those who would like to rent off-season may find themselves stymied by the lack of insulation and heating in many of the cute cottages. No restaurants stay open off-season, either; though, happily, the distance to Town is only a tad over seven miles, and mid-Island dining is easy to reach.

THE SUMMER HOUSE–SCONSET

Manager: Susan Manolis.
508-257-4577,
fax 508-257-4590;
summerhouse@
nantucket.net.
www.thesummerhouse.com.
17 Ocean Ave., PO Box 880,
Siasconset, MA 02564.
Open: Late April–Oct. 31.
Price: Very Expensive.
Credit Cards: AE, MC, V.
Special Features:
Restaurant; cottages;
swimming pool; tennis
privileges at the Casino
private club; continental
breakfast; no pets.

Here you can see the rose-trellised cottage where James Cagney stayed and which has been named in his honor. As the only true inn in Sconset for decades, the Summer House has been the sometime residence of celebrities in arts and politics. Nantucket Film Festival guests stay here now. It has a lovely setting on the bluff overlooking the Atlantic, with its own beach amid the dunes below and a beachside swimming pool where you can have lunch if you like. The cottages are adorable, with Dutch doors, white curtains, English pine furniture, and Jacuzzi tubs. Summer House also operates two inns in Town: **Summer House Fair Street** and **Summer House India Street.** A jitney service brings the Townies out to the Sconset beach.

WADE COTTAGES
Owners: Wade and
  Susanne Green.
508-257-6308
  (winter 212-989-6423);
  seamail@wadecottages.
  com.
www.wadecottages.com.
Shell St., PO Box 211,
  Siasconset, MA 02564.
Open: late May–mid-Oct.
Price: Moderate to Very
  Expensive.
Credit Cards: AE, MC, V.
Special Features:
  Continental breakfast.

Built in the late 1920s, the inn has belonged to the same family for more than fifty-five years. The owners for the last two decades are an artist and a writer as well as innkeepers. The Greens have a B&B, apartments, and cottages right on the north bluff overlooking the dunes and the sea. Some of the baths are shared but are priced accordingly. If you call and tell them what kind of lodging you have in mind, the Greens will very likely be able to comply. Just do it early, possibly using their New York telephone number.

LODGING EVERYWHERE ELSE

**NANTUCKET INN &
  CONFERENCE
  CENTER**
Manager: Suki Hall.
508-228-6900, 800-321-8484,
  fax 508-228-9861;
  ackinn@nantucket.net.
www.nantucket.net/lodging
  /nantucketinn.
27 Macy's Ln., Nantucket,
  MA 02554.
Opposite the airport.
Open: Apr.–Oct.; Christmas
  Stroll.
Price: Moderate to
  Expensive.
Credit Cards: AE, D, MC, V.
Special Features: Full-
  breakfast; complimentary
  transfers to Town and
  Surfside Beach; airport
  and ferry pick-up;
  indoor/outdoor
  swimming pool; two lit
  tennis courts; whirlpool
  spas; fitness center;
  packages; 1-night stays
  (excluding holidays and
  special events); parking.

With one hundred rooms, this resort on three landscaped acres across from the airport is one of Nantucket's largest inns. It's new (as such things are measured here), comfortable (all rooms have air-conditioning and private baths), and the inn's own shuttle makes commuting to the historic district easy.

Airport location and parking as well as Island central location have made the inn a natural for conferences and sales meetings, but groups don't dominate, and families fit right in. Children under eighteen stay free in their parents' room.

Rob Benchley

Once the "Star of the Sea" life-saving station, this American Youth Hostel is on the National Register of Historic Places.

ROBERT B. JOHNSON MEMORIAL AYH-HOSTEL (Star of the Sea)
508-228-0433, 800-909-4776 x29, fax 508-775-2970, out-of-season 617-531-0459, nantuckethostel@juno.com.
www.hi-travel.org.
31 Western Ave., Nantucket, MA 02554.
Surfside Beach.
Open: Apr.–Oct.
Price: Very Inexpensive.
Credit cards: MC, V.
Special Features: Dormitory; kitchen; linen rental; groups welcome; five-night limit.

Built in 1874 as the Star of the Sea lifesaving station, this American Youth Hostel (AYH) facility is on the National Register of Historic Places. In fact, you'll see it replicated off Polpis Road in the Life Saving Museum. Many of its guests get here via the Surfside bike path, and reservations are essential. For $15 to $19 a night plus light chores, you get one of the hostel's forty-nine bunks in a dorm room and meet hostelers from all over the world. In 1921 the lifesaving station became a radio compass station for the U.S. Navy. Purchased by AYH in 1963 to replace the hostel at the airport, it was named for a former AYH executive instrumental in establishing eastern Massachusetts hostels. Guests range in age from six to seventy-six, and there's an 11pm curfew along with some other rules. Families with teenagers might consider letting the kids stay here rather than taking an extra room or bringing in rollaway beds in an inn. The experience can't be beat.

THE WAUWINET
Owners: Jill and Stephen Karp.
Managers: Russ and Debbie Cleveland.
508-228-0145, 800-426-8718; email@wauwinet.com.
www.wauwinet.com.
120 Wauwinet Rd., PO Box 2580, Nantucket, MA 02584.

Combining luxury with environmental awareness is the way of the Wauwinet, a country inn built in the 1850s and once operated as a get-away-from-Town restaurant serving lobster and seafood "shore dinners." It became a summer hotel, declined, and closed down, only to be awakened and rebuilt in 1986 to the tune of some $3,000,000 by Stephen and Jill Karp, who were summer visi-

Rob Benchley

The Wauwinet presides over the quiet east end of the Island.

Off Squam Rd.
Open: May–Oct.
Price: Very Expensive.
Credit Cards: AE, D, DC,
  MC, V.
Special Features:
  Restaurant; no smoking;
  no pets; complimentary
  transfers to Town; full
  breakfast; family
  cottages; parking;
  afternoon wine and
  cheese; tennis; launch;
  boats and bikes to
  borrow; beaches.

tors and lovers of Nantucket. Now the inn is a member of Relais & Châteaux and the Island's class act, with a two-to-one ratio of staff to guests, thirty-five gorgeous rooms and suites, and even family cottages, all at the quiet east end of the Island. This is the "Haulover," where boats were once dragged across the sand to save time going from harbor to sea around the point; now guests have a choice of beaches: bay on one side and ocean on the other.

Beyond the Wauwinet lies only the wildlife sanctuary and the far reaches that lead to Great Point lighthouse. In midseason the Wauwinet adds wonderful extras such as nature and history tours, visits to the studios of craft artisans, bird-watching excursions, and the like — often transporting guests in "Woody," the inn's classic 1936 station wagon. Topper's, its award-winning restaurant, attracts appreciative diners from all over the Island, but it's exclusively for guests at the breakfast hour. At 4pm those guests not out on boats or beaches gather in the library for sherry, port, and cheese. After dinner many choose videos from the Wauwinet's selection and have them delivered to their room accompanied by hot buttered popcorn.

Handicap Access

While few of the old restored houses that have become inns or B&Bs are equipped to handle wheelchairs, many cottages can do so. Island realtors offer house rentals as well as sales and will be happy to suggest appropriate places (see "Real Estate Rentals" at the beginning of this chapter). Here, however, are some lodgings with full or limited access for your consideration; see the individual listings for descriptions of each property. When you telephone, be sure to explain your needs in full — only the most recently restored places completely meet all the requirements. For a copy of *Nantucket Island: Guide for Visitors with Special Needs*, call Nantucket Commission on Disability, 508-228-8085. See also www.nantucketchamber.org.

<u>Nantucket Town:</u>
   Beachside at Nantucket (508-228-2241, 800-322-4433); **Easton House** (508-228-4759); **Harbor House** (508-228-1500, 800-ISLANDS); **Jared Coffin House** (508-228-2400, 800-248-2405); **1739 House** (508-228-0120, 800-672-0908); **Pineapple Inn** (508-228-9992); **Point Breeze Hotel** (508-228-0313, 800-365-4371); **The White Elephant** (508-228-2500; 800-ISLANDS).

<u>Everywhere Else</u>:
   Nantucket Inn (508-228-6900, 800-321-8184, fax 508-228-9861; ackinn@nantucket .net; www.nantucket.net/lodging/nantucketinn/cobblestone; 27 Macy's Ln., Nantucket, MA 02554); **The Wade Cottages** (508-257-6308, 212-989-6423 (winter); sea mail@wadecottages.com; www.wadecottages.com; 35 Shell St., PO Box 211, Siasconset, MA 02564).

CHAPTER FOUR
Mind, Matter, and Monuments
CULTURE

While the early settlers of Nantucket were literate and quick to set up home schooling for their sons and daughters alike, we have no evidence that they were intellectuals in any formal sense nor particularly conscious of the high culture of their day. The Island's early entry into international commerce brought a degree of sophistication, however, and the great wealth of the whaling industry tempered by the strict understatement of Quakerism led to a steady if not meteoric rise in appreciation of the arts.

Rob Benchley

The Jethro Coffin house, also known as the Oldest House, was built in 1686 on Sunset Hill

Porcelain dinnerware was considered an appropriate and practical gift to bring home from Asia, and occasionally purely decorative things slipped by, as well. On the years-long voyages, whaling men created their own art, too: wood sculptures, boxes inlaid with whale ivory, pictures incised as scrimshaw in whale teeth. The level of skill and taste improved with practice.

The simplicity of Quaker style contributed to the spare and handsome architecture, and Quaker restrictions against music and theater elevated the demand for books and lectures. The outspoken and early position against slavery put Nantucket squarely in agreement with New England philosophical ferment, and soon an invitation to speak at the Nantucket Atheneum was an indication of prominence in the world of letters.

As Quakerism declined, the strictures against the arts relaxed, and Nantucket style became more aesthetically adventurous, especially among those who could afford to import home furnishings, fabrics, and silver. Yet the centuries of simplicity kept opulence in check. The interiors of the mansions along Upper Main Street did not reach the garish hodgepodge of wealthy mainland residences. Commercial buildings came under this influence, too. For an example of pure Federal architecture, note the Pacific National Bank on Main Street, now a branch of Fleet. Incidentally, the bank was named for the Pacific Ocean where Nantucket whalers were making fortunes for the shipowners and is worth visiting for its murals and old teller cages.

When Nantucket was discovered by the New York theater crowd as a summer retreat in the late 19th century, Nantucket Town was rejected as far too proper. The actors, comedians, playwrights, and their friends and support systems, arriving as soon as the theaters closed for the season, settled in Siasconset. They built summer homes and the Casino theater where they could entertain themselves not only with dances and parties but also with their own little shows. The orchestra alternated its gigs between the Casino and the Point Breeze Hotel in Town. The old fishing village was declared downright fashionable, and the message was relayed instantly to the Smart Set. Overnight, mainland popular culture came to the Island full-blown (if not full year).

Inside the vintage Siasconset Casino, the beat goes on.

Betty Lowry

As Nantucket's business community rallied to embrace economic salvation in the form of tourism, the mainstream residents were cautious about changing their lives on behalf of the off-Island visitor. The time came when Nantucket had to decide whether to reach for tourist volume and risk becoming just another ticky-tacky holiday island, or whether to limit access (by reducing the size and number of ferries, for instance) and risk accusations of elitism. Here, again, however, ingrained reticence worked in the Nantucketer's favor. The highest rollers were attracted to more flamboyant places ashore, and Nantucket's steady clientele increasingly drew from a segment of society that was happy with good music, good talk, good company, good food, and good beaches. Consequently, the Island incorporated the taste of its summer people without losing any of its own character. Unlike other resort areas where the past was retrieved and rewritten as a tourist attraction, Nantucket has never lost touch with its own history.

ARCHITECTURE

In 1836 Joseph Starbuck built three identical houses side by side for his three sons. The Three Bricks, as they are known, are all privately owned, though occasionally one is open to the public for a benefit house tour.

Rob Benchley

It is not stretching a point to call Nantucket Town an outdoor museum of original American domestic architecture of the 17th, 18th, and 19th centuries. By and large it was spared the ravages that decimated other historic New England communities. Nearly eight hundred houses built before the Civil War are still standing, a situation unmatched anywhere else in New England, including Boston and Salem. In fact, the Island itself is one of the largest and finest official historic districts in the United States.

A walk about **_Nantucket Town_** is social history as well as architectural. The neo-Georgian, Federal, and Greek Revival homes of the wealthy shipowners are mostly along upper Main Street and Pleasant Street. The sea captains built shipshape houses "cheek-by-jowl" on Orange Street, using ships' carpenters as architects. Fishermen lived near their boats in shanties made of shipwreck debris and the like. Lumber was valuable.

When the Great Fire of 1846 burned down one-third of the Town, the wharves and shops were gutted, but the noncommercial two-thirds were saved. The lower downtown, therefore, dates from the mid-1800s. The fact that the **Atheneum**, the Town's dignified if rather pretentiously named public library and lecture hall, was rebuilt in much grander style within six months after the fire says a great deal for the Island's attitude toward education and culture.

The three-story brick **Pacific Club** survived the fire, though more than a century later owners were still blaming "four feet of wet ash left over from the Great Fire" for structural problems. It was built in 1772 as a counting house for the man who owned two of the three ships involved in the Boston Tea Party. When it became the Pacific Club, its membership was limited to ship captains who had gone whaling in the Pacific Ocean and wanted a place to swap old stories. It now holds commercial offices and is currently undergoing extensive structural repairs to restore it to its club days. Meanwhile, this building together with the iron horse fountain in the middle of Main Street across from its door have come to be a recognized motif of Nantucket Town.

The "Oldest House" is the **Mary and Jethro Coffin House** (1686) on Sunset Hill, now owned by the Nantucket Historical Association (NHA) and open to the public at regular hours in the summer and special times the rest of the year. Its architectural style is straight out of medieval England, a post-and-beam frame two stories high with a steeply pitched roof. The fisherman's cottage called Auld Lang Syne at 6 Broadway in *Siasconset* claims to be older still: dating to 1675, the year the village was settled.

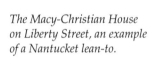

The Macy-Christian House on Liberty Street, an example of a Nantucket lean-to.

Betty Lowry

When Thomas Macy and friends arrived at *Madaket* in 1659, winter was coming on, and they were happy to learn from the resident Wampanoags how to build a functional tepee-style shelter. When other settlers arrived with their families the following spring, they expressed dismay at the primitive dwelling and set to work at once putting up houses that were not much warmer but at least had a familiar Anglo-civilized look to them. These grew into the simple lean-tos of the early 1700s, added on to as families grew and required more space. A good example of the lean-to is the **Christopher Starbuck House** (c. 1690) at 105 Main Street, as is the **Macy-Christian House** (1745) at 12 Liberty Street, another NHA property. Because of the lack of usable timber on the Island, houses were more often moved than taken down, and some, like the **Dreamland Theater**, 17 South Water Street, have quite a track record. That they survived shows the special care taken in the original construction, in turn mandated by the high cost of imported building materials. Despite the expense, the number of new houses raised in Nantucket between 1740 and 1840 is said to have exceeded every other town of comparable size in the country.

Typical Nantucket houses are considered to be the plain, weathered, gray-shingle two-and-a-half story homes of Quaker days (1760–1830), and you will see these both as original houses and as copied by vacation-home builders. (Restrictions limit builders to shingles and cedar clapboard.) Walk by the **Thomas Starbuck II House** (c. 1761) at 11 Milk Street and stop in at the **1790 Hezekiah Swain House**, 1 Vestal Street, preserved as the birthplace of Maria Mitchell. It stands next to the headquarters of the Maria Mitchell Association and is open to the public in summer.

The next architectural step was the two-story house with center chimneys and a roof walk. These, too, are credited to Quaker inspiration, but the fact is that the most devout Quakers of their day considered them ostentatious. These fronted directly on the street and stood close together like the town houses of Philadelphia — which was, of course, also a Quaker settlement but worldly by Nantucket standards. About 270 houses built during this period still stand. Late-colonial houses include the **Peter Foulger II House** (c. 1765), 52 Centre Street, and the **Thomas Macy House** (1770), 99 Main Street.

The really imposing residences began with the big money from whaling. The earliest brick mansion was **Moors End** (1829–34), at 19 Pleasant Street. It was the first of two houses built by Jared Coffin in trying to please a socially unhappy wife. She declared Moors End too far out of Town, so his next attempt was the Island's first three-story house, now the **Jared Coffin House** Inn. Alas, she didn't like that either — particularly since soon after the Coffins moved there, in 1845, the Great Fire destroyed most of the town surrounding their new home. Eventually, she moved back to the mainland. The elegant **Three Bricks**, at 93, 95, and 97 Main Street, were all built in an identical style by Joseph Starbuck in 1836 for his three sons. Their total cost — $40,000 — shocked everyone. The "Bricks" are privately owned, but across the street at 96 Main Street, **Hadwen House** (1840–45), belongs to the NHA and is open to view. It's one of the **Three Greeks**, at 92, 96, and 100 Main (the houses where Starbuck's daughters lived).

Along Cliff Road are the estates the wealthy off-Islanders of the 1920s and 1930s — called "cottages" following the Newport, Rhode Island, and Berkshire County, Massachusetts, custom of grandly overstated modesty. In *Siasconset*, the showy neo-Victorian beach houses built by summer people at the turn of the century and the gentrified shanties alike were given names instead of street numbers, a custom that persists, street numbers or no.

Fishing shacks have become art galleries on Old South Wharf, and the warehouses and blacksmithies on the waterfront hold gift shops, boutiques, and cafés. The 1840s spermaceti whale-oil candle factory on Broad Street is now the **Whaling Museum.** Private homes with fascinating histories have become antique shops, restaurants, and bed & breakfast inns.

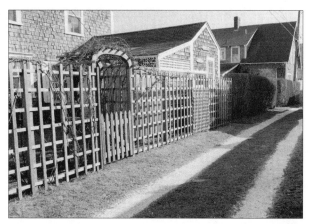

The village of Sconset is about 7 miles from Nantucket Town, but its residents and return visitors say it's light-years away.

Rob Benchley

It was the acute financial depression that followed the end of the Civil War that saved the Town architecturally. When the profits of worldwide whaling ceased, the population of the Island dropped by one-third, and there was no money to update or replace existing structures with the new and fashionable Gothic Revival and Victorian styles. Nantucketers made do or did without in the accepted New England way. The few gingerbread-trimmed houses that slipped through the net of austerity show what might have been but thankfully was not.

Architecture is key to the history of Nantucket. The Nantucket Historical Association, in its more than a century of care, has preserved and protected gems of colonial and post-colonial architecture, holding diverse structures in trust for the future. Many are open to the public. Also, since 1955, the Historic District Commission has monitored repair and renovation of existing structures and has enforced authority over new construction. (Even the size of a sign in front of a business and the color of a house or trim are subject to NHA approval.)

In the late 1950s the Nantucket Historical Trust was established by summer Islanders Walter Beinecke and Walter Beinecke Jr. Out of this grew Sherburne Associates (1964), formed to rebuild the dilapidated waterfront and provide capital for the Town's historical preservation needs. Though hotly debated at the time, the Beinecke long-term formula of preservation and conservation over exploitation and immediate profits is liturgy today.

HOUSE TOURS

Members of the NHA and those who purchase visitor passes or tickets at the door can create their own tours or follow the NHA walking tour. However, while the main museums are open year-round, during the off-season the houses are staffed and open only on holiday weekends. From Memorial Day through Columbus Day, Hadwen House, the Macy-Christian House, and the Jethro Coffin House observe regular museum hours.

During special events such as the Daffodil and Harvest Festivals, inns and bed & breakfasts open their doors to self-conducted tours for a donation to a designated Island cause. Historical houses are open certain days during the Nantucket Noel, which begins Thanksgiving weekend and continues through Christmas.

At other times of the year, churches and charities arrange house and garden tours as fund-raising events. *The Nantucket Garden Club House Tour* (508-228-9644) has been opening doors on upper Main Street in August for more than forty years. *Friends of the Nantucket Public Schools* (508-325-0669) sponsor a Christmas House Tour 4pm–7pm the first Friday in December. For listings of annual and impromptu tours, see the calendar columns of the free and regular newspapers and online: www.nantucket.com and www.nantucketchamber. org.

ARTS CENTERS, COUNCILS, AND SCHOOLS

Nantucket may be one vast Art Colony. "If you're not an artist when you come here you soon learn to be," one painter told me. Whether it is the sweep of the bogs at cranberry harvest, the ever-present panorama of sailboats, or roses climbing the trellises of weathered gray Sconset cottages, the scene begs to be captured. Individual artists drifting over from the mainland, saw the Island's natural beauty, found work, and quietly stayed on.

Artists' Association of Nantucket (508-228-0294; aan@nantucket.net; www. nantucketarts.org; 19 Washington St., Nantucket, MA 02554) More than half a century of exhibiting the works of its members and representing them in community decision making. It also holds classes in many media and for all ages and serves as an art information clearinghouse.

Nantucket Arts Alliance (508-228-4922, PO Box 2823, Nantucket, MA 02584) Brings together all the artistic disciplines to the Island, from sketching to film and including an international concert series, and sponsors the Island-wide Arts Festival in October.

Nantucket Island School of Design & the Arts (508-228-9248; nisda@nantucket.net; www.nantucket.net/art/nisda; 23 Wauwinet Rd., Nantucket, MA 02554) NISDA and its Sea View Farm Barn Studios are way out of Town but easy to reach by bike or bus. Every August, NISDA co-produces the popular Sand Castle and Sculpture Day with the Chamber of Commerce, and every day in summer classes are held on its out-Island premises. NISDA also offers workshops, one-week Teachers Institutes, and college credit programs through affiliation with Massachusetts College of Art, Boston, as well as enrichment offerings in all media to children and adults. The school also has lodgings on Washington Street (at the harbor).

Preservation Institute: Nantucket (508-228-2429; 11 Centre St., Nantucket, MA 02554) A summer program of the University of Florida College of Architecture focusing on documentation of historic structures, planning and design in historic context, and preservation technology. Students earn nine graduate or undergraduate credits for coursework completed during the seven-week session.

Shredder's Studio (508-228-4487; 3 Salros Rd., Nantucket, MA 02554) Classes from preschool through adult; basket making to painting, sculpture, and drawing. Most courses run on a monthly basis, but a variety of one- and two-day intensive workshops are also offered. Shredder is the name of the founder's cat, by the way.

Private Lessons: Individual artists, sculptors, and artisans also teach. You can get referrals by describing your needs to the Artists' Association (listed above). Island-specific arts and crafts such as making lightship baskets and doing scrimshaw are taught both in classes and one-on-one.

CINEMA

Dreamland movie theater is for Saturday night dates as well as the Nantucket Film Festival.

Betty Lowry

Nantucketers go to the movies in the pleasant old-fashioned way of family entertainment and Saturday night dates. They don't demand premiers or cutting-edge films except as demonstrated during the Film Festival (see "Special Events," below). Two of the three movie houses are open only in summer, and the movies are listed in the papers.

FILMS MADE IN AND ABOUT NANTUCKET

The cost of producing a major film on the Island appears to be the inhibiting factor. Even the hilarious movie *The Russians are Coming! The Russians are Coming!* (1966), adapted from the book *The Off-Islanders* by Nantucketer Nathaniel Benchley in Nantucket about Nantucket and — to some extent at least — for Nantucket Islanders, was shot in northern California. *To Gillian on her 37th Birthday* (1996) was made on the Island, however, and is a virtual Island tour from Hy-line Ferry to Madaket. *Moby Dick* (1956) could have been made nowhere else, but alas it was. Most of the action was filmed in Wales and Madeira.

Looking Back

More than any other single individual, Walter Beinecke Jr. was responsible for the redevelopment of the waterfront, the retention of historical integrity downtown, and the shaping of present-day Nantucket. In 1988 Ronald Reagan, president of the United States, presented him with one of the first individual awards ever given under the National Historic Preservation Act for his twenty-five years of work.

Beinecke first came to Nantucket in 1923 at the age of five. In 1998 on his eightieth birthday he described what it was like getting to Nantucket from New York in the 1920s:

"It was easy and enjoyable. . . .You took a boat right from the foot of Manhattan at the end of a business day, ate a good dinner, slept in a cabin, and woke up in New Bedford. You walked from one gangway to another and were on a boat bound for Nantucket arriving at half past ten in the morning. I can still remember the porters from the hotels waiting on the dock and calling out 'Ships Inn! Point Breeze Hotel!' My father spent weekdays in his office and weekends with us in Sconset."

THE MOVIE HOUSES

Going to the movies on Nantucket is a night out as vintage as the Island. Even the name of the summer downtown theater — **Dreamland** (508-228-5356; 17 S. Water St., PO Box 547, Nantucket, MA 02554) — seems like a throwback to the '30s and '40s, though the theater has been in this spot since 1905. Constructed as a Quaker meetinghouse on Main Street after the Great Fire, it became a hat factory and was moved to Brant Point as part of a hotel. Its transport to the present location was by boat across the harbor, which attracted a great crowd of onlookers.

The **Casino** in *Siasconset* (508-257-6661; New St., Siasconset, MA 02564) was built in 1899 to provide a stage for the New York drama and vaudeville stars who summered there, and is a summer theater still. Movies are shown three nights a week June–September. The only year-round movie house is the Town's **Gaslight Theatre** (508-228-4435; gaslighttheatre.@aol.com, 1 N. Union

St., PO Box 599, Nantucket, MA 02554), which seldom makes the deadline for listing its shows in the newspaper. If you care, you have to phone.

DANCE

The Boston Ballet sends a troupe to perform every summer as a fund-raiser for an Island cause, and Nantucket has its own dancers, too, with performances year-round. Training programs from preballet through professional are offered year-round by the **Giovanna La Paglia Studio of Ballet** (508-228-4979; etcetera@nantucket.net; Twin Street Barn, 7 Twin St.; mail: 5 Atlantic Ave., Nantucket MA 02554), which also has a resident company, the **Backstage Ballet Ensemble**. Performances are frequent, and the ensemble has a very good reputation for both classic and innovative dance.

GARDENS

Nantucket basket topiary outside a basketmaker's home.

Betty Lowry

In keeping with the English tradition of the 18th- and early 19th-century Nantucket houses also had "Secret Gardens," though here they were more often categorized as "Hidden Gardens." Many of the historic houses have these little gems tucked out of sight but visitable when the houses are open to the public. **Hadwen House Garden**, 96 Main Street, has an 1850s garden with lily of the valley, herbs, and other fragrant plants. The garden is maintained by the Nantucket Garden Club. The garden club also maintains the colorful garden of the **Atheneum** library, an alcove where you can drop down on a bench to read a book as well as admire the pink azaleas.

Also in Town is **Garden of the Sea Nursery** at 10 Candlehouse Lane (508-

228-0714), specializing in heather, ornamental grasses, and daylilies, set in a group of shingle cottages. The **Garden at Greater Light** at Howard Street off Gardner belongs to the Nantucket Historical Association and is open to the public, though the house is not. The quiet spot with its wrought- iron benches and chairs is maintained in the memory of Betsy Palmer.

Siasconset's gardens can hardly be called hidden. Rather, in mid-June, the gardens (pink and red roses) climb all over the houses. Front gardens are also vintage style: delphiniums; hollyhocks; forget-me-nots, wallflowers, and bachelor buttons.

Gardening by the sea has its own limits and rewards. Hydrangeas do well in the Nantucket climate, so it's no surprise to see them the specialties of the nurseries. The perennials of Nantucket can be found at **Perennial Gardens** (508-228-5608; 165 Hummock Pond Rd., Nantucket, MA 02554), **Moors End** Farm (508-118-2674; 40 Polpis Rd., Nantucket, MA 02554), **Bartlett's Ocean View Farm & Greenhouses** (508-228-9403; www.BartlettsOceanViewFarm.com; Bartlett Farm Road, Nantucket, MA 02554), **Surfing Hydranagea Nursery** (508-228-6828; Somerset Rd., PO Box 2819, Nantucket, MA 02584), Serenity Farm (508-825-9032; 8 Skyline Rd., Nantucket, MA 02554) and **Arrowhead Nursery** (508-228-1961; 13 Arrowhead Dr., Nantucket, MA 02554). For wildflowers visit **Nantucket Wildflower Farm** (508-228-5551; 84 Old South Rd., Nantucket, MA 02554; at Egan Lane). Packets of seeds make good packable take-home gifts.

Incidentally, those white-picket fences capped with a horizontal rail that set off Nantucket gardens so admirably are called ship-rail fences and are descended from the rail needed on board a ship to help brace anyone standing on a rolling deck. Since many of the Island's early structures were built by ships' carpenters, the rail went on as a matter of course.

HISTORIC BUILDINGS AND DISTRICTS

All Nantucket Island was declared a historic district by the Massachusetts Legislature in 1970, but that wasn't nearly enough. Nantucket Town and Siasconset were officially named Old Historic Districts in 1956; Nantucket Town became a National Historic Landmark in 1966, and structures of all kinds continue to be named to the National Register of Historic Places with amazing regularity. For more information: **Nantucket Historic District Commission** (508-228-7231; 10 South Beach, Nantucket, MA 02554).

While many significant buildings are preserved by the Nantucket Historical Association (NHA) as museums, others are private homes (occasionally on view as part of a charity house tour), and others continue to serve their original function as bank, library, church, and store. Today's inns and bed & breakfasts (see Chapter Five, *Lodging*) were the homes and hostelries of a century or two ago.

WALKING TOURS

In a survey by the *Inquirer and Mirror*, "downtown" was voted Nantucket's "Best Place to Walk." Your first afternoon's stroll around Town will show you why. Nevertheless, serendipitous wandering can be enhanced by a small-group walking tour with a guide who is not only well informed on history but who also has a genius for trivia and the urge to tell a good story. Walking tours are generally a May through October activity but often take place on off-season weekends, as well. Call and see if there's room. Reservations are necessary.

Nantucket Town

During the warmer months, the Congregational Church on Centre Street opens its tower to provide sweeping views of the island.

Rob Benchley

First Congregational Tower Tours (508-228-0950; 62 Centre St., Nantucket, MA 02554) It's the best view in Town of the entire Island and also a good way to start any self-conducted tour. Tours of the North Church tower are scheduled 10am–4pm daily except Sundays mid-June through mid-October and during special events. Hours are posted at the gate.

Dirk Gardiner Roggeveen Walking Tours (508-221-0074; PO Box 1827, Nantucket, MA 02554)

Nantucket Historical Association (508-228-1894; 15 Broad St., Nantucket, MA 02554) See below, under "Museums."

The Nantucket Ghost Walk (508-325-8855) Bill Jamieson meets the fearless outside the Atheneum at 7pm from Daffodil Weekend through Christmas Stroll. July and August, every night; the rest of the year varies, so call first. Halloween for sure. The one-hour-and-forty-five minute walking tour is replete with tales. Adults $10; children 6–12, $5.

Old South Church (Unitarian Universalist Church) (508-228-5466; 11 Orange St., PO Box 1023, Nantucket, MA 02554) The golden dome of the tower is a point of orientation anywhere in Town. The Portuguese Bell was cast in

The Black Heritage Trail

Slavery was abolished on Nantucket in 1770, largely because of the influence of the Island's Quaker principles. Thus Nantucket became a refuge for escaping slaves and free blacks alike. In the 19th century they were joined by Portuguese-speaking natives from the Cape Verde islands and Angola, who came to Nantucket as members of whaling crews recruited on the coast of Africa, and by a small number of Polynesians who joined Pacific voyages. Approximately three hundred people of color lived and worked on Nantucket at various times (not counting the Wampanoag).

Black Heritage Trail, a pamphlet prepared by Friends of the African Meeting House on Nantucket, is a self-conducted tour through Nantucket Town and the area south of Town known as **New Guinea.** New Guinea (the name was commonly applied to black neighborhoods much as the term Chinatown identified districts occupied by Chinese) is now considered to have been roughly bounded by Silver and Orange Streets, Williams Lane, and Prospect Street, plus the cemetery.

Rob Benchley

The African Meeting House at Five Corners was built as a segregated school in 1820 and is the second oldest building in the United States built by free African-Americans for their own use.

In the 19th century it was a thriving community, with its own stores, churches, and social organizations centered around Five Corners. At its heart stood the **African Meeting House**, built as a segregated school in 1820 by the African Baptist Society and also serving as church, community center, and meeting place for abolitionist and other groups. Now called **The African School and Church on**

Nantucket, it is considered to be the second oldest public building still standing in the United States built by free African Americans for their own use.

Long neglected and ignored, the restored building was opened to the public in 1999. It was saved thanks to a woman who first came to the island as a fifteen-year-old household servant. Florence Higginbotham, who lived beside the Meeting House at 27 York Street, bought the property when it came up for sale and added it to her own. The modest post-and-beam structure had been used as a garage, bicycle repair shop, and storage shed.

Always regretting that she could not afford to rebuild it, Higginbotham wanted the Meeting House to be somehow kept as a memorial to the people it had once served. When she died in 1972, her son and only heir sought to honor her request. Others were concerned, too. The man who had stored his bicycles there began research that led to its inclusion in the National Register for Historic Places. In 1989 the property was acquired by Boston's Museum of Afro-American History, and the site was rededicated as an integral part of Nantucket history. It is open daily in July and August and by appointment.

The house appears as it did in 1880 — remarkably enough, nearly 75 percent of the structure is original — and contains the beginnings of a museum as well as providing a venue for meetings, cultural programs, and classes. Scholarly research on Nantucket's black and Cape Verdean communities is ongoing. One of the builders was Captain Absalom Boston, son and grandson of slaves, who became the captain of a whaling ship with an all-black crew in 1822. Boston lived at 3 Atlantic Avenue (now a private home) and owned both a store and an inn at Five Corners. In 1846 he effectively ended de facto segregation in the Nantucket public schools when he sued the Town on behalf of his daughter, Phebe Ann, who had been denied admission to the high school because of her race after easily passing the entrance examinations. Another black student who had passed her exams a few years before but had been denied entrance, Eunice Ross, was also finally accepted and attended the school, as a result of the Boston suit.

The **Black Heritage Trail** begins at the **Whaling Museum**, where a formal portrait of Captain Boston is exhibited next to the story of his voyage as a whaling captain. Also on display are examples of the "Temple Toggle Harpoon" invented in 1848 by Lewis Temple of New Bedford. Temple, an African-American blacksmith, unfortunately never patented this important technical tool of the whaling industry.

The **Peter Foulger Museum** next door has a portrait of the Reverend Arthur Cooper (d. 1853), who escaped from Virginia along with his wife, Mary, and arrived in Nantucket in 1820. Disguised and hidden from slave catchers by Quaker Oliver Gardner, in time Cooper became the minister of the African Methodist Episcopal (AME) Church established on the island in 1835.

Next stop is the **Atheneum**. Here in 1841 the young Frederick Douglass (1817–1895), a former slave who was on the island for an antislavery convention, made his first public speech. Encouraged by the response from an integrated audience, he went on to become a leading black abolitionist, writer, and orator. He returned to the island many times, often sharing the podium with Booker T. Washington (1856–1915). Both spoke at the **Unitarian Universalist Church** (Old South Church) where, incidentally, Absalom Boston was married. The interior of the church (at 11 Orange Street) is unchanged from the mid-19th century.

You can walk by **Sherburne House**, 30 Orange Street, a guesthouse where Douglass stayed, and **Anna Gardner's home** at 40 Orange Street, though both are privately owned and not open to the public. Anna was the daughter of Oliver Gardner and lived her Quaker principles to the fullest. She taught in the African School, was secretary of the Abolitionist Society at the time of the Island's first anti-slavery convention in 1841, and, during Reconstruction, went south to teach in the schools of the Freedmen's Aid Society.

New Guinea is a twenty-minute walk from the wharves and is on the loops of two NRTA shuttles. The **cemetery** behind the hospital off Prospect Place is where members of the Boston and Cooper families are buried, along with Eunice Ross. Other prominent members of the African-American community whose graves are here include Sampson Pompey Dyer (1830–1909), who served in the Union navy during the Civil War, and Reverend James Crawford (d. 1888), a minister of the African Baptist Church and an escaped slave who gave lectures to raise money to purchase freedom for his sister.

Five Corners (Atlantic Avenue, York Street, and Pleasant Street) has other houses of the same design and vintage as the African Meeting House, though none are presently open to the public. Number 5A Atlantic Avenue is thought to have been the house of Seneca Boston, father of Absalom and a weaver.

Although the Black Heritage Trail is essentially a self-conducted walk, guided tours of two and a half hours are offered from time to time and on request. The charge is $10 for adults. For more information, contact: Friends of the African Meeting House on Nantucket (508-228-4058; 23 York St., PO Box 1802, Nantucket MA 02554) or the Museum of Afro-American History (617-742-1854; 46 Joy St., Boston MA 02114).

Lisbon in 1810; the Town clock was installed in 1832. The interior of the church is little changed from the days when it gave speaking room to famous abolitionist leaders. If you are walking by looking at the whaling captains' houses on Orange Street, drop in.

LECTURE SERIES

The 19th century might well be called the Age of Oratory. The lecture circuit was entertainment and education — vaudeville and public television combined. People who had never read his books quoted Mark Twain. John Greenleaf Whittier and Horace Greeley were household names. The poets and authors who represented the "flowering of New England" were as well known on Nantucket as they were in Concord and Boston. And why not? Almost all of them came to the Island sooner or later.

Everyone who was anyone in the circle of important literary figures found an appreciative audience at the Atheneum or the church halls of Nantucket: Ralph Waldo Emerson, Henry David Thoreau, Daniel Webster, Herman

The Portuguese Bell

The bell in the gold-domed tower of the Unitarian Universalist Church, 11 Orange Street, was cast in Lisbon, Portugal, in 1810, during the Napoleonic Wars. It was one of a set of six destined for the Shrine of the Good Jesus in Braga, Portugal, but was in danger of being melted down for cannons. Captains Cary and Clasby of Nantucket heard about the bell and decided — with true Island gallantry — to rescue it on behalf of the still-empty tower of the Town's new South Church. The thousand-pound bell was bought and stored until it could be shipped on the *William & Nancy* in 1812.

Even though the bell had escaped Napoleon, it was not yet out of danger. The United States government had its own cannon-casting needs for the War of 1812. When the bell arrived in Nantucket, it was promptly hidden — "lost" was the word used — until 1815 when it was "found" and hung with appropriate ceremony. It served as fire alarm and a signal of shipwreck. For nearly two centuries it has tolled a full three minutes (that's fifty-two times) at 7am, 12 noon, and 9pm every day of the year.

Melville, as well as Twain, Whittier, and Greeley. John James Audubon came to sell subscriptions to his *Birds of America*. A young Frederick Douglass made his first public speech before a racially mixed audience at an abolitionist rally here and was so encouraged by the response that he went on to become one of the leading spokesmen for his people.

Nantucket's affinity for the spoken word unfiltered by radio or television continues today. The **Atheneum** was conceived as a lecture hall as much as a public library, and it still is. The line-up of speakers' names on the popular summer lecture series often reads like a list of best-selling authors, and this continues at a somewhat reduced pace off-season. Important science writers and researchers speak regularly in the auditorium of the **Maria Mitchell Museum of Natural Science**, while experts on the sea appear every week in summer under the auspices of the **Egan Institute of Maritime Studies** at the Coffin School. Contemporary Nantucket historians have a forum at the Whaling Museum. The Nantucket Life Saving Museum on Polpis Road presents lectures on maritime drama and disasters. Children's book authors and illustrators speak and read aloud to audiences of all ages in the Atheneum's Weezy Wing for Children.

The **Old South Church (Unitarian Universalist Church)** has hosted controversial speakers since the early 1800s. Frederick Douglass appeared here and so did Booker T. Washington when even the Atheneum was pulling back from what was felt to be a potential incitement to riot.

See also the section on "Museums" below.

LIBRARIES

The public Nantucket Atheneum and its attached Weezie Children's Library are at the center of the Island's culture.

Rob Benchley

Nantucket's **Atheneum** (508-228-1110; atheneum@nantucket.net; 1 India St., Nantucket, MA 02554) is a byword in public libraries, a total success story. The 1834 original burned to the ground in 1846, together with its 3,500 books. An appeal to the country for replacements resulted in a much larger and enriched selection to be shelved in the new building on Lower India Street that was completed only six months after the fire. Ralph Waldo Emerson gave the dedication speech in 1847. In 1996 expansions and renovations enabled additional materials including audio-visual to be made available. Its newly enlarged children's wing (the Weezy Wing for Children) with regularly scheduled story hours and activities make it a magnet for the young, especially on days when it's too foggy for the beach.

Checkout privileges are free to residents, property owners, and Massachusetts public library card holders; there's a $5 seasonal fee for visitors. Special collections include Nantucket history and historical newspapers. The Atheneum is closed Sundays (in winter Sun.–Mon.) but otherwise open 9:30am–5pm daily in summer and 9:30am–8pm Tues.; 9:30am–5pm Wed. and Sat.; noon–5pm Thurs.–Fri. in winter.

The **Maria Mitchell Science Library** (508-228-9219; www.mmo.org; 2 Vestal St., Nantucket, MA 02554) is open Tues.–Sat. 10am–4pm June 25–Sept. 15 and Wed.–Fri. 2pm–5pm, Sat. 9am–noon the rest of the year. Special collections include historic documents, research journals, science books, and displays, including Maria Mitchell's own papers. Library privileges are free; book checkout is two weeks. There is a cozy children's nook, and Internet and computer access are available to patrons.

The **Edouard A. Stackpole Library and Research Center** (508-228-1894; www.nha.org; Peter Foulger Museum, 17 Broad St., Nantucket, MA 02554) is open Mon.–Fri. 10am–3pm year-round. Contains ship logs, books, charts, and audio-visual materials related to Nantucket history. $5 per visit; $10 for two visits or visitor's pass; free to NHA members.

MONUMENTS

While you will find plaques aplenty around the Island marking the homes of significant historical figures and the places of vanished structures, these deserve note:

Abiah Folger Fountain on Madaket Road. Abiah was the daughter of Peter Foulger and the mother of Benjamin Franklin. Nearby is the site of the homestead where she was born.

Civil War Monument on Upper Main Street, listing the Nantucket men who died in the Civil War.

Forefathers Burial Ground, west of Wannacomet Rd.

Miacomet Indian Burial Ground, Surfside Rd.

Old Polpis Burial Ground, Polpis Rd.

MUSEUMS

Nantucket's museums are both specific and varied, well supported by the community and by the funds of nonprofit organizations.

Nantucket Town

The African School and Church on Nantucket (508-228-4058; 23 York St., PO Box 1802, Nantucket, MA 02554) This 1827 historic landmark is the only public structure remaining on the Island that is central to the African-American community of the 18th and 19th century. Now owned by the Museum of Afro-American History in Boston, it serves as a cultural and educational center as well as museum. (See "Black Heritage Trail.")

Aquarium (508-228-5387; 28 Washington St., Nantucket, MA 02554; by the Town Pier) Life in Nantucket waters, with hands-on exhibits for children, in a waterfront shack downtown. Marine ecology trips can be accessed here. Open early June through August, Tues.–Sat. 10am–4pm.

Birthplace House (508-228-2896;www.mmo.org; 1 Vestal St., Nantucket, MA 02554) Maria Mitchell original portraits, scientific instruments, and memorabilia. This traditional old Nantucket house with its roof walk and painted decor is fascinating as well as historic.

The Coffin School contains the **Egan Institute of Maritime Studies** (508-228-2505; eganinst@nantucket.net; www.marinehomecenter.com/eganinstitute;

*Admiral Sir Isaac Coffin's school is now home to the Egan
Foundation for Maritime History.*

Betty Lowry

4 Winter St., Nantucket, MA 02554) The school's brick Greek Revival building was completed in 1854. It was called Admiral Sir Isaac Coffin's
Lancasterian School and was founded in 1827 to give "a good English education to the youth who are descendants of the late Tristram Coffin . . . as
long as they have a drop of Coffin blood" — which at that time included just
about every child on the Island. Nautical skills were emphasized, and the
Admiral also provided the first training ship in America, the *Clio*, an eighty-
seven-foot brig that took Nantucket boys as far as Rio de Janeiro. Visitors see
"Visions of Nantucket's Past, 1659–1900" by British maritime artist Rodney
Charman as well as a short film on the life of Admiral Sir Isaac Coffin,
American Tory and British naval officer. The Admiral's Reading Room has
paintings, ship models, books and periodicals on American maritime history, and art. The **Egan Institute of Maritime Studies** supports a notable
lecture series with speakers on maritime science and history. General admission fee $1; free to NHA members and pass holders.

Hinchman House Natural History Museum (508-228-0898; 7 Milk St.,
   Nantucket, MA 02554; corner of Milk and Vestal Streets) Exhibits of
   Nantucket flora and fauna; headquarters for nature walks; shop.

Loines Observatory (508-228-9273; 59 Milk St., mail: 4 Vestal St., Nantucket
   02554) Open for public viewing through a fine old telescope on a regular
   schedule in summer and for special astronomical events — always depending on the weather, so always call ahead.

Maria Mitchell Association (508-228-9198; www.mmo.org; 4 Vestal St., Nantucket, MA 02554) Named for Nantucket's famous first American woman
   astronomer, this amalgam of science-related buildings and programs memo-
   rializes most appropriately a 19th-century woman who was not only a scien-
   tist and discover of a comet but also a librarian (the Atheneum) and educa-
   tor (Vassar College). The facilities, lectures, bird walks, nature walks, marine
   ecology walks, children's educational programs, and classes are open to the

public. An activity-filled "Discovery Day" for children and adults is held at the Vestal Street Campus and Aquarium in August.

The Nantucket Historical Association (508-228-1894; www.nha.org; 15 Broad St., PO Box 1016, Nantucket, MA 02554) With more totally preserved buildings in the National Register of Historic Places than Boston, Salem, or Plymouth, Nantucket has a viable claim to being the preeminent historic center of the northeastern United States. The Town became a National Historic Landmark in 1966, and the entire Island has been a historic district since 1971. The Nantucket Historical Association (NHA), incorporated July 9, 1894, is the owner of much and, in a very real sense, the keeper of all.

In addition to serving as the resource center for Island history, the NHA also sponsors lectures, changing exhibitions, children's educational projects, and special events for the public as well as its own members. The NHA has self-guided walking tours of historic Nantucket available at Visitor Services, 12 Federal Street, as well as at the Whaling Museum.

Not all NHA properties are currently open to the public. Some are in process of renovation or restoration — these are, after all, very old structures. And the public sites are not all houses; the operating windmill is the last of four that once stood on this particular hill, and the old jail ("gaol" to use the old English spelling) and fire hose cart house played significant roles in Nantucket history.

You can visit the properties listed below in summer and on weekends midseason. In July and August, children from six to ten can participate in two-hour Living History programs. Watch the newspaper for times and days. Lectures, slide presentations, exhibits, concerts, book signings, demonstrations, and tours happen almost daily. All sites are open 11am–3pm; the Whaling Museum and Peter Foulger Museum are open 10am–5pm. Admission to each ranges from $2 to $5 for adults and $1 to $2 for children, payable at the door. Best buy is the $10 Visitor Pass, which allows you to visit all of them.

Touring the properties takes about two-and-a-half to three-and-a-half hours on foot. The Whaling Museum has limited hours spring and fall and closes in winter. Handicap access to the Whaling Museum is through the Museum Shop.

Fire Hose Cart House (8 Gardner St.) This 1886 structure houses old fire equipment brought out annually for the Antique and Classic Car parade of Daffodil Weekend.

Friends Meeting House, 1838 and **Fair Street Museum**, 1904 (both at 7 Fair St.) Originally built as a school, this structure was converted to a meetinghouse in 1864, and it is still used for regular meetings of the Religious Society of Friends. The museum is the site for changing exhibitions from the NHA's permanent collections.

Hadwen House (96 Main St.) One of the "Three Greeks," this elegant Greek Revival house was built in 1845 for a Starbuck daughter and contains

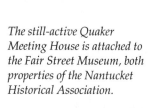

The still-active Quaker Meeting House is attached to the Fair Street Museum, both properties of the Nantucket Historical Association.

period furnishings, fabrics, and decorative accessories, many original to the house. The garden is maintained by the Nantucket Garden Club.

Macy-Christian House (12 Liberty St.) 18th- and 19th-century furnishings, including decorative arts and crafts. The guide explains the changes made by successive owners from its construction in 1740. These have been retained to show such aspects as the 20th-century Colonial-Revival style.

Oldest House (Sunset Hill) Built in 1686 for Jethro and Mary Coffin (see "Making Love, Not War, on Nantucket" in Chapter One, *History*), the house is a rare remnant of early Nantucket.

Old Gaol (Vestal St.) Built in 1805, this jail held prisoners accused of diverse crimes — but in the early days they were allowed to go home at night. In 1933 the last few prisoners escaped, and the Town built a new jail.

Old Mill (Prospect St.) The 1746 mill, said to be the oldest operating mill in the country, still functions in peak season, using wind power to grind corn into meal, much to the delight of children attending the NHA's Living History programs. It has handcrafted wooden gears and is one of several mills that once stood along the hills west of Town.

Peter Foulger Museum (17 Broad St.) His descendants use the Folger spelling but asked that the original be used in naming the museum. Changing exhibits. The Edouard A. Stackpole Library and NHA Research Center on the second floor has a collection of manuscripts, letters, ship's logs, and genealogical materials as well as books.

Whaling Museum (15 Broad St. at Steamboat Wharf) In the 1840s this was a factory for making spermaceti whale oil candles. Its vast rooms lend themselves well to such objects as a full-size whaleboat and the skeleton of a forty-three-foot whale. The memorabilia of the Whaling Age is well displayed and includes a renowned collection of scrimshaw. Programs and lectures are held here, and exhibitions change regularly. A delightful museum shop is next door.

The Whaling Museum houses an extensive exhibit of whaling artifacts, a full-size whaleboat, and the skeleton of a finback whale (pictured).

Rob Benchley

Out of Town on the Madaket Road is the **Abiah Folger Franklin Memorial.** The stone trough placed by the Nantucket chapter of the Daughters of the American Revolution is a tribute to Abiah Folger, mother of Benjamin Franklin, who was born nearby. Across the pasture to the north is a boulder with a plaque commemorating the site of the Folger house lot laid out in 1600 and one of the first homestead sites on the Island.

Nantucket Lightship Basket Museum (508-228-1177, 49 Union St., Nantucket, MA 02554) This museum dedicated to Nantucket's famous art-craft opened in 2000 in a building formerly known as the 1821 House. Highlight is the workshop of Jose Reyes, the man who designed the lightship basket handbag, moved from its original place at 18 York St. Original baskets made aboard the New South Shoal Lightship are among the permanent exhibits. Classes and seminars, too. Open Wed.–Sun. 10am–5pm.

Vestal Street Observatory (508-228-9273; 3 Vestal St., Nantucket, MA 02554; off Upper Main St.) Hosts young scientists. Solar system models and children's astronomy classes. Open all year.

Science Library (508-228-9219; 2 Vestal St., Nantucket, MA 02554) Personal papers of Maria Mitchell and an academically significant collection of natural science and astronomy, historical documents, current periodicals, and even a special children's section. The building is the schoolhouse where William Mitchell once taught celestial navigation. Open all year.

Everywhere Else

Nantucket Life Saving Museum (508-228-1885; mo72506@nantucket.net; www.nantucket.net/museums/lifesaving; 158 Polpis Rd., Nantucket, MA 02554; at Folger's Marsh) The world's only lifesaving museum, it's a copy of the old Star of the Sea Life Saving Station at Surfside Beach (now the youth hostel). Exhibits include one of only four known Massachusetts Humane Society

The Life Saving Museum off Polpis Road is a duplicate of the original "Star of the Sea" station at Surfside (now a youth hostel) and commemorates the U.S. Life Saving Service.

Rob Benchley

surfboats and the only beach cart left in existence. Also on display are artifacts of the Revenue Cutter Service, Lighthouse Service, and United States Coast Guard, plus the original 1856 Fresnel lens of the Brant Point lighthouse and the restored upper portion of the 1818 Great Point lighthouse with its 1857 Fresnel lens. The poignant but little-known motto of the United States Life Saving Service and the United States Coast Guard is: You have to go out, but you don't have to come back. Nantucket's shoals are still referred to as the "graveyard of the Atlantic." The museum makes an ideal break for a tour and picnic along the new Polpis Bike Path. Open June 15–Oct. 31, 9:30am–4pm. A museum shop has many unusual and even original treasures for sale.

MUSIC

In the newspaper listings of one summer week arbitrarily chosen, a recent visitor found the following: a noontime concert at the Unitarian Universalist Church (Chopin to jazz presented by a pianist and dancer); a chamber music concert in the bandstand at Children's Beach one night and a band concert another, part of the Harbor View Music Festival; three nights of ballet; the Nantucket Jazz and Folk Festival at Island Marine; a gospel concert in the North Vestry of the First Congregational Church; a ballad singer at the Cross Rip Coffeehouse; plus live dinner music at restaurants and evening musical entertainment — folk, jazz, and rock and roll — in the pubs and night spots. During the October Arts Festival, the churches even produce an "organ crawl."

Major concerts by internationally known performers such as the Boston Pops are held under the summer stars on Jetties Beach. Band concerts are held every week in season in the bandstand at Children's Beach, and the Christmas Stroll could hardly exist without roving bands of carolers.

Music festivals and organizations on Nantucket:

Harbor View Music Festival (508-228-7213; Children's Beach) 6pm Thursdays and Sundays in summer sponsored by Parks & Recreation Commission.

Nantucket Arts Council Concerts (508-228-2190, PO Box 554, Nantucket, MA 02554) Internationally known performers on tour come to Nantucket.

Nantucket Community Music Center (508-228-3352; 11 Centre St., PO Box 1228, Nantucket, MA 02554) Chamber music fits nicely into small spaces.

Nantucket Jazz & Folk Festivals (508-228-6874; PO Box 929, Nantucket MA 02554). Look for these in summer and holiday weekends.

Nantucket Musical Arts Society Concerts (508-228-1287; First Congregational Church, 62 Centre St., PO Box 897, Nantucket MA 02554). Fine musicians from all over the world perform on Tuesday evenings at 8:30pm during July and August at the First Congregational Church. At 8:30pm on Mondays in July and August, join informal get-togethers with artists and/or composers at the Meetinghouse of the Unitarian Church in preparation for Tuesday concert.

Noonday Concerts (508-228-5466; Unitarian Universalist Church, 11 Orange St., PO Box 1023, Nantucket, MA 02554) A spectacular series of international talent offer concerts on Thursdays during July and August.

NATURE CENTERS

It's tempting to say that all Nantucket is a nature center, since it contains not only specific centers of study like the Maria Mitchell Association's facilities (see above under "Museums") but also acres of conservation land. For more information, see Chapter Seven, *Nature and the Environment*.

NIGHTLIFE

Nantucket readily admits to being an early-to-bed sort of place. Even the liveliest spots don't go much past midnight, must close by 1am, and are rarely loud enough to annoy the neighbors. Evening entertainment is plentiful: movies, theater, lectures, concerts, dance performances, miniature golf, and plenty of special events at the museums; but if you're thinking "nightlife," even in high season you will find Nantucket's offerings of blues, funk, and jazz on the light side. Some name rock and blues bands do play weekends in-season at the Island's three nightclubs, the Muse, the Box, and the Rose & Crown (see below).

Nantucket Town

The Brotherhood of Thieves (no phone; 23 Broad St., Nantucket, MA 02554) Weekend entertainment is usually a duo or maybe a single good guitarist and attracts a young crowd. There's inevitably a line outside on the street waiting to get in. Stays open to 12:30.

Cross Rip Coffee House (508-325-7741; United Methodist Church, 2 Centre St., Nantucket, MA 02554) Good fall to spring entertainment from folk music to comedy acts in an alcohol-free environment. Venue for Nantucket performing artists of all ages.

Rope Walk (508-228-8886; 1 Straight Wharf, Nantucket, MA 02554) Live jazz Monday nights.

Rose & Crown (508-228-2595; 23 S. Water St., Nantucket, MA 02554) A pleasant pub popular with Islanders and off-Islanders alike. Live entertainment of the folk-singer-and-small-jazz-ensemble type nightly in summer and Saturday nights all year.

The Tap Room at the Jared Coffin House (508-228-2400; 29 Broad St., Nantucket, MA 02554) Downstairs you can actually talk as well as hear the music.

Everywhere Else

Chicken Box (508-228-9717; 14 Dave St., PO Box 2122, Nantucket, MA 02554) "The Box" is mid-Island in the direction of Surfside Beach. Live bands every night from Memorial Day to Labor Day; weekends the rest of the year. A bar, not a pub.

The Muse (508-228-6873; www.museack.com; 44 Surfside Dr., PO Box 2549, Nantucket, MA 02554) Popular year-round hangout, with bands on tour in summer and other live entertainment on weekends. This is the liveliest spot on the Island year-round, though off-season you're likely to sometimes find DJs. Keno and trivia games, too. The Muse sponsors most of the Island's new music events. Recently it added a pizzeria and even serves coffee and muffins midmorning.

SPECIAL EVENTS

The harbinger of springtime on Nantucket is Daffodil Weekend, followed by the Nantucket Wine Festival. Summer comes in with a flair at the Film Festival, then explodes on Independence Day. The Sandcastle and Sculpture Day is mid-August. Autumn has its own color — deep red — especially during the Harvest Festival, which includes Cranberry Harvest weekend and comes right behind the Arts Festival. Winter is the frosty month of Nantucket Noel that begins the day after Thanksgiving and runs through December. The famous Christmas Stroll is the first Saturday of the last month. In many cases the multilayered events grew around a traditional Island happening rather than being a made-for-tourist project by the ever-enthusiastic chamber of commerce.

Although the early settlers were cool toward religious holidays, they built a major party around a day of sheep shearing. Everyone on the Island came to socialize and dine as well as relieve the sheep of their winter coats. The event continued through the 19th century. Harvest Home, the tradition of English villagers and early American colonists, was glorified on the Island, too, especially in connection with the annual cranberry gathering.

The very nature of Island living mandated homegrown celebrations. Things are more organized now, though not so much so that changes don't occur at the last minute. One predictable: The iron horse fountain in the middle of lower Main Street, made originally so the animals could have a stand-up drink of water, will be appropriately decorated for every occasion.

DAFFODIL WEEKEND

The annual Daffodil Festival features an antique car parade from downtown out to Siasconset.

Rob Benchley

The last weekend in April, Nantucket goes for the gold in a big way. This harbinger of spring on the Island began more than a quarter century ago when Jean MacAusland, a long-time Islander and cofounder of *Gourmet* magazine, gave a million Dutch bulbs to beautify Milestone Road for the annual Classic Car Parade. The first hundred thousand turned out to be a learning experience. Hand planted in stiff rows by volunteers and schoolchildren, they were mowed down before they had time to store up sufficient food for the following year.

The lost bulbs were replaced and, every year since more have been donated by local merchants, organizations, and private individuals. Straight lines have given way to naturalized drifts; deceptively random clusters skirt the trees. You will see daffodils blooming irrationally beside sand dunes and poking coyly from dry fountains as well as window boxes and cottage gardens.

Saturday morning's Antique and Classic Car Parade, begun in 1964, is now limited to pre-1962 vehicles, and well over one hundred participate. Many of the drivers wear period costumes, and nearly all of the cars are elaborately decorated with daffodils. (Purists refuse to put anything on a restored automobile that wasn't there in the first place — flowers, for example — but such eccentricities are in the minority and politely overlooked.) The spectators wear flowers, too, and even the dogs sport yellow ribbons.

After assembling on Main Street, the parade heads out daffodil-enhanced Milestone Road to Sconset for the noontime Tailgate Picnic. Some people bring their own lunches; if hotel guests, they dine al fresco from buffets. The spreads are judged both for decor and food, then marked with prize ribbons.

There's a contest for the best decorated shop windows, too, and if you arrive by noon on Friday, you can follow the judges around. At the Nantucket Garden Club's Annual Daffodil Show, amateurs and pros alike compete for the best floral arrangements.

Nantucket's historic houses open for the weekend, and inns invite the public on informal tours. Special events, gallery shows, exhibits, and music tend to pop up at the last minute, rather like the flowers themselves.

Daffodils have few diseases, grow in full sun or dense shade, and can make do with thin, rocky soil. Perhaps that's why they seem so appropriate in sea-captain country — people or flowers that require pampering have forever been scorned hereabouts.

While only the foolish or exceptionally hardy would swim in the Atlantic before the fourth of July, spring is an ideal time to walk or wheel about the Island. Daffodil Weekend signals the reopening of those hotels and restaurants that were closed for the winter. Bird-watching tours begin about now, and conditions are prime for a seal cruise. The weather is cool to mild, and the flowers last five to six weeks.

The Nantucket Wine Festival, held at the Siasconset Casino, attracts connoisseurs from around the country.

Rob Benchley

For more information, contact: Nantucket Chamber of Commerce (508-228-1700; 48 Main St., Nantucket, MA 02554).

NANTUCKET WINE FESTIVAL

This mid-May event attracts more than a hundred wineries for exhibitions and tastings. The festival also emphasizes Nantucket's restaurants and food products, a long and proud list of gastronomic achievement. It's a wonderful time to come. The Island is not yet awash with tourists, and off-season rates still prevail in the inns. (See also Chapter Five, *Restaurants and Food Purveyors*.) For more information, program, and reservations, contact: Nantucket Wine Festival (508-228-1128, fax 508-228-7830; winetone@nantucket.net; nantucketwinefestival.com; PO Box 306, Nantucket, MA 02554) or the Nantucket Chamber of Commerce (508-228-1700; 48 Main St., Nantucket, MA 02554).

THE NANTUCKET FILM FESTIVAL

Though there had been another before it, the first serious and fully realized Nantucket Film Festival was held in 1997. It proved to be such a success that it was promptly put into the permanent calendar of Island events for the third week in June. The idea was to celebrate what was called "the Other Hollywood" — that is, the emerging screenwriters, producers, actors, and filmmakers who create independent films. Naturally this attracted film creators from Los Angeles and New York as well as Boston, first to a party for eight hundred in a private summer home on Cliff Road and then to a week of morning coffees, seminars, panel discussions, stage readings, and film showings open to the public. For information, contact: The Nantucket Film Festival (212-708-1278) or the Nantucket Chamber of Commerce (508-228-1700; 48 Main St., Nantucket, MA 02554).

The annual sandcastle contest, sponsored by the chamber of commerce and the Nantucket Island School of Design and the Arts, is held every August at Jetties Beach.

Betty Lowry

THE ANNUAL SANDCASTLE AND SCULPTURE DAY

Nantucket's answer to mid-August blahs (if there is such a thing) is the more than a quarter-of-a-century-old Jetties Beach sandcastle spectacular cosponsored and organized by the Nantucket Island School of Design & the Arts.

Check-in is from 12 to 12:30 at Jetties Beach, but unless you have registered

Nantucket Limericks

Some names lend themselves to limericks, and "Nantucket" definitely has what it takes. Recently the publication *Yesterday's Island/Today's Nantucket* resurrected these from a 1924 edition of a Nantucket newspaper.

> There once was a man from Nantucket
> Who kept all his cash in a bucket
> But his daughter, named Nan
> Ran away with a man,
> And as for the bucket, Nantucket.
> > — *Princeton Tiger*

> But he followed the pair to Pawtucket,
> The man and the girl with the bucket,
> And he said to the man
> He was welcome to Nan
> But as for the bucket, Pawtucket.
> > — *Chicago Tribune*

> Then the pair followed Pa to Manhasset
> Where he still held the cash as an asset,
> But Nan and the man
> Stole the money and ran,
> And as for the bucket, Manhasset.
> > — *Exchange*

> Of this story we hear from Nantucket
> About the mysterious loss of a bucket,
> We are sorry for Nan
> As well as the man —
> The cash and the bucket, Pawtucket.
> > — *Pawtucket Times*

> Oh, what to do with the bucket,
> Now that it's back on Nantucket?
> Nan & Pa will refill it
> And try not to spill it,
> And pretend that the man never tucket.
> > — *Native Islander*, Nantucket

in advance at the chamber of commerce office, you will be on standby for the space of a no-show. You may use tools, aids, ornaments, and decorations. Anything not biodegradable must be hauled away afterward.

Sculptors work in teams, with the age group determined by that of the oldest member. A family is considered a team if adults participate, but no unregistered helpers are permitted. When registering, you must give the name of your sandcastle or sculpture, the name of your team, and designate a team captain. Each team may have up to eight members, and their full names also go on the registration form.

Divisions are 10 & Under, 11–16, Family Team, and Adult Team. Ribbon prizes for first, second, third, and honorable mention are awarded in each division (there are no losers). Entry fee is $5 per person. For more information, contact: Nantucket Chamber of Commerce (508-228-1700; 48 Main St. Nantucket, MA 02554).

THE NANTUCKET ARTS FESTIVAL

The first week in October is reserved for the arts in all media in venues throughout Town. These include meeting the authors as well as attending the concerts; viewing the films, plays, and performances; listening to the storytellers; watching the craft demonstrations; and touring Nantucket's many, many galleries. Children are included, too, with handcrafts such as making sailors' valentines and activities from treasure hunts to skateboarding. Buying an Arts Festival button enables the wearer to attend a week of events free or with discounted admissions.

The popular "Wet Paint Auction" is a fund-raiser for the Artists' Association of Nantucket. It works this way: On Sunday morning several artists begin to paint on location in Town and around the Island. At 4pm they bring their wet paintings to the Artists' Association Gallery at 19 Washington Street, where there is a short preview of the work and a grand auction. If the paint isn't quite dry, you can arrange to pick up your purchase the next day. For information, contact: Artists' Association of Nantucket (508-228-4922; 19 Washington St. 02554).

NANTUCKET NOEL

Snow is relatively unusual on Nantucket, and when it falls is more often than not melted by noon. No matter — with or without a White Christmas, Nantucket Town is a Christmas card come true for a full month from the day after Thanksgiving until December 31.

From the enormous wreath hung by the coast guard on the side of the Brant Point lighthouse to the three hundred or more decorated trees on the streets of Town, to the welcoming doorways of the historic houses, Nantucket never looks lovelier. The churches put on Christmas pageants. Carolers sing. The Lighting of the Trees ceremony takes place the day after Thanksgiving, with

The U.S. Coast Guard brings Santa to Straight Wharf during the annual Christmas Stroll.

Rob Benchley

the decorating completed by the Christmas Stroll the first weekend in December. Colored lights are reserved for Main Street, white lights for the rest.

The Nantucket Historical Association sponsors a Festival of the Trees in the Fair Street Museum and with it a silent auction of decorated wreathes. Hadwen House and the Thomas Macy House across the street are open for a Victorian holiday, right down to the harp and cello playing in the parlors. There are raffles, craft shows, bazaars, drawings, giveaways, and contests, including one for the best gingerbread house. The art galleries have special exhibits and sales. Merchants decorate their shop windows and homeowners their front doors.

The Christmas Stroll began in 1973 and has grown to a three-day event. Every inn is full that weekend, and reservations are firmed up months in advance. Community singers, bell ringers, and musicians in Victorian costume appear downtown. The Christmas trees have been decorated by shopkeepers and by community groups, from the chamber of commerce to the Cub Scouts. A benefit house tour opens the doors of private historic homes. In the "Stroll Food" tent at the bottom of Main Street, the Girl Scouts offer a bake sale all day, and lunch is served by various organizations.

On Stroll Saturday, the Town crier officially rings in the festivities all the way down Main Street to meet the ferry. Santa arrives by coast guard cutter and leads a procession up Main Street, then settles in on the doorstep of the Pacific Bank not far from where the Magical Talking Christmas Tree has been delighting and mystifying youngsters. A parade of giant puppets starts at the iron horse fountain and proceeds up to the United Methodist Church, where the puppets will give a matinee performance.

The evening activities begin at the Atheneum with the recitation of something appropriate, perhaps *A Child's Christmas in Wales*. Music all around Town follows. There are candlelight services at the churches, evensong, plays, and concerts.

Christmas stroll is the busiest weekend of the year.

Rob Benchley

When the crowds leave on Sunday night, Nantucket holds its own Christmas. Events and music continue, though at a calmer pace. The other December weekends have their own concerts and contests. On the Saturday before Christmas, the Jared Coffin House holds a traditional Boar's Head Processional Dinner; that Sunday there's a retelling of the Christmas story, featuring an ecumenical choir, at the Old South Church. Christmas on Nantucket was not always so overtly celebrated. Those first settlers, though not Puritans themselves, came out of the severe Oliver Cromwell Protestantism that flatly forbade the holiday. The Quakers were nearly as abstemious. On the whaling ships far from home, Christmas was just another working day, more often than not.

By the mid-1800s, though, things had changed. Christmas dinners were served on the ships as well as at home, especially on ships where the captains' wives were along. Ships in port were decorated with greens, and Christmas trees were hoisted and attached to the mainmasts. At home Yule logs burned, and Christmas trees were hung with gifts and candy. Santa came with the predictable "Ho, ho, ho!"

Maybe — just maybe — it will snow on Christmas. Then the powers-that-be will close Main Street to traffic, and the children will get out their sleds or whatever they can invent on the spot that will slide. The artists will grab their sketchbooks and brushes to record the event. Everyone will take pictures. It will be remembered and talked about for years.

THEATER

Live theater on Nantucket is a blend of professional, neo-professional, and amateur talent performing a wide range of light and serious drama, adap-

Coming to Terms

Nantucket (land far out to sea), *Siasconset* (near the great bone), *Madaket* (bad land), *Quidnet* (at the point), and most other places on the Island have names taken from the purely descriptive Algonquin language. On occasion a real person is honored: *Gibbs Pond* was named for John Gibbs, a Wampanoag who was a special friend to the first settlers, a Christian pastor to his people, and studied at Harvard College. *Tom Nevers*, another Wampanoag, once watched for shipwrecks and whales off a south shore headland that now bears his name. *Wauwinet* was the name of a legendary sachem of great integrity, and his name means "Witness my hand." The name for *Dionis Beach* — Dionis being the wife of first-purchaser Tristram Coffin— came later and is considered to have been an attempt to cozy up to the thousands of Coffin descendants.

On Nantucket you'll find none of those English place names repeated in every New England state (sometimes modified by "New") memorializing some former home shire or town. Following a flurry of outrage when John Gardner, half-share holder, persuaded the governor of New York Colony to name the main settlement "Sherburne" for his own English hometown, Nantucket's settlers were shrewd enough to eliminate this potential competition within their group. They changed the name of the place the Wampanoag called Wesko (for a white rock in the harbor) to Nantucket Town, ignored Sherburne, and kept the other place names Algonquin. This was all right with the Wampanoag, who naturally preferred to keep whatever they could, including the names they had bestowed upon the land.

The working vocabulary of whaling has lingered here, too, as well as other words of obscure origin. A few pithy word-pictures of more modern days have also caught on. These are just a few of the terms you are likely to encounter on Nantucket:

Gam: A visit and exchange of news and tales between whaling ships. The two captains would meet on one ship and the two first mates on the other to forestall mutiny. The term is now used for any get-together.

Rantom scooting: An unstructured cruise or wandering without definite destination or purpose.

Squantum: A picnic or outing with specific location.

Right whale: As in "the right whale to catch" because it did not sink when killed.

Quahog: Pronounced KO-hog, this is a variety of clam, almost a synonym for Nantucket chowder. (You have to be on Island at least once to know how to pronounce it.)

Nantucket sleigh ride: What the riders in a whaleboat got when a harpooned whale took off, pulling the boat behind it. Speeds were estimated as twenty to twenty-five miles per hour.

Camel: A floating dry dock invented in 1842 to carry ships over the hump of the blocking sandbar and into Nantucket Harbor. It was a good idea — but not good enough to keep up with sandbar growth. A loaded whaling ship was a great weight; eventually Nantucket lost out to the more accessible and deeper harbor of New Bedford.

"Thar-e-bl-ooo-os!" A distinctively Nantucket cry recognizing the sight of a whale. New Bedford whalemen shouted "Ah-blo-oo-o, blow, blow."

Historic, historical, old: Adjectives of praise to be used with equanimity on everything you see.

America: The mainland. The Revolution was known in some quarters as "America's War." When Islanders talk about spending a few days in Boston or Hyannis, they are likely to say they are "going to America."

Day-tripper: Those who cross over from America and do not stay long enough to contribute significantly to the Island economy.

Tourists: Those who stay a while, spend a lot, and, it is hoped, will leave their automobiles in America.

Stand-by: Someone attempting to bring a vehicle larger than a bicycle to Nantucket without a firm reservation made months ahead.

Around-the-Point: Year-round residents not born on Nantucket, hence coming from somewhere "around the point." (Usually applied to a previous generation; current settlers establishing themselves year-round are called "Washashores.")

Off-Islanders: Those who inhabit America as well as other diverse places on earth.

Islanders: Those born on Nantucket Island and descended from at least three generations of island-born people. A grandfather from the Cape knocks you out of the definition, according to some people.

Summer people: Those who reside on Nantucket for the season, including property owners (no matter how rich and famous), renters, and the working college students. Does not include day-trippers or tourists.

The Inky Mirror: Nantucket's two-century-old newspaper, the *Inquirer and Mirror.*

"Oil! Oil!" Old whalers and their spiritual descendants will raise their glasses in this toast.

Island: There is only one — the Island of Nantucket.

Town: There is only one — the Town of Nantucket.

tations, originals, and children's theater. On a summer's evening no one worries about what the critics will say the next morning, and everyone has a good time. It can be tryout time for well-known actors and playwrights, too. Yet there's a certain magic to seeing, say, Orson Welles's *Moby Dick* performed on Nantucket. Auditions go on all year — one intriguing notice recently was: SMALL DOG NEEDED FOR THREE-NIGHT PERFORMANCE — and are announced in the newspaper. Casting for children's theater often draws on summer residents as well as locals. Theater performances continue through the fall.

Actors Theatre of Nantucket (508-228-6325; www.nantuckettheatre.com; United Methodist Church, 2 Centre St., Nantucket, MA 02554) A professional theater company with shows from Memorial Day through Columbus Day. The intimate theater is in the lower level of the Methodist church. ATN has had some smashing one-person shows and stand-up comedy routines, with Broadway actors trying out their ideas. There are also 5pm family matinees of familiar tales and a 10pm Late Night Theatre After the Mainstage Show.

The Children's Theatre of Nantucket (508-228-7257, ext. 1576; kidstars@ nantucket.net; 10 Surfside Rd., PO Box 2284, Nantucket, MA 02584) Community

School's Children's Summer Theatre asks a minimum commitment from aspiring students eight to eighteen. "Join Monday and perform by Wednesday," is the invitation. Shows in the auditorium of Nantucket High School or in the Sconset Casino.

In one form or another, theater is alive year-round on Nantucket. Here, Grace Noyes (left) and Marcela Jones rehearse a scene during the Nantucket Short Play Festival.

Rob Benchley

Nantucket Theatrical Productions – Short Play Festival (508-228-5002; PO Box 2177, Nantucket, MA 02584) Entries come from all over the country. Readings of the four finalists are held on successive nights at the end of August in the Brock Conference Center on Main Street and in the garden of the Atheneum on India Street.

Theatre Workshop of Nantucket (508-228-4305; www.theatreworkshop.com; johnm@nantucket.net; 62 Centre St., PO Box 1297, Nantucket, MA 02554) The National Shakespeare Company comes to Nantucket's Bennett Hall on Centre Street.

CHAPTER FIVE
Chowder to Fiddleheads
RESTAURANTS AND FOOD PURVEYORS

Dining out is what everybody does on Nantucket — Islanders as well as visitors — because the restaurants are so uniformly good. Since ingredients are either local (straight from the sea, the moors, or Bartlett's Farm) or brought from the mainland at great trouble and expense, nothing second-rate slips by. The cost of obtaining these ingredients is passed on to diners, however, so food is more

Robert Benchley

Garden dining and a high-caliber menu are just part of the experience at the Chanticleer Restaurant in Sconset.

expensive as a result — yet not extraordinarily so, especially when compared with dining out in comparable resort or city restaurants. Few things are better value or more delicious on a foggy day than a Nantucket staple: a cup of quahog chowder (often pronounced and sometimes even spelled "chowdah") with puffy crackers for less than $4. And in springtime freshly gathered fiddlehead ferns are so plentiful, they are served as a vegetable instead of a garnish.

A good many restaurants are partly or entirely chef-owned. The result is a personal investment in seeing that, say, the seafood is same-day fresh. Your chef was probably down at the dock making the selection or maybe even out on the boat. When the cook does more than merely prepare, cookery becomes a matter of personal pride and style.

As you might guess from Nantucket's long history of international connections, the cuisine is not limited to hearty New England or even American fare. You can dine well on authentic French, Asian, Italian, and more. The Island's beauty and way of life have enticed gifted chefs away from enviable positions on the mainland for the stress-free pleasures of Nantucket. So you will find innovative cookery as well as classic, responding to the tastes of upscale visitors and sophisticated residents alike.

Of course, you can also get good hamburgers, pizza, and ice cream cones. Full-menu take-out is commonplace as are sandwiches to go and plain-to-elegant box lunches.

The restaurants themselves are distinctive. A number are in what were once private or even historic homes, so you will find a series of small dining rooms rather than one large space. Perhaps this arrangement itself contributes to the sense of being guests rather than customers. Yet you see none of the studied quaintness common to the "step-back-in-time" hostelries of theme-park villages. And while Nantucket is not a late-night town even in midsummer, food is available in the pubs and in the restaurant bars that stay open long after the dining rooms have closed.

Restaurant wine lists are impressive and repeatedly marked as excellent by *Wine Spectator, Wine Enthusiast*, and similar publications. In addition, the Island has its own Nantucket Vineyards where a "Shipwrecked Cider" is produced as well as limited amounts of wine using off-Island grapes. There's a microbrewery next door, and you are welcome to visit both (seasonally) between 11am and 6pm daily (Sunday noon–5pm).

Except in the fast-food take-out places near the beaches, bare feet and swimsuits are not acceptable in Island restaurants any time of day. But slip on sandals and pull a cover on over your bareness, and you'll pass. At the dinner hour the best restaurants probably won't even put you behind a potted palm if you look raunchy, but you will find most people dressed in what has come to be called "smart-casual" — jackets for men and skirts or pants (but not jeans) for women. At lunch the criterion seems to be "whatever goes on the golf course" — but note that Nantucket golf courses have dress codes.

Local purveyors make food shopping fun. Fruit and vegetable stands are set up on Main Street, and there are just-off-the-boat seafood markets. Portuguese bread is an item Nantucket has taken to with particular enthusiasm, and it is baked on-Island. (Nantucket's Portuguese associations include its 1812 church bell and 20th-century immigration from the Azores.)

Ready-prepared meals, one-course take-outs, and creatively combined sandwiches make impromptu dining a breeze. Since taking along a picnic lunch for a biking expedition or a day at the beach is part of the fun, it's good to know the choice goes far beyond the ubiquitous ham and cheese on rye (although you can get that, too, along with peanut butter and jelly). And Island caterers will provide you with everything from a wedding reception to a clambake.

So food is taken seriously but not too seriously. Case in point: On the second Friday in July there's the ultimate summer shenanigan: the Waiter/Waitress Race. Carrying trays bearing a glass of water and a can of beer from South Water Street to Main to Centre to Broad to South Water (that is, a rectangle of both paved and cobblestone streets) victory goes to the nimble, quick, and steady.

We have also included a limited list of breakfast and lunch places. While B&Bs provide at least a continental breakfast, often expanded from juice and rolls to include fresh fruit and cereals, you may want to take advantage of a

The Island Appellation

Culinary specialties from or associated with Nantucket have a reputation to uphold. Throughout the Northeast — New York, Boston, Hartford, and Providence — the small plump Island scallops are always designated "Nantucket" on menus to justify price as well as to indicate their quality. However, you will not see the Nantucket appellation applied cavalierly, for all its cachet. The direct Nantucket connection is mandatory, though at times it seems to have been stretched rather thin. "Nantucket Nectars," the fruity beverages sold all over New England, were originated on Nantucket by a pair of Brown University graduates (known locally as "Tom and Tom, the Juice Guys") who started their vending from a boat in the harbor — and who ultimately sold a percentage of their company to the giant Ocean Spray cooperative. The product, however, is bottled on the mainland. "Nantucket, Naturally," the designer spring water, is not from any Island spring — that comma says it all, apparently. It may be our imagination, but the dried cranberries (cranraisins and even craisins to some) sold here in the gourmet shops seem less dehydrated than the standard supermarket packaged stuff.

Jams and jellies made with beach plums, cranberries, blueberries, and currants are literally a cottage industry, and cranberry honey is gathered from the hives of moorland bees. Island-grown herbs go into the blends of **Island Herbs** (508-228-9851, 800-472-7110; 11 Deer Run Rd., Nantucket, MA 02554) that you buy in pack and jar. **Nantucket Coffee Roasters** (508-228-6862, 800-432-1673; www.nantucket-coffee.com; 15 Teasdale Circle, PO Box 2977, Nantucket, MA 02554) and **Nantucket Coffee Co.** (508-228-5267; 52 S. Shore Rd., Nantucket, MA 02554) roast and blend if not grow right here, and the chocolates of **Sweet Inspirations** (508-228-5814, 888-225-4843; www.nantucketclipper.com; 26 Centre St., PO Box 966, Nantucket, MA 02554) designated "Nantucket" are made right on the premises. Lastly, some restaurants have their own lines of salsa and sauces often named for the Island.

full Nantucket repast (blueberry pancakes or eggs benedict, say) now and then, especially after an early run or bird-watching trip. We tell you where food is available from 5:30am on. As for lunch, we've singled out a few especially useful places for when you don't want a long midday break.

At present there are no solely vegetarian eateries on Nantucket, but many places serve vegetarian dishes, and a few have menus more vegetarian than not. You will find most of these noted under the "Special Features" of each restaurant. Meatless pastas are even more widely available, and chefs are very accommodating.

The number of fine restaurants is remarkable for a small island. Many — but not all — are in or on the fringes of Nantucket Town. Some are mid-Island or not far from the beaches. Good food is also available both near and at the airport. Sconset is home to several excellent restaurants and a catering service that handles impromptu picnics as well as major functions of the rich and famous residents. In summer, the Wauwinet Inn's renowned Topper's restaurant offers transportation by boat between the Town wharf and the resort at the far bend of the Island. In the off-season, some mid-Island restaurants will pay for your taxi one way. Your innkeeper is an invaluable resource both for the current hot spots and the precise cuisine or price range you have in mind. Most B&Bs have a rack of current menus for you to look over or even a book where recent guests have jotted down their good (and not-so) dining experiences.

Nantucket restaurants and cafés alike have taken a cue from the European tradition and post their menus and prices outside the door. If they have a Web site, menus will be online, as well. Since the restaurants are small, during July and August reservations are necessary a day or even two days in advance. Many close at the end of October. Those that are open after that may decide to close an extra day for no apparent reason except that the chef has other things to do. Save yourself disappointment by telephoning.

In addition to a price code signifying the approximate cost of a single three-course meal, not including cocktails, wine or tip, we have tried to give you a view of the place as well as the food. Reviews are organized by section of the Island, then alphabetically by restaurant name. Food purveyors are grouped by type, then alphabetically by name of the establishment. Every entry appears in the general index, too. Do call ahead for a table. Diners are not rushed no matter how long the line is outside, and being in is infinitely better than being out.

Dining Price Ranges

Very Inexpensive	Up to $20
Inexpensive	$20–$30
Moderate	$30–$50
Expensive	$50–$60
Very Expensive	Over $60

Credit cards are abbreviated as follows:

AE	American Express
CB	Carte Blanche
D	Discover Card
DC	Diners Club
MC	MasterCard
V	Visa

Meals

B	Breakfast
Br	Brunch
L	Lunch
SB	Sunday Brunch
D	Dinner

DINING IN NANTUCKET TOWN

Dining on the patio at the Boarding House restaurant on Federal Street.

Rob Benchley

AMERICAN BOUNTY
508-228-3886, 228-4886.
www.tuckernuckinn.com.
60 Union St., Nantucket,
    MA 02554.
At the Tuckernuck Inn four
    blocks east of Main St.
Open: Apr.–Jan.
Serving: B, D.
Cuisine: American
    regional.
Price: B, Inexpensive;
    D, Moderate to Expensive.
Credit Cards: AE, MC, V.
Reservations:
    Recommended.
Handicap Access: Yes.
Special Features:
    Nonsmoking; vegetarian
    selections; patio dining;
    parking.

The restaurant in the century-old inn is bright and cheerful, and the food is hearty. Chef John Cataldi has an inspired touch. Families will find the service patient and friendly and the menu broad enough to appeal to a range of tastes.

All entrées are available in half portions so you can accommodate small appetites and/or share. The Bounty Bouilabaisse is remarkable (phone ahead for this), and the sternest vegetarian will cheer the farfalle pasta with wild mushrooms. Breakfast is a real bargain — as low as $4 — and for just a tad more you can have a Bounty Omelet with fillings to order. Drop in for this after your morning brisk walk on the beach or bike path, and the day will be off to a fine start.

AMERICAN SEASONS
508-228-7111; amerseas@
    nantucket.net.
www.americanseasons.com.
80 Centre St., Nantucket,
    MA 02554.
Open: Apr.–Dec.
Serving: D.
Cuisine: New American.

The menu of this chef-owned restaurant is divided geographically into Pacific Coast, Wild West, Down South, and New England. For instance, you can have slow-roasted California rabbit and wild-mushroom tart with black-pepper goat cheese, red-onion comfit, and a grilled-apple salad as on the coast; or you could go for Wyoming

Price: Expensive.
Credit Cards: AE, MC, V.
Reservations: Required.
Handicap Access: Yes.
Special Features:
    Vegetarian dishes; patio.

golden trout with refried pinto beans in a smoked tomato and sage broth for the West. Sautéed silk red snapper with Carolina rice and scallion risotto, smoked-bacon collards with a sauce of fire-roasted onions will more than satisfy the South; while New England fans can dine on Nantucket oysters, Maine blue-crab salad, fresh Vermont quail, or local monkfish. The dining rooms of the 19th-century house overflow into the patio on summer evenings, or maybe it's the other way around.

Arno's at 41 Main Street is a cozy bistro popular with Islanders and Off-Islanders alike.

Betty Lowry

ARNO'S AT 41 MAIN STREET
508-228-7001; akdiamonds @nantucket.net.
41 Main St., Nantucket, MA 02554.
Open: Daily Apr.–Dec.
Serving: B, Br, L, D.
Cuisine: Eclectic American.
Price: Inexpensive to Moderate.
Credit Cards: AE, D, DC, MC, V.
Reservations: Accepted in summer.
Handicap Access: Yes.
Special Features:
    Nonsmoking; children's menu; take-out; vegetarian.

You may have to wait for a table at Arno's. It's a standard favorite with locals as well as being convenient for visitors pausing halfway up cobble-stoned Main Street. The atmosphere is chummy, with original brick walls as background for original works by Island artist Molly Dee. If you can get a window table, it's a perfect place for people-watching. Jeanne Diamond, who owns Arno's together with her husband, Richard, modestly admits to winning numerous awards in local dining competitions. Quahog chowder and lobster bisque are done with éclat, as are a range of other dishes: lobster and boursin cheese omelets or pancakes filled with bananas, walnuts, and chocolate chips for breakfast; lunch, a cranberry BBQ pork sandwich; and for dinner, deviled sautéed crab cakes. Desserts include lots of decadent chocolate dishes, too.

ATLANTIC CAFÉ
508-228-0570;
  theac@nantucket.net.
www.atlanticcafe.com
15 South Water St.,
  Nantucket, MA 02554.
Open: Daily 11:30am–
  11:30pm; closed Dec. 25.
Serving: L, D.
Cuisine: Seafood,
  American, sandwiches.
Price: Very Inexpensive to
  Inexpensive.
Credit Cards: AE, D, DC,
  MC, V.
Reservations: No.
Handicap Access: Yes.
Special Features:
  Nonsmoking section;
  children's menu.

BLACK-EYED SUSAN'S
508-325-0308.
10 India St., Nantucket, MA
  02554.
Open: May–Oct.
Serving: B, D; except no
  Sun. D.
Cuisine: New American.
Price: Moderate.
Credit Cards: None.
Reservations: Accepted for
  6pm only.
Handicap Access: Yes.
Special Features: BYOB;
  counter service;
  nonsmoking; vegetarian
  dishes; some outdoor
  tables.

BOARDING HOUSE
508-228-9622.
12 Federal St., Nantucket,
  MA 02554.
Open: Daily.
Serving: D.
Cuisine: Contemporary
  classic.
Price: Moderate to
  Expensive; bistro menu:
  Moderate.

Very busy, very popular, and often very crowded, the Atlantic Café is one of those drop-in places with a full bar where no one seems to mind waiting for a table at noon. It's right down in the Historic District, for one thing. For another, the chowder is full of clams, the hamburgers are cooked to order, and the sandwiches are generous enough to share. This is a very good place to take the family after a morning in the Whaling and Peter Foulger Museums diagonally across the street. Turnover is rapid, so you'll barely have time to look around at the ship models, original seagoing-theme art, and nautical decor before you're squeezed in somewhere.

Starting with the fact that the Susan, who greets you at the door, has blue eyes, this tiny chef-owned restaurant beloved by the boomer generation is a bit of an enigma. If you don't want to sit on a stool and watch the cooks grilling dinner a few feet away, you need to reserve for dinner; but as sometimes there's no operating phone, the only way to make a reservation is to stop by early in the day or even the day before and leave your name. The menu, too, is a puzzle. No such thing as a small à la carte salad to go with a main course, for example. Whatever, the flavors are well balanced on the plate, and the menu changes every two weeks. Susan's is always packed, and the steady customers love it. Maybe you will, too. And bring your own bottle as well as cash.

Not your average boardinghouse, even on Nantucket. The dining room is candlelit, fresh flowers are on the tables, and original art is on the walls. (The delightful flower shop next door, Flowers at the Boarding House, is one of the most photographed places in Town, by the way.) It's family-owned (he's the chef, she's the manager) by two alums of the New England Culinary Institute who were recently named "Graduates of the Year." The

Credit Cards: AE, MC, V.
Reservations:
  Recommended.
Handicap Access: In the
  café.
Special Features:
  Nonsmoking; outdoor
  dining; bar open
  5pm–1am.

food has decided Asian and Mediterranean overtones never dreamed of in the place's boardinghouse days. Among the entrées: rare yellowfin tuna with wasabi aïoli and soy ginger glaze; ginger sautéed prawns with jasmine rice, yellow Thai curry cream, and fried shallots. Bistro fare includes a Japanese Bento Box of the Evening, an Asian noodle sampler (soba, peanut, Thai pesto), or lobster tempura with Japanese soba noodles and ginger broth. Since the menu changes often, call for the night's specialties.

The stylish bar is a favorite with both locals and summer "high-rollers."

Next door in the Flowers at the Boarding House cottage and under the same management is **The Pearl** (508-228-9701, 14 Federal), specializing in seafood. Opens Daffodil Weekend through summer, and reservations are necessary.

BRANT POINT GRILL
508-228-2500.
50 Easton St., Nantucket,
  MA 02554.
At the White Elephant.
Open: Apr.–Dec.
Serving: L, D.
Cuisine: cContemporary
  American; seafood.
Price: Expensive to Very
  Expensive
Credit Cards: AE, D, DC,
  MC, V.
Reservations:
  Recommended.
Handicap Access: Yes.
Special Features: Patio
  dining; parking.

After dinner on a summer evening at this airy and elegant restaurant on the harbor, you can stroll down to the Brant Point lighthouse and watch the fishermen trolling. Brant Point Grill, elegant and revised like its White Elephant Hotel home, has a new executive chef, Don Kolb. You might start with the chilled shellfish sampler (lobster, oysters, clams, and shrimp) or lobster fritters with mizuna, radish, and lemon-pepper aïoli. Move on to delicious entrées like pan-roasted dayboat scallops. The harbor-side terrace lunch has a range of delicious lighter offerings. Picnic coolers to go, too.

The line begins to form outside the popular Brotherhood of Thieves restaurant.

Rob Benchley

BROTHERHOOD OF THIEVES
No listed telephone.
23 Broad St., Nantucket, MA 02554.
Up from Steamboat Wharf.
Open: Daily except Feb.
Serving: L, D.
Cuisine: American.
Price: Inexpensive.
Credit Cards: None.
Reservations: No.
Handicap Access: Yes.
Special Features: Weekend entertainment all year; nightly in summer.

You will know the Brotherhood of Thieves by the line snaking down Broad Street. This authentic 1840s whaling bar is a hangout for the young and hungry, and the den-of-rogues atmosphere adds to the fun. Several rooms, all with low ceilings and brick and timber walls, hold more diners than you might guess, and the service is fast and friendly. The super-size hamburgers and thick sandwiches come with curly shoestring fries (the fries are the first thing mentioned if you ask anyone under twenty what they like about the place). Actually, there's more — salads, pasta, and seafood, for example — but you get the picture. The whole-grain poppy-seed buns are a plus. The sandwiches are named for Nantucket streets and the burgers for other places, like Texas and Boston. Desserts are limited to cheesecake and chocolate cake. In winter a fire burns cheerily on the hearth. Also in winter the menu enlarges to include full dinners. Open daily except February with continuous service from 11:30am to midnight (Friday and Saturday to 12:30am) plus a guitar and folk singer or maybe a trio every night in midsummer and weekends the rest of the year. It's a good family place, too, if you go for an early dinner or off-season so the kids don't have to stand in line.

CAP'N TOBEY'S CHOWDER HOUSE
508-228-0836.
Straight Wharf, Nantucket, MA 02554.
Open: Mid-May–mid-Oct.
Serving: L, D (continuously 11am–10pm).
Cuisine: New England, seafood.
Price: Inexpensive to Moderate.
Credit Cards: AE, MC, V.
Reservations: Accepted.
Handicap Access: Yes.
Special Features: Early-bird specials 5pm–6:30pm; take-out; children's menu; upstairs and downstairs dining rooms.

Cap'n Tobey's has been under the same management for more than forty years, and they have casual dining down to a tee. They take the "chowder house" in the name seriously, too, and make a mean meal-in-itself bowlful. Or settle for a cup and save your appetite for the other seafood on the menu and the extensive salad bar. Lobster is always a good choice, but there are daily specials to consider. Furthermore, you can literally eat all day starting at 11:30am. Luncheon moves directly to dinner, which goes on until 10pm. The salad bar is included with all entrées, and if you're not all that hungry (you may change your mind once you get there, though), there's a "grazing menu," too. For dessert, try the Indian pudding with ice cream. If "famous" means being listed in just about every guidebook to Nantucket and the name leaps to mind when any Islander says "chowder," this is a famous place. It's especially nice to sit upstairs and look out on the wharf and watch the people go by, but anywhere you sit you'll know how near you are to the waterfront by the nautical theme of boat gear and sailing art.

**CENTRE STREET
  BISTRO**
508-228-8470.
www.nantucket.net/food/
  bistro.
29 Centre St., Nantucket,
  MA 02554.
At the rear of the Meeting-
  house Shops complex.
Open: Year-round (closed
  Mon. and Tues.in winter)
Serving: B, L, D.
Cuisine: New American.
Price: Moderate.
Credit Cards: None.
Reservations: Suggested for
  dinner.
Handicap Access: No.
Special Features:
  Vegetarian dishes; inside
  and outside seating; no
  cell phones.

You can walk right by on Centre Street and not know this trendy little restaurant is there because it is off-off Centre . . . sort of. Persevere — some interesting combinations of food are waiting tucked in the back of the Meetinghouse Shops complex on the first floor of the Meetinghouse Inn. Tom and Ruth Pitts, the chef-owners, have made a name for themselves over the past four years. Sometimes when the diners outnumber the tables, people have found the take-out option a bonus. After all, the Atheneum garden-park is only a block away. One of the Bistro's specialties on their seasonally evolving menu is their smoked salmon platter. There's also a "risotto of the evening" plus fresh home-baked breads and desserts.

**CHANCELLOR'S ON
  EASTON STREET**
508-228-8674; ptbreeze@
  nantucket.net.
www.pointbreeze.com.
71 Easton St., Nantucket,
  MA 02554.
At the Point Breeze Hotel.
Open: May–Sept.
Serving: B, D.
Cuisine: Continental.
Price: Moderate to
  Expensive.
Credit Cards: AE, M, V.
Reservations:
  Recommended.
Handicap Access: Yes.
Special Features:
  Nonsmoking; parking;
  outdoor dining;
  children's menu;
  vegetarian salad bar.

Some may remember when this restaurant was the Whale and the Point Breeze was Folger's Hotel. It's a big, rambling place, and on a summer's night you can sit on the veranda sipping your cocktail and pretend to be an Islander in the 1920s and 1930s. All was rebuilt in 1926, though the hotel first opened in 1891, and the porch was added in 1912. There's even a ballroom where more likely than not you'll find a wedding reception in progress. Another high point: The food has become considerably more sophisticated (consider Nantucket bouillabaisse with local finfish and shellfish and roasted-garlic crostini, lemon sorbet topped with candied lemon peel).

**CIOPPINO'S
  RESTAURANT & BAR**
508-228-4622; cioppino@aol.
  com.

The Cioppino is San Francisco-style using local seafood, a winning combination. Personalized service is emphasized, with owners Tracy and Susi

www.cioppinos.com.
20 Broad St., Nantucket,
  MA 02554.
Open: May–Nov., plus
  Christmas Stroll.
Serving: SB, L, D.
Cuisine: Continental.
Price: Moderate.
Credit Cards: D, DC, MC,
  V.
Reservations:
  Recommended in
  summer.
Handicap Access: No.
Special Features: Twilight
  menu 5:30–6:30; patio
  dining; small but lively
  bar area.

Root on the premises at all times. You'll find three dining rooms in this hundred-year-old house and a dining patio, as well. Try the Nantucket bay scallops niçoise and chilled fresh oysters in a red wine mignonette, lobster-and-asparagus salad with a lemon-herb vinaigrette, hazelnut-crusted salmon filet fish, and pastas of the day. Wind up with raspberry crème brûlée or a chocolate fantasy cake, which is walnut torte with Kahlua buttercream. The house Bloody Mary (the "Bloody Cioppino") is so popular, you can take it home—the mix concentrate, anyway.

Rob Benchley

The Club Car restaurant at 1 Main Street, with its attached car from the old Nantucket Railroad.

THE CLUB CAR
508-228-1101; fax 508-228-
  8740.
www.theclubcar.com
1 Main St., PO Box 1852,
  Nantucket, MA 02554.
Open: mid-May–mid-Oct.,
  plus Thanksgiving and
  Christmas Stroll
  weekends.
Serving: L, D.
Cuisine: Continental.
Price: Expensive.
Credit Cards: MC, V.
Reservations:
  Recommended.
Handicap Access: No.

The Club Car is not just a name. This is the last remnant of the Nantucket Railway, the one car that missed the great sell-off of 1917. The restaurant began as a diner, expanded in 1977, and actually the club car is now just the lounge, but never mind. There's a piano in the lounge area in the evening, and you can stop in anytime for a chowder-and-sandwich lunch or a brew. The main dining room is the much more elegant room to your right as you enter: white tablecloths, fresh flowers, and such. The dinner menu of renowned Island chef Michael Shannon is a long way from the railway picnic basket, too, with a number of specialties like Maryland Crab Cake Club Car with mustard cream sauce and some unexpected items such as Bangkok-style Japanese squid with enough peppers to blow the ears if not the mind. The menu varies with the season, and there are off-season Sunday night specials that are major bargains (beef Wellington for $30) until the end of June.

COOK'S SIDEWALK CAFÉ

508-228-8810.
6 S. Beach St., Nantucket, MA 02554.
Serving: L, D.
Cuisine: Natural New Age.
Price: Inexpensive.
Credit Cards: MC.
Handicap Access: Yes.
Special Features: Outdoor dining; vegetarian; delivery; all-day juice, smoothie, and yogurt bar.

A "designer drink" at Cook's may be a blend of echinacea, astragalus, and golden seal mixed with a Very Berry smoothie (this is called "Immune Booster") or something similar with ginseng, spirulina, kava kava, etc. All sorts of wraps are available, too, from "Very Veggie" to turkey and other ideas too numerous to mention from the Cooks' travels in Asia. You can also have a fresh fruit blend and a bran muffin or a nonfat bagel. This is New Age on the Beach, so it should be no surprise that you can coordinate your take-out with your mountain-bike or kayak rental. Cook's connects with Cook's Cycles, delivering bikes and boats to any location. Families with kids playing on the beach can conveniently feed them healthy snacks or an energy-enhanced lunch.

DE MARCO

508-228-1836,
fax 508-228-5587.
www.nantucket.net/food/demarco
9 India St., Nantucket, MA 02554.
Open: Apr.–Nov.
Serving: D.
Cuisine: Northern Italian.
Price: Expensive to Very Expensive.
Credit Cards: AE, MC, V.
Reservations: Recommended.
Handicap Access: Yes.

The healthful aspects of the Mediterranean diet seem beside the point in this intimate 19th-century two-story restaurant with its candles and flowers on the tables. The menu is resolutely northern Italian (with translations), from antipasti to primi and secondi. Consider fresh watercress tossed with Gorgonzola cheese, citrus fruits, and toasted pecans; steamed clams in a broth of vermouth, garlic, vegetables, and fresh herbs over angel-hair pasta; grilled veal chops with wild mushrooms over creamy polenta. Try the petto di pollo ripiene con spinaci, or osso bucco d'agnello con verdure glasate. Over one hundred Italian wines await in the De Marco cellar, and all breads and desserts are made fresh on the premises. When you ask a resident for the names of the best restaurants on the Island, De Marco always makes the list.

THE GALLEY AT CLIFFSIDE BEACH

508-228-9641.
54 Jefferson Ave., Nantucket, MA 02554.

You are watching the sun go down from beneath an awning on Nantucket Sound. Someone unobtrusively lights a candle on the table, signaling that the stars are now expected to appear in the

At Cliffside Beach.
Open: June–Oct.
Serving: L, D.
Cuisine: Seafood,
  international.
Price: Expensive.
Credit Cards: AE, MC, V.
Reservations:
  Recommended.
Handicap Access: No.
Special Features:
  Waterfront; jazz piano;
  vegetarian dishes.

THE HEARTH
508-228-1500.
5 S. Beach St., Nantucket,
  MA 02554.
At the Harbor House.
Open: Apr.–Dec.
Serving: B, SB, L, D.
Cuisine: American,
  seafood.
Price: Moderate.
Credit Cards: AE, D, DC,
  MC, V.
Reservations:
  Recommended.
Handicap Access: Yes.
Special Features: Parking;
  live music; late-night
  snacking; children's
  menu; take-out; outdoor
  dining.

INDIA HOUSE
508-228-9043.
37 India St., Nantucket,
  MA 02554.
At the India House Inn.
Open: Apr.–Dec.
Serving: D.
Cuisine: French, Thai,
  Caribbean.

sky. Try the gazpacho with avocado puree and herb crostini; the pistachio-crusted rack of lamb; the grilled tuna with Asian stir-fry. The menu emphasizes Nantucket fresh produce and seafood. Even the mussels are steamed in Nantucket Sleighride Riesling, and the breast of duck has a sun-dried cranberry demiglace. The cookery has overtones of Asia as well as the Mediterranean. You may well resist the call of other restaurants and return tomorrow.

The Hearth also appears in its ads as "The Hearth Pub & Patio at the Harbor House" and adds a significant slogan: Vita, Libertas, Felicitas. At the Hearth, this means that among its several rooms you can find what you want, whether it's a family dinner or an on-the-Town supper. Sunday brunch is an event as well as a bargain. In fact, it's so famous locally, it's a good idea to make reservations. The buffet is long and replete with seafood, roasts, omelets made to order, salads, and desserts.

At any meal the Hearth's servings are generous and the cookery is hearty. It's a good place to bring the family, especially if you have hungry teenagers to fill. The menu is long, with steaks, chicken, pasta, rotisserie ribs, and seafood, both local and Maine. The New England bouillabaisse with thick egg noodles is not what you would get in Marseilles, but this is Nantucket, after all. You can start with the raw bar and combine your appetizer with two each of oysters, clams, mussels, or shrimp. Lighter eaters will find soups and salads or such seafood selections as mussels in tomato-garlic broth tempting alternatives. In Harbor House but with its own entrance, the Hearth has the same open atmosphere as the rest of that friendly downtown resort complex.

Accolades from magazines for its fine dining and wine are matched by comments by diners. A honeymooning couple recently recommended it for a "one big splurge." Don't expect curry. The name comes from the street and from the fact that the wealth of the Indies contributed to the comforts of sea captains living there. The inn itself dates from 1803, when it was built by a wealthy rope

International fare at the India House restaurant includes French, Thai, and Caribbean dishes.

Frederick G. S. Clow

Price: Expensive.
Credit Cards: AE, MC, V.
Reservations: Required.
Handicap Access: No.
Special Features: Garden
 café in summer.

maker and trader, and has been preserved much as it was in those halcyon days.

The cuisine, however, is both innovative and truly international, and the menu changes every two weeks. In summer you can enjoy the formal garden with its fountain, blooming cherry tree, and roses galore.

The Jared Coffin House is home to Jared's, an Island favorite.

Betty Lowry

JARED'S
508-228-2400.
www.jaredcoffinhouse.net.
29 Broad St., Nantucket,
 MA 02554.
At the Jared Coffin House.
Open: B, 7:30–10:30am weekdays, 7:30–11am weekends
 year-round; D, 6–9pm.

This large, airy dining room, the signature restaurant of the 1843 Jared Coffin mansion-cum-inn, is a solid favorite with Islanders and off-Islanders alike. *Cape Cod Life* magazine has endowed it with a whole series of culinary "bests," from breakfast to pub to inn to outdoor dining. The cuisine is innovative without being overpoweringly so: The potato-crusted halibut is served over sautéed arugula and

Serving: B, year-round; D, through Oct.
Cuisine: American.
Price: Moderate.
Credit Cards: AE, CB, D, DC, MC, V.
Reservations: Suggested for dinner; off-season, call for times.
Handicap Access: Yes.
Special Features: Nonsmoking; seafood buffet seasonally Wed., Sun.; parking; children's menu.

spinach with red-pepper coulis; the lemon-thyme roasted duck has a Madeira-wine pan gravy. Desserts are simple. Try the coffee crème brûlée or the chocolate torte with raspberry sauce. The full country breakfast is served all year.

KENDRICK'S AT THE QUAKER HOUSE
508-228-9156.
www.nantucket.net/lodging /quakerhouse.com.
5 Chestnut St., Nantucket, MA 02554.
In the Quaker House, corner of Centre and Chestnut Sts.
Open: Apr.–Jan. Thurs–Mon.
Serving: L, B Sat. and Sun., D.
Cuisine: Fusion.
Price: Moderate to Expensive.
Credit Cards: AE, MC, V.
Reservations: Recommended.
Handicap Access: Yes.
Special Features: Bar menu served daily 6pm–11pm; dinner 6pm–10pm; weekend brunch 8am–2pm; vegetarian dishes; wine bar.

The restaurant has two intimate dining rooms, and because there are so few tables, you really must reserve. Once a tearoom, then a chef-owned restaurant, it has moved on to another chef-owner and an entirely different menu. The cusine is now fusion, as in sesame-crusted salmon with sweet-soy glaze and Asian greens and jasmine rice. For dessert, try chocolate crème brûlée or apple-tart Tatin. There is also a bar menu in case you can't get a regular table or you come in after the movie.

LE LANGUEDOC
508-228-2552.
www.lelanguedoc.com.
24 Broad St., Nantucket, MA 02554.
At Le Languedoc Inn.
Open: May–Christmas Stroll.
Serving: D.
Cuisine: French, continental.
Price: Moderate to Expensive.

This is a dual restaurant, since the menus of café and dining room do not really overlap. The café — and outdoor garden — provides a cheeseburger (albeit Black Angus, with hand-cut fries) as well as duck-leg comfit with balsamic and onion sauce, and braised lentils and apples. Dinner in the dining room, however, is a matter of, say, lobster bisque with chive blossoms, or porcini-dusted sweetbreads, celery-root puree, and white truffle oil, or even a

Credit Cards: AE, MC, V.
Reservations:
  Recommended for dining
  room; not accepted for
  café.
Handicap Access: No.
Special Features: Wine bar.

LOBSTER TRAP
508-228-4200.
23 Washington St.,
  Nantucket, MA 02554.
Open: Mid-May–mid-Oct.
  4–9:30pm.
Serving: D.
Cuisine: Seafood.
Price: Moderate.
Credit Cards: AE, MC, V.
Reservations: Suggested.
Handicap Access: Yes.
Special Features: Home
  delivery "Meals on
  Keels" and private
  clambakes; take-out;
  early-bird specials.

ORAN MOR
508-228-8655.
www.nantucket.net/food/
  oranmor.
2 South Beach St.,
  Nantucket, MA 02554.
Behind the Whaling
  Museum.
Open: Mon.–Sat. in season;
  Fri.–Sun. off-season.
Serving: D; SB off-season.
Cuisine: New international.
Price: Expensive.
Credit Cards: AE, MC, V.
Reservations: Yes.
Handicap Access: No.
Special Features: Full menu
  available at the bar.

THE ROPEWALK
508-228-8886.
www.theropewalk.com.
1 Straight Wharf,
  Nantucket, MA 02554.
At end of wharf on
  Nantucket Harbor.
Open: May–mid-Oct.

short stack of foie gras, potato brioche, and duck rillettes followed perchance by roasted hickory-scented salmon with fresh peas, lobster broth, and crisp polenta, or mustard-and-herb-crusted rack of lamb with white bean cake and roasted-red-pepper demiglaze. Obviously a place for serious diners.

If you watch carefully, you may see the fishermen delivering their catch at the rear of the restaurant. The specialty is fresh lobster, but that doesn't mean clams, mussels, and other shellfish are overlooked. Only dinner is served here, but they will also send a clambake with you to the West End beach to enjoy a private sunset repast or deliver to your home, guesthouse garden, or yacht.

Peter Wallace, the chef-owner of Oran Mor, opened his own restaurant after a decade with Topper's at the Wauwinet Inn. Dinner is the only meal served (except Sunday brunch during off-season), and the menu changes its regional influence frequently. The result is always surprising. For example: Italian brings grilled local oysters wrapped in pancetta with balsamic beurre; hand-hauled bay scallops with fire-roasted tomatoes and pappardelle; eggplant rollatini with house-made ricotta and spinach; chocolate and espresso pudding. The ambiance is intimate and decidedly European. A small and special place. (*Oran mor* is Celtic for "great song.")

As soon as you touch the rope on the walk, you feel as if you are boarding a yacht. The Ropewalk has seafood as basic as beer-batter fish and chips (the lunch menu) and "Nantucket Clam Chowda" (any time), but it also does osso bucco with pasta gnocchi and sautéed shrimp and scallops with cob-smoked bacon, wild mushrooms,

Serving: L, D.
Cuisine: American,
  seafood.
Price: Moderate.
Credit Cards: MC, V.
Reservations: No.
Handicap Access: Yes.
Special Features:
  Vegetarian burger; on-
  the-water dining; patio;
  raw bar.

ROSE & CROWN
508-228-2595.
www.theroseandcrown.com.
23 South Water St.,
  Nantucket, MA 02554.
Open: Daily 11:30am–1am
  mid-May–Christmas
  Stroll.
Serving: L, D.
Cuisine: American casual,
  seafood.
Price: Inexpensive.
Credit Cards: AE, MC, V.
Reservations: No.
Handicap Access: Yes.
Special Features:
  Vegetarian dishes;
  children's menu, early-
  bird specials;
  entertainment.

SHIPS INN
508-228-0040, 888-872-4052.
www.nantucket.net/lodging
  /shipsinn.
13 Fair St., Nantucket, MA
  02554.
At the Ships Inn, 1-1/2
  blocks off Main St.
Open: May–Christmas
  Stroll; closed Tues.
Serving: D.
Cuisine: California-French.
Price: Expensive.
Credit Cards: AE, D, MC, V.
Reservations: Suggested.
Special Features: Gourmet
  vegetarian dishes.

and Madeira sauce. The Nantucket steamed lobster with new potatoes, vegetable, drawn butter, and lemon is ever ready at the day's market price, and Nantucket swordfish with smoked corn and black beans and chili sauce is a staple menu item. You can easily make a meal with two first courses, like the pan-fried crab cake with smoked corn-tomato salsa and Dijon mustard cream or Portuguese-style mussels with linguiça, tomato, and saffron. Plain grilling is always available. Thursday is Barbecue Night, and Sunday night is Clambake Special. Incidentally, the Raw Bar is open from 3pm–10pm.

While waiting for your pizza, pasta, seafood, salad, burger, or chicken wings (house specialty), you can crayon on the white paper covering the tabletops. (No prizes, but on this art-aware Island, it may only be a matter of time.) The Rose & Crown is a pub with a children's menu and a family feeling. Its chowder has devoted fans, but then this is a place of steady customers. Late at night it can get a little loud — the action begins at 10pm with live music Thursday through Saturday, DJ dancing Monday and Tuesday, and karaoke Sunday and Wednesday.

Built in 1831 for whaling captain Obed Starbuck, the house has been an inn for fifty years. The restaurant is on the lower level, and dinner is the only meal served. The white-linen tablecloths, hurricane lamps on the table, and the chinaware collectibles in the cabinet and on the windowsill are presumably a cut above what the good captain had on his whaler, the *Loper*. As for the food — well, doubtless he did not have a chef like Mark Gottwald, trained in Paris and apprenticed at Spago in Los Angeles and Le Cirque in New York. Mark, who owns the inn with his wife, Ellie, calls his cuisine California-French ("like Nantucket we're halfway between France and California"). Try, for example, the crispy salmon with celery root purée, Niçoise vegetables, and Cabernet sauce. The roast duck is with mushroom ragout and plum wine jus. The soufflé of the evening never disappoints.

STRAIGHT WHARF RESTAURANT
508-228-4499; straightwharf @nantucketonline.com.
6 Harbor Square, PO Box 388, Nantucket, MA 02554.
At Straight Wharf
Open: June–Sept. 30, closed Mon.
Serving: D.
Cuisine: Seafood, New American.
Price: Moderate to Expensive.
Credit Cards: AE, MC, V.
Reservations: Recommended for dining room.
Handicap Access: Yes.
Special Features: Grill menu in bar; waterfront dining.

The atmosphere here directly on Nantucket Harbor is strictly boats and more boats. The twin menus of dining room and bar are so international in concept and execution it's hard to see why the proprietors call the cuisine "New American." Once you've worked your way through Nantucket lobster stew with pasta, wild leeks, fava beans, and champagne or sauté of Atlantic halibut with lobster morels and spaetzle, you won't mind waiting fifteen minutes for some spectacular desserts: warm Valrhona chocolate tart with mango gelato or crème brûlée Napoleon with berries.

SUSHI BY YOSHI
508-228-1801.
www.nantucketsushi.com.
2 East Chestnut St., Nantucket, MA 02554.
Opposite the police station.
Open: Daily June–Oct.; Wed.–Sun., Mar.–May and Oct.–Dec.; closed Jan.–Feb.
Serving: L, D.
Cuisine: Japanese.
Price: Inexpensive to Moderate.
Credit Cards: None.
Reservations: Recommended.
Special Features: Nonsmoking; vegetarian; take-out; BYOB.

The specialty in this small chef-owned restaurant is the seven-course Japanese dinner including tempura at a reasonable price. Miso soup is a great bargain. Look for sushi, noodles, teriyaki, and curry, too. In short, this is authentic Japanese cuisine as prepared by Yoshi Mabuchi. Considering the number of whalers who stopped at ports in Japan once it was reopened to foreigners by Matthew Perry in 1853, dining on sushi by Yoshi is as much a part of Nantucket history as moor-gathered blueberry pie. (Except in Yoshi's case dessert will be banana tempura.) Only six tables, so it's prudent to make your reservation early.

TAP ROOM
508-228-2400.
www.jaredcoffinhouse.net.

Tucked downstairs beneath the famous and venerable Jared Coffin House, the Tap Room is what you like to think snug eateries were like during whal-

29 Broad St., PO Box 1580,
Nantucket, MA 02554.
Downstairs at the Jared
Coffin House.
Open: Daily, 11:30am–9pm.
Serving: L, D.
Cuisine: American.
Price: Inexpensive to
Moderate.
Credit Cards: AE, D, DC,
MC, V.
Reservations:
Recommended.
Handicap Access: No.
Special Features: Daily
vegetarian specials; patio
in season; children's
menu; take-out; smoking.

ing days. The food is hearty and straightforward —
in short, a good place to bring a whetted appetite.
Consider the New England–style scrod baked with
lemon butter and seasoned bread crumbs or the
grilled swordfish served with citrus butter. Roast
prime ribs au jus with popover comes in two sizes,
and this is so popular you might want to reserve your
favorite cut when you make your reservation. Lunch
in the Tap Room can be as classic as codfish cakes
with Boston baked beans, brown bread, and coleslaw
or the "Great Point Lobster Roll" — lobster on a soft
roll with Cape Cod potato chips. Executive chef
Wendy has named a vegetarian garden sandwich
after herself, so you know it's a winner.

Frederick G. S. Clow

Dining out has a curbside meaning at the Tavern at Straight Wharf, Harbor Square.

THE TAVERN
508-228-1266,
fax 508-228-6168;
signet@nantucket.net.
www.nantucket.net/food/
signet/tavern.html.
1 Harbor Square, PO Box
388, Nantucket, MA 02554.

This is prime people-watching territory right
on the dock at Harbor Square, and you may
want to get there a little ahead of the lunch-hour
crowd. The Tavern opens at 11am. Fortunately
service is fast as well as cheerful, and the menu is
uncomplicated with sandwiches, steaks, and local
seafood. The Tavern doesn't advertise much, since

At Straight Wharf.
Open: mid-May–Columbus
Day.
Serving: L, D.
Cuisine: Regional American.
Price: Moderate.
Credit Cards: AE, M, V.
Reservations: Large parties
only.
Handicap Accessible: Yes
Special Features: Outdoor
dining; children's menu;
late-night pub menu.

21 FEDERAL
508-228-2121
fax 508-228-2962.
www.21Federal.net.
21 Federal St., PO Box 1409,
Nantucket, MA 02554.
Open: mid-Apr.–mid-Dec.,
bar service 11:30am–1am,
dinner 6pm–10pm.
Serving: D.
Cuisine: New American,
seafood.
Price: Moderate to
Expensive.
Credit Cards: AE, MC, V.
Reservations:
Recommended.
Handicap Access: Yes.
Special Features: Wine bar;
patio.

VINCENT'S
RESTAURANT
508-228-0189.
21 S. Water St., Nantucket,
MA 02554.
Across from police station
and Town Hall.
Open: Apr.–Nov. from 8am.
Serving: B, L, D Apr.–Oct.
Cuisine: Italian specialties,
pasta, burgers, seafood.
Price: Very Inexpensive to
Moderate.
Credit Cards: D, MC, V.
Reservations: No.
Handicap Access: Yes, in
downstairs dining room.

nearly everyone exploring the wharf comes across it without help. The great American pastime of People Watching is secondary only to the catch-of-the-day.

Respected for its creative cookery as well as its snug romantic ambiance, 21 Federal is a contemporary restaurant in a 1847 Greek Revival building. It's where Islanders go on special dates, but you don't have to wait for that occasion. The menu changes daily to take advantage of the freshest and best foods available. Even the pasta is made on the premises. The unusual but delicious combination of flavors in every dish is the overall specialty of the house, such as pan-seared salmon with champagne cabbage or the asparagus with beet butter. The 21 Federal Bistro has a limited but no less interesting menu at low to moderate prices and does not accept reservations. The beautiful cherry-wood bar is beloved by Islanders as is the house special cocktail the "Cosmo" (a.k.a. "Cosmopolitan"): vodka with a dash of Cointreau and a splash of cranberry juice.

Vincent's, the cheerful family restaurant in the middle of downtown, has an unexpected history. The building was a "House of Refuge" established by the Humane Society of the Commonwealth of Massachusetts in the days before the U.S. Life Saving Service to store the boats and gear required to save the lives of shipwrecked mariners. Volunteers manned the boats, and their last use from this building was in 1904. Vincent Arno started the restaurant in the 1950s, making pizza and other Italian specialties along with fresh seafood entrées. Today the owner-chef is John Arno, and over the years the menu has grown to include veal, chicken, Nantucket lobster, and more.

Special Features:
Nonsmoking; children's menu; take-out and free delivery service 5–10pm in season; cappuccino bar.

WHITE DOG CAFÉ
508-228-4479;
whitedogcafe@aol.com.
1 N. Union St., PO Box 599, Nantucket, MA 02554.
Off Main St. in the garden patio at the Gaslight Theatre.
Open: Summer only.
Serving: Light dinners before the movie.
Cuisine: American light.
Price: Inexpensive.
Credit Cards: AE, MC, V.
Handicap Access: Yes.

THE WOODBOX
508-228-0587; woodbox@ nantucket.net.
www.woodboxinn.com.
29 Fair St., Nantucket, MA 02554.
1 1/2 blocks from Main St.
Open: Daily except Mon. (B 8:30–10:30am; D 6:30pm–9pm).
Serving: B, D.
Cuisine: Gourmet continental.
Price: Moderate to Expensive.
Credit Cards: None.
Reservations: Recommended.
Handicap Access: No.
Special Features:
Nonsmoking, small dining rooms; wine dinners.

Upstairs the bar-lounge has a late-night menu, cappuccino, Italian pastries, and entertainment in season. Take-out is straight from the kitchen entrance next door to the main entrance. Early-bird specials 4:30pm–5:30pm are very inexpensive.

First you call 508-228-4435 for the film listing at the Gaslight Theatre, and then you decide which of the two evening screenings you want to take in. You can go into the theater by the side door directly from the café. The children's menu is available all day, and so is the coffee bar, fresh-squeezed orange juice, quahog chowder, salads, bites, and wines or microbrews. Sangria is the house specialty. Pastries and desserts are home-made. Nothing fancy here, just a pleasant and slightly old-fashioned Nantucket way to spend a summer evening.

The Woodbox was built in 1709 and is the oldest dining room you'll find on Nantucket or nearly anyplace else. The walls are pine paneled, and the beamed ceilings are low. People were shorter in those days, and they didn't eat nearly as well. Nowadays beef Wellington and rack of lamb are house specialties as is seafood in all its forms. Chef Oakman is inventive enough to bring to his menu such fare as native albacore tuna with pineapple risotto, popcorn chutes, and balsamic vinegar reduction. He also creates a special pasta of the day. The hot popovers alone, though, are enough to bring diners here and back again.

DINING IN SIASCONSET

THE CHANTICLEER
508-257-6231.

The chef-owned Chanticleer often appears on "best French restaurant" lists and has received

www.thechanticleerinn.com.
9 New St., PO Box 601,
  Siasconset, MA 02564.
Open: Mid-May–mid-Oct.;
  every night. No lunch
  served Monday.
Serving: L, D.
Cuisine: Traditional French.
Price: Very Expensive.
Credit Cards: AE, MC, V.
Reservations:
  Recommended.
Handicap Access: Yes.
Special Features: Three
  public dining rooms;
  vegetarian entrée;
  parking; jackets required
  in main and upstairs
  dining rooms.

the *Wine Spectator*'s Grand Award since 1987 for "one of the best wine lists in the world." There is garden dining as well as three formal dining rooms, each uncrowded, different, and equally elegant. The weathered gray-shingled restaurant (the original was constructed in 1895) is covered with climbing roses in summer, the epitome of Sconset style. Although the owners, Anne and Jean-Charles Berruet, call the food "traditional French," it is a quantum leap beyond what that term has come to mean. You will find truffles, foie gras, and shallots. You won't find heavy sauce, and there's more than a touch of Provence, especially in the treatment of fresh vegetables. Try the lobster-and-truffle soup baked in puff pastry, the simply roasted duckling served with a currant sauce, the hot Valrhona chocolate soufflé with a bitter-chocolate sauce. The menu is choice rather than overwhelming, but there is always lobster, rack of lamb, a fresh fish of the day, and Black Angus rib. To be sure of a table, reserve well in advance. Many guests do this even before they leave for the Island. The Bastille Day party is limited, but maybe if you reserve a year in advance . . .

THE SCONSET CAFÉ
508-257-4008.
www.sconsetcafe.com.
8 Main St., Siasconset, MA
  02564.
On Post Office Square.
Open: Daily mid-May–mid-
  Oct.
Serving: B, L, D.
Cuisine: American "with
  world accents."
Price: Moderate.
Credit Cards: No.
Reservations: Accepted for
  6pm dinner only, wait
  list after 6:15pm; call
  ahead for take-out.
Handicap Access: No.
Special Features:
  Nonsmoking; BYOB;
  take-out dinners.

The tiny Sconset Café is as much a part of the village center as the post office, the general store, and the Casino, all within steps of if. There are only nine tables, but villagers who can't squeeze in at dinner happily carry home the entrées of owner-chef Rolf Nelson. Who wouldn't walk a mile (or drive seven from Town) for lamb tenderloins marinated in dark-red wine, Dijon mustard and herbs de Provence, served with a vegetable medley plus roast-garlic-and-scallion mashed potatoes? The individual rich chocolate cakes are served warm and ooze chocolate when cut. Don't plan on an eat-and-run evening, and bring you own wine.

THE SUMMER HOUSE
RESTAURANT
508-257-9976, 508-825-7563.
www.spiceoflifeonnan
  tucket.com.

You turn in and walk past rose-covered cottages to the main house, all on a bluff above the dunes and the sea. The dining room is large, with plenty of space between tables. Yes, you can imagine the movie stars

Betty Lowry

Whether you're dining in or taking out, Sconset Café fare is justly popular.

17 Ocean Ave., Siasconset, MA 02564.
At the Summer House.
Open: Daffodil Weekend to Columbus Day.
Serving: L, D.
Cuisine: American.
Price: Expensive; L Moderate.
Credit Cards: AE, DC, MC, V.
Reservations: Dinner.
Handicap Access: Yes.
Special Features: Bar menu 6–10pm; lunch at pool restaurant mid-June–Labor Day.

of yesteryear staying and dining here. Lunch is served in summer at the Ocean Restaurant overlooking the Atlantic from 12:30pm–3:30pm. The main restaurant has a 6–10pm menu reminiscent of fine country-club dining. You can order pan-seared fois gras with warm fruit compote and port jus or roast rack of spring lamb with a hazelnut crust, baby spinach, and beet risotto. Smoked meats and fish as well as all desserts and breads are made here. The Moby Dick Bar has a limited light menu from 6–10pm.

DINING EVERYWHERE ELSE

A. K. DIAMOND'S
508-228-3154.
www.akdiamonds.net

Here is mid-Island family dining with hearty portions and a huge salad bar. Bring your

---

Vegetarian Victuals

Although no Nantucket restaurant defines itself as solely vegetarian, few if any are without meatless dishes from simple to gourmet. We have noted those with consistent vegetarian menus under the Special Features of each restaurant listed, but this does not rule out others. When you call for reservations, you might ask what is meatless on the menu of the evening.

When asked to name their favorite Island dining spots, local vegetarians most often mentioned **American Bounty**, the **Fog Island Café**, **Kendrick's at the Quaker House**, the **Ropewalk** (for the vegetarian burger), **Ships Inn**, the **Tap Room at the Jared Coffin House**, the **Sea Grille**, **Sushi by Yoshi**, and the **Chanticleer in Sconset**. The prepared dishes from Bartlett's Farm and the sandwiches of **Something Natural from Nantucket** were also cited.

---

16 Macy's Lane, Nantucket,
 MA 02554.
Near the airport.
Open: Daily 11:30am–
 10pm; bar to 12:30am.
Serving: L, D.
Cuisine: Steaks, seafood,
 pasta.
Price: Inexpensive to
 Moderate.
Credit Cards: AE, D, MC, V.
Reservations: Accepted.
Handicap Access: Yes.
Special Features: 25 percent
 off dinner entrées before
 6pm; children's menu;
 parking; nonsmoking
 dining room.

CAFFÈ BELLA VITA
508-228-8766.
7 Bayberry Court,
 Nantucket, MA 02554.
Lower Orange St. at
 Nantucket Commons.
Open: Year-round Tues.–
 Fri. L, Tues.–Sun. D.
Serving: L, D.
Cuisine: Italian, pasta,
 seafood, steak.
Price: Moderate.
Credit Cards: MC, V.
Reservations: For parties of
 five or more.
Handicap Access: Yes.
Special Features: Smoke-
 free; parking; children's
 menu, wheelchair access.

starving teenagers before 6pm, and it's even more reasonable. Prime rib, swordfish, surf & turf, shrimp scampi, sirloin steak — served with all the trimmings. Full dinners are served upstairs, while quick bites are in the lounge. They have wonderful chowder out here and an amazing list of starters such as steamed pot stickers, pizza sticks, and "killer onion straws." Entrées include great pepper tenderloin, BBQ baby-back ribs, and baked stuffed sole, all with the salad bar, fresh vegetables, and potatoes. Your hosts also own Arno's at 41 Main Street. The bar area is a local hangout.

Forget rushing. This is not the place to go if you're trying to make a movie or a concert. Everything is cooked to order, and it all takes time. They make their own pasta, too (but not while you wait of course. You will know Caffè Bella Vita by its green awning, and you should seek a table beneath it on a balmy evening.

FAREGROUNDS RESTAURANT
508-228-4995.
www.faregrounds.com.
27 Fairgrounds Rd.,
Nantucket, MA 02554.
Open: Year-round
11:30am–midnight.
Serving: L, D.
Cuisine: American.
Price: Inexpensive to
Moderate.
Credit Cards: AE, MC, V.
Handicap Access: Yes.
Special Features: Sports bar
Pudley's Pub adjoining;
parking; dining deck;
children's menu;
vegetarian dishes; full-
menu take-out.

The Faregrounds used to be the family-favorite Pines Restaurant, and while much is the same (the extensive menu, for example), much is different. Pudley's Pub is an eighty-seat sports bar named for the owners' pet pot-bellied pig. The walls are covered with photos of Island sportsmen from the '50s and earlier. The menu is heavy on appetizers, and there's a Sunday- and Monday-night-football schedule. The adjacent Faregrounds is one of the Island's larger dining rooms, capable of feeding one hundred hungry patrons pizza, pastas, platters, prime rib, and more. Starving teenagers can be filled up here without maxing out your credit card.

HUTCH'S
508-228-5550
At Nantucket Memorial
Airport inside the
terminal building.
Open: 6am–8pm every day
but Christmas.
Serving: B, Br, L, D.
Cuisine: American.
Price: Very Inexpensive to
Inexpensive.
Credit Cards: D.
Reservations: None.
Handicap Access: Yes.
Special Features: Take-out
all items on menu;
children's menu;
smoking; parking;
breakfast served all day.

If you usually pass right by airport eateries after too many unfortunate involuntary meals at various ports of call, you'll be pleasantly surprised at Hutch's. The food is fresh, uncomplicated, and well prepared. Islanders not in need of airport services come out here for dinner. This is a family restaurant with reasonable — no, make that low — prices. Owner Bill Hutchinson explains the menu as being "like a diner" in that he serves breakfast, sandwiches, soups, salads, appetizers, and dinner entrées "no matter what meal time it is." There are daily "Blue Plate Specials" like fish & chips (Friday), meat loaf (Tuesday), and prime ribs (Saturday). Deplaning Island residents can be seen picking up their dinners-to-go-home-with at the take-out counter. While you dine, you and the kids can watch the planes take off and land or even cast an eye on the giant screen TV. Oh yes, if you watched the TV series *Wings*, you saw Hutch's.

THE SEA GRILLE
508-325-5700.
www.theseagrille.com
45 Sparks Ave., Nantucket,
MA 02554.
Far enough at the south
end of Town to be called
mid-Island.

Robin and E. J. Harvey have owned and operated the thirty-table Sea Grille (E. J. is the chef) for a decade, long enough for it to become one of the Island's most popular restaurants. Accolades have ranged from awards of excellence from the *Wine Spectator* to popular-vote winner of the Nantucket Chowder Fest.

Open: Year-round.
Cuisine: Creative regional
  seafood.
Serving: L Mon.–Sat.
  11:30am–2pm, light bar
  2pm–5:30pm; D nightly
  6:30pm on.
Price: Moderate to
  Expensive.
Credit Cards: AE, MC, V.
Reservations:
  Recommended.
Handicap Access: Yes.
Special Features:
  Nonsmoking; vegetarian
  platter; parking.

The Sea Grille unabashedly specializes: Nantucket scallops in season (November to April) and native striped bass (July and August) are augmented by Nantucket bouillabaisse (half lobster, shrimp, scallops, clams, mussels, and swordfish in vegetable bouillon) plus much more. Lobster bisque with dilled pastry crust is an appetizer that has become a signature dish. For dessert try the chocolate mousse topped with white chocolate sauce. There's an extensive bar menu, too, and for lunch, house specialties include homemade crab cakes with half a Caesar salad.

Sea Grille Quahog Chowder

This chowder recently won the Harborfest Chowder Contest by popular vote. Many thanks to Robin and E. J. Harvey, co-owners of the Sea Grille Restaurant.

1/2 cup butter
2 strips bacon, diced
3/4 cup diced onions
1/2 cup diced celery
1/2 cup all-purpose flour
1 bay leaf
2 pinches dried thyme
1/4 teaspoon freshly ground white pepper
1 pint sea clam juice
1 pint quahog clams, ground with juice
1 quart heavy cream, or desired consistency
1 pound potatoes, diced and cooked
3 dashes Worcestershire sauce
Salt and freshly ground black pepper to taste
8 teaspoons butter
Ground paprika
Oysterette crackers

In a large pot, melt the butter and bacon together. Add the onions and celery, and let sweat. Stir in the flour and cook as a roux. Add the bay leaf, thyme, white pepper, clam juice, and clams and stir until heated through. Add the cream, potatoes, Worcestershire sauce, salt, and black pepper, and continue to cook on low heat for 10 to 15 minutes or until hot. Adjust the seasonings and consistency to taste.

Ladle the chowder into bowls, top each bowl with 1 teaspoon butter, and sprinkle with the paprika. Serve with the crackers.

Yield: 8 servings.

TOPPER'S
508-228-8768.
www.wauwinet.com.
120 Wauwinet Rd., PO Box
  2580, Nantucket, MA 02554.
At the Wauwinet.
Open: Daily May–Oct.
Serving: L, SB, D.
Cuisine: Regional American.
Price: Very Expensive.
Credit Cards: AE, MC, V.
Reservations: Highly recom-
  mended; required for boat
  transportation.
Handicap Accessible: Yes.
Special Features: Non-
  smoking; summer compli-
  mentary transfers on the
  Wauwinet Lady from
  Straight Wharf and back;
  men require jackets at din-
  ner; light menu in the bar.

On warm evenings you dine on the deck looking out at the bay; when it's cool, by the wood-burning fireplace. Either way the wines are extraordinary, service is exemplary, and the food justifies the raves of critics. Say you begin with lobster-crab cakes with smoked corn and mustard sauce or seared foie gras with rhubarb and black pepper marmalade. Then there are choices such as pan-roasted Nantucket lobster with Spice Island butter, spinach, and oyster mushrooms; roasted Chatham cod on a warm golden-beet-and-leek salad with lobster vinaigrette, or maybe grilled dry-aged lamb with morels and fiddleheads. For dessert: a fresh-fruit or berry sorbet made in the Wauwinet kitchen or possibly the planet's best lemon custard.

Even the 11am–2pm Sunday brunch is unique. The set price is for three courses, and one of the most popular entrées is Wauwinet wild turkey hash with poached eggs and hollandaise. It's a memorable meal that attracts residents from all over the Island.

The historic Wauwinet dates from the 1800s and, though now a country inn, was once a famous Island restaurant specializing in lobster and bringing crowds from Town for the weekend Shore Dinners. The traditional way of getting there by boat has been revived with the complimentary motor launch cruise from Town to Topper's on the *Wauwinet Lady,* both at lunch and dinner. It's a scenic as well as a comfortable way to go, but you need to make your meal reservations in advance. Topper, by the way, is the name of the terrier beloved by owners Jill and Stephen Karp. His portrait is in his namesake restaurant.

WEST CREEK CAFÉ
508-228-4943.
11 West Creek Rd.,
  Nantucket, MA 02554.
Between Lower Orange
  and Lower Pleasant, far
  south end of Town.
Open: Year-round; closed
  Tues.
Serving: D.
Cuisine: New American.
Price: Moderate to
  Expensive.
Credit Cards: MC, V.
Reservations: Recommended.
Handicap Access:
Special Features: Nonsmoking;
  parking; patio.

Three dining rooms share the same eclectic menu. There is a great chilled cucumber soup with dill crème fraîche and lobster ravioli over creamy leeks with shrimp butter. Much is grilled, sautéed, or pan seared, whether fish or meat.

WINDSONG RESTAURANT
508-228-6900.
www.nantucket.net/lodging /nantucketinn.
29 Macy's Lane, Nantucket, MA 02554.
At the Nantucket Inn across from the airport.
Open: Apr.–Oct.
Serving: B, D.
Cuisine: Traditional American.
Price: Inexpensive to Moderate.
Credit Cards: AE, D, DC, MC, V.
Reservations: Recommended.
Handicap Access: Yes.
Special Features: Complimentary van service from Town; vegetarian dishes; children's menu; clambake.

Dinner specialties like the Traditional Nantucket Clambake (cup of clam chowder, tossed green salad, one-and-a-quarter pound lobster, grilled chicken, steamers, corn on the cob, and potato) and the Nantucket Cut Prime Rib Dinner (chowder, salad, twenty-two-ounce cut of prime rib, vegetable, and potato) are certified bargains at the price. But there's a full à la carte menu, too, including a vegetarian strudel, meal-size salads, and sandwiches — even a cheeseburger. It's a good place to take the family, and the kids can watch the planes come in at Nantucket Airport, only a clamshell's throw away.

BREAKFAST AND LUNCH

Breakfast time before a midsummer fishing expedition might be barely past dawn, so when you show up at 5:30am, expect that your fellow diners probably will be serious boat folks. Later risers might savor a Nantucket specialty breakfast midmorning. We've selected a few true early-bird spots (some in unlikely nests) and others with breakfasts into the afternoon. See the listings of bakeries below, too; on Nantucket they provide counter service and carry-out from early morning. Lunch is served in many Nantucket restaurants, though not all. Others (Arno's at 41 Main Street, for instance) serve an extensive breakfast menu until 2pm, overlapping the lunch menu. Here are a few suggestions for both the early and midday meals.

Aunt Leah's Fudge (508-228-1017, 800-824-6330; Lower Main St., PO Box 981, Nantucket, MA 02554, next to Cap'n Tobey's in the Courtyard) In July and August, coffee, juice, bagels, doughnuts, and muffins from 5:30am.

Downyflake Restaurant (508-228-4533; 18 Sparks Ave. Nantucket, MA 02554; across from the supermarket and fire station) Possibly the biggest bargain on Nantucket and surely, after more than fifty years in operation, a fixture in the dining firmament. You'll be hard put to find a modern novel set on the Island where the main characters don't have blueberry pancakes at the

The Wauwinet Cranberry Scones

The Wauwinet Inn is at the eastern end of the Island, just beyond the cranberry bogs. Breakfast there is a feast, made all the more sumptuous by these delicious scones. Try them at afternoon tea, too. Whatever the time of day, serve them warm with sweet butter.

3 cups all-purpose flour
1 tablespoon baking powder
1/3 cup granulated sugar
1/2 teaspoon salt
4 tablespoons (1/2 stick) cold unsalted butter, cut into small pieces
2 large eggs
1/2 cup plain yogurt
3/4 cup buttermilk
3/4 cup dried cranberries
1 teaspoon grated orange zest
1 tablespoon water
Cinnamon sugar (8:1 ratio sugar to cinnamon) for dusting

Preheat oven to 425°F.

In a large bowl, mix together the flour, baking powder, sugar, and salt. Cut the butter into the flour mixture until the texture is mealy.

In another bowl, lightly beat 1 egg, and then blend in the yogurt and buttermilk. Add the cranberries and zest, and stir together well. Stir the wet ingredients into the dry ingredients.

On a lightly floured board, knead the dough a couple of times to complete mixing (do not overmix). Roll the dough to one-half inch, cut with a floured cutter, and place on an ungreased baking sheet. In a small bowl, slightly beat together the remaining egg and the water. Brush the egg wash over the tops of the scones. Sprinkle with the cinnamon sugar and bake for 15 minutes (do not overbake). Serve warm, straight from the oven.

Yield: 22 scones.

Downyflake. Breakfast is served all day, and lunch fits in. It's a diner-concept restaurant with home-style cookery and all bakery goods and doughnuts made in-house. Open Mon.–Sat. 5:30am–2pm and Sun. 6am–noon. Nonsmoking; children welcome (you'll find peanut butter and jelly sandwiches among others); take-out; no credit cards; good, friendly service; and very inexpensive. Can't beat this one.

Expresso Café (508-228-6930; 40 Main St. Nantucket, MA 02554) A European-style café with a garden patio in mid-Town. Fine for breakfasts and coffee breaks for weary shoppers. At lunch you can get sandwiches, salads, soups, and quiche; coffee, baked goods and/or desserts at any time. Open daily year-round, this busy café has a brisk turnover, and you won't have to wait long to find a place to sit.

Nantucket Bagel Company (508-228-6616; 5 West Creek Rd., Nantucket, MA 02554; far south end of Town) Bagel specialties (cranberry-orange, spinach, and Cajun, among others), muffins, scones, cookies, and coffee from 5:30am. For lunch you can also get made-to-order sandwiches, soups, and hot-lunch specials (turkey chili is reportedly a local favorite).

Centre Street Bistro (508-228-8470; 29 Centre St. Nantucket, MA 02554) Many Island hostelries get their morning selection of breads and pastries from here. If you come in, you can get fresh fruit popovers, huevos rancheros, and break-fast burritos as well as conventional buttermilk pancakes and great cinnamon rolls. No credit cards, prices are reasonable, and it's open all year. Brunch is also served. The bistro is tucked in the back of the Meetinghouse Shops.

Something Natural from Nantucket (508-228-0504, 877-762-8875; www.some thingnatural.com; 50 Cliff Rd, Nantucket, MA 02554; north end of Town; Mon.–Fri. 9am-5pm in season) The number-one supplier to those heading off on the bike trail to picnic at the beach. Yet it's more than a provider of sophisticated sandwiches on home-baked bread with appropriate garnishes. You can also dine on picnic tables in the garden. The variety reaches from salads ("Lisbet's Favorite" is turkey, sprouts, cucumber, and sunflower and sesame seeds with balsamic honey vinaigrette) to comfort food (peanut but-ter with grape jelly) to desserts. You can ship baked goods home, too, though there's a six-loaf minimum for bread.

ROAD FOOD AND QUICK BITES

Henry's (508-228-0123; Steamboat Wharf, PO Box 1077, Nantucket, MA 02554) and **Henry Jr.** (508-228-3035; 129 Orange St., Nantucket, MA 02554; south end of Town) Sub and sandwich shops on a grand and friendly scale. All sandwiches are made to order and come with your choice of innumerable fixings. Henry's has been a Nantucket institution for more than twenty-five years and consistently wins accolades from Townies in the "Best of Nantucket" voting. No credit cards. Inexpensive.

The Juice Bar (508-228-5799; 12 Broad St., Nantucket, MA 02554; Steamboat Wharf across from the Whaling Museum; daily 7am–10pm; closes earlier off-season) Opens with bagels and pastries, and the sundaes, frappes, smooth-ies, and nonfat frozen yogurt as well as homemade ice cream will give you a tasty break any time. The waffle cones get raves.

The Juice Guys (508-228-4464; 4 Easy St., Nantucket, MA 02554) Deluxe teas and juices like hot cranberry-ginger by the guys who brought you Nantucket Nectars. A juice bar opens mid-March to mid-October and week-ends to mid-December.

Provisions (508-228-3258; Straight Wharf, Nantucket, MA 02554; at Harbor Square) A gourmet take-out with specialty sandwiches, coffees, fresh breads and cookies, and deli specials. In summer you can get pâtés, cheeses, olives, dips, and salads; in spring, fall, and winter, hearty homemade soups, clam chowder, and pizza. Among the salads is a veggie with cucumber, artichoke hearts, carrots, sprouts, lettuce, onions, and tomato with a choice of hummus or goat-cheese spread. The Wharf Rat Club is smoked turkey, Swiss, bacon, lettuce, tomato, onion, and mayo. The tuna salad is labeled "dolphin-safe," and you may find yourself devouring the whole loaf of onion dill bread before you get to wherever else you're going.

The Rotary (508-228-9505; Milestone Rotary, Nantucket, MA 02554) An inexpensive family place with take-out as well as dining-room and outdoor seating. In summer, breakfast is served from 6am Monday–Saturday (Sunday, too, from May 23 until September), you can get lunch and dinner from 11am–8pm. The regular menu is burgers, fried chicken, seafood, subs, and sandwiches, but they've added a dinner menu with prime rib, steak, pasta, swordfish, and the like.

Tacos Tacos (508-228-5418; 10 Broad St., Nantucket, MA 02554; at Steamboat Wharf; 11am–2am Mar.–Dec.) Nachos, burritos, tacos, and other Mexican favorites. Anything can be prepared vegetarian, too. All items are made fresh to order and packed for traveling or instant dining.

FOOD PURVEYORS

BAKERIES

While home baking is the watchword in many Nantucket restaurants, and the variety in the average restaurant breadbasket is remarkable, the Island also has old-fashioned bakeries where you will be overcome by aromas and dazzled by the infinite number of cookies. Here are a few of the notables, but be aware that great baked goods are also available at other, more general, purveyors.

Daily Breads (508-228-8961; 147 Lower Orange St., Nantucket, MA 02554; south end of Town; 6am–6pm seasonally) The whole line of baked goods, morning pastries, cookies, pies, cakes, and savory snacks may carry you beyond temptation to rapture. Hearth-baked organic varieties are house specialties, and there are seasonal changes. If you have a special request, the proprietors urge you to call or stop by.

Nantucket Bagel Co. (508-228-6461; 5 West Creek Rd., Nantucket, MA 02554; south end of Town between Lower Orange and Lower Pleasant) Home-baked muffins and bread as well as a zillion kinds of bagels; breakfast and lunch as well as carry-out.

The Nantucket Bake Shop (508-228-2797,800-440-BAKE; bakeshop@nantucket.net; www.nantucketbakeshop.com; 79 Orange St., PO Box 539, Nantucket, MA 02554; south end of Town; 6:30am–5pm Mon.–Sat., closed

Christmas eve to April) Provides the hungry customer with more than a dozen kinds of bread, some ten kinds of pie, five kinds of croissants, plus rolls, cakes, pastries, doughnuts, quiches, cookies, and even cranberry granola in addition to hot and cold beverages. If you're celebrating a birthday in Nantucket, let it begin here. If you must leave the Island (or want to please an off-Island friend), the Bake Shop ships wonderful combos.

CANDY

Chocolates are handmade the old-fashioned way at the Sweet Inspirations Chocolate Workshop.

Frederick G. S. Clow

These shops have never been observed to be without customers. If you want to bring a gift to anyone with a sweet tooth, give it a truly Nantucket touch. The shops also ship their goodies anywhere you like.

Aunt Leah's Fudge (508-228-1017, 800-824-6330; Straight Wharf, Nantucket, MA 02554; at the Courtyard) More than thirty varieties of homemade fudge, including a prize-winning Cranberry Chocolate Nut Supreme available only October through June. You can even join the "Fudge-of-the-Month Club." Aunt Leah makes preserves and marmalades, too. Her own bottled spring water, "Naturally, Nantucket," is wholesaled to a lot of prestigious Manhattan locations.

Sweet Inspirations (508-228-5814, 888-225-4843; www.nantucketclipper.com; 26 Centre St., PO Box 966, Nantucket, MA 02554) One of the world's great chocolatiers. Everything but the jellybeans is handmade right here, including the mouthwatering cranberry chocolate truffles. The packaging is Nantucket-enhanced, too: lighthouses; Sconset cottages — roses and all — are reproduced on tins, and miniature cranberry crates are filled with Island treats, including preserves as well as confections.

COFFEE SPECIALISTS

Nantucket Coffee Roasters (508-228-6862, 800-432-1673; www.nantucketcof fee.com;hotbeans@nantucket.net; 15 Teasdale Circle, PO Box 2977, Nantucket, MA 02584; near the airport) You will see the coffees of this Island company specified on menus around Nantucket. They are also for sale in grocery and specialty shops.

Looking for a coffee shop for a cup and something to munch? Try **Expresso Café** (508-228-6930; 40 Main St., Nantucket, MA 02554) with a patio; **Fast Forward** (508-228-5807; 117 Orange St., Nantucket, MA 02554); **Fog Island Café** (508-228-1818; 7 South Water St., Nantucket, MA 02554); **Nantucket Bagel Co.** (508-228-6461; 7 West Creek Rd., Nantucket, MA 02554); **Centre Street Bistro** (508-228-8470; 29 Centre St., Nantucket, MA 02554).

FARM, ORCHARD, AND PRODUCE MARKETS

Beginning in early spring, the farm trucks and barrows on Main Street are as charming as they are practical. Who wants to wait for a parking space in the supermarket when the best and freshest are where you are working or walking, anyway? Look for just-picked berries, herbs, and veggies. All the main farms are out of Town, naturally, and they sell to the public as well as to restaurants.

Bartlett's Ocean View Farm (508-228-9403; www.bartslettsoceanviewfarm.com; 33 Bartlett Farm Rd., PO Box 899, Nantucket, MA 02554) If ever there was a produce institution, this is it. Restaurants state on their menus that the lettuce they serve is from Bartlett's. Stopping at Bartlett's for produce or for prepared soups, appetizers, one-dish meals (mostly meatless), and desserts is part of a day at Cisco Beach, though more often than not it's worth a special trip. Bartlett's has greenhouses as well as fields on its hundred acres, and it's thor-

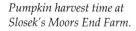

Pumpkin harvest time at Slosek's Moors End Farm.

oughly dependable if not cheap. During the Harvest Festival, tours of the farm are on the agenda.

Moors End Farm (508-228-2674; 40 Polpis Rd., Nantucket, MA 02554; daily Apr.–Nov.) Moors End is both expanded nursery and produce market. They also make table arrangements.

Nantucket Cookbooks

Where there are good cooks, there are cookbooks. Island bookstores stock the *Cranberry Cookbook*, *Harborfest Cookbook*, and *Daffodil Festival Cookbook*, and you can also buy them on site at festivals and special events. Tastings and cookery competitions among both amateurs and professionals are inevitably part of the scene. At some event or other you will find restaurants vying for recognition in specific dishes such as the great restaurant chowder contest. A highlight of April's Daffodil Festival is the judging of the best tailgate picnic lunch at Sconset.

For general Nantucket cookery there is *Home Cooking from Nantucket*, by nutritionist Nancy Ivas; *The Nantucket Open House Cookbook* and *Cold Weather Cooking*, both by Sarah Lea Chase, founder of a former Island gourmet shop; *Bartlett's Ocean View Farm Cookbook*, compiled by Dorothy Bartlett of the Island's famous farm; *Sconset Café – A Kitchen Collection* by Pam McKinstry, owner-chef of the Sconset Café; *Nantucket Recipes from the Fog Island Café*, by Mark and Anne Blake Dawson, owners-chefs of the Fog Island Café; *Once More at Cy's*, by Zelda Kaufman Ziotin, which has anecdotes of famous diners as well as recipes from the one-time Cy's Green Coffee Pot; and *Bluefish Cookbook*, a specialized compilation of recipes and tips from Greta Jacobs and Jane Alexander Sherin. (See Chapter Nine, *Information*, the "Book List" section, for more titles.) You can find any and all in the Nantucket Room at Mitchell's Book Corner (508-227-1080; 54 Main Street, Nantucket, MA 02554) and most other bookstores and kitchen shops, as well.

FISH AND POULTRY MARKETS

Glidden's Island Seafood (508-228-0912, 508-228-0913; 115 Pleasant St., PMB 174, 2 Greglen Ave., Nantucket, MA 02554) Provides and delivers lobsters live or steamed; shellfish; even quahog chowder base. Been here, done that since 1898.

Sayle's Seafood (508-228-4599; 99 Washington St. Ext., PO Box 1062, Nantucket, MA 02554) Promises local and worldwide delivery of everything that swims in the sea (except mermaids). Take-out platters with all the trimmings; clambakes; lobster dinners, too. Call them and they'll cook a lobster to order for you to eat on the beach or maybe on the ferry going home.

Souza's Seafood (508-228-9140; www.souzaseafood.qpg.com; 23 Trotters Lane, PO Box 742, Nantucket, MA 02554; year-round 9am–7pm) You need only to look for the lobster flag to find Souza's. In addition to the fresh native lobster, quahogs, flounder, scallops, littlenecks, cherrystones, etc., they also carry the Island delicacy, smoked bluefish. Souza's does travel packs of lobster to take home to the mainland; on Island they deliver to your door.

Straight Wharf Fish Store (508-228-1095; 4 Harbor Square, Nantucket, MA 02554; on the dock behind the bandstand; daily: 9:30am–7pm during season) Lest you think Nantucket's seagoing days are history, the ads read "Try our fresh harpooned swordfish!" You can phone your order in ahead (perhaps allowing time to sharpen the harpoons?).

GOURMET AND DELI MARKETS; CATERERS

While nearly every restaurant also caters on request, and places like the Lobster Trap do a major business in off-site clambakes ("Meals on Keels"), this is a sampling of the special gourmet food shops not associated with specific restaurants. Gourmet is a fighting word on Nantucket — every food emporium on the Island claims the adjective as its own. There are also private chefs who will come to your home with prepared meals or use your kitchen to cook their specialties or yours.

Claudette's (508-257-6622; Main St., Siaconset, MA 02564; Open in season) You can ask for a box lunch or a wedding reception. Just call ahead. There's a tiny deck outside if you want to eat on the spot.

Fahey & Formaggio (508-325-5644; www.faheywines.com; 49A Pleasant St., 5 Corners, Nantucket, MA 02554; daily, Wed. until 7pm) Co-owners Michael Fahey and Valerie Guirdal left top restaurants to start their own gourmet food business. They do cheeses, salads, pâtés, sandwiches, pastas, pasta salads, specialty items, and have a perfect-temperature wine cellar.

Fishers Fiddle Catering (508-228-9047; 73 Orange St., Nantucket, MA 02554) Stephen Bender specializes in seafood and raw bars.

L'Ile de France (508-228-3686; 18 Federal St., Nantucket, MA 02554) You can plan your next trip to Paris while buying the ingredients for a coq au vin à la bourguignonne in this wonderfully fragrant emporium across the street from the Visitor Information Center. Just looking in the window will make you hungry. They bring the baguettes in fresh daily — from France.

Nantucket Clambake Co. (508-228-9283, 72 Skyline Dr., Nantucket, MA 02554) Susan M. Warner also does "Unforgettable Feasts."

Nantucket Cuisine (508-257-4621; cuisine@nantucket.net; www.nantucketcuisine.com; PMB 213, 2 Greglin Ave., Nantucket, MA 02554) Picnics, gift baskets and more by cookbook author Ellen Brown.

Nantucket Gourmet (508-228-4353; ngourmet@nantucket.net; www.nantucketgourmet.com; 4 India St., Nantucket, MA 02554) An all-round shop with gifts, gadgets and pottery as well as food specialties like cranberry bog honey and rose hip jelly.

Summer 'N Smoke (508-257-9982; smoker@nantucket.net; www.summer-n-smoke.com; Arlington St., PO Box 921, Siaconset, MA 02564; at Tom Nevers Head) Bluefish the way it ought to be done plus other good things.

Via Provence (508-325-4800; 6 Amelia Dr., Nantucket, MA 02554; at the Nantucket Trading Emporium, mid-Island toward the airport between Old South Rd. and Ticoma) This place will take you back — all the way across the Atlantic. Have you had Carpegna prosciutto lately? Chatelain camembert? The fragrances of the south of France will transport you as you enter the shop.

HEALTH AND NATURAL FOOD STORES

ACKnatural (508-228-4554; www.acknatural.com; 95 Washington St., Nantucket, MA 02554; across from Island Marine; open daily) A whole natural food market (formerly Light Generation Market) where you can buy organic produce, free-range chickens, bulk grain and pasta, herbs, and vitamins and supplements. You can also get smoothies and raw juices. Parking.

Nantucket Natural (508-228-3947; www.nantucketnatural.com; 29 Centre St., Nantucket, MA 02554) One of the Meetinghouse Shops and conveniently located downtown. It has a fresh-juice bar, tofu meals, natural medicines, and vitamins and supplements.

ICE CREAM

Eating ice cream while browsing and shopping along Main Street.

Rob Benchley

Massachusetts is one of the nation's most ice-cream-eating states — though, given the frosty winters, no one is quite sure why. Nantucket's restaurants all have ice-cream specialties on their dessert menus, and food sellers from one end of the Island to another tout their frozen yogurt, sorbets, and rich ice creams as being without parallel. However, your best bet on Nantucket is to do what your parents and grandparents did where they were growing up: Go to the Main Street drugstore soda fountains. The Soda Fountain is in the

Nantucket Pharmacy (508-228-0180; 45 Main St., Nantucket, MA 02554) and David's Soda Fountain is in **Congdon's Pharmacy** (228-0020; 47 Main St., Nantucket, MA 02554). You won't do any better than these. The waffle ice-cream cones at the **Juice Bar** (508-228-5799; juicebar@nantucket.net;12 Broad St., Nantucket, MA 02554) are an Island institution, too.

SUPERMARKETS

The **A&P** on Salem Street at South Wharf and the **Stop & Shop** on Pleasant St., mid-Island, have parking lots and are the basic supermarkets of the Island, providing all the everyday items you expect. Nothing fancy. For super but small, try **Allserve General Store** (508-228-8170; www.juiceguys.com; 44 Straight Wharf, Nantucket, MA 02554).

WINE AND LIQUOR; PACKAGE STORES

Cisco beer is Nantucket's home brew.

Betty Lowry

Cisco Brewers (508-325-5929; brewers@nantucket.net; www.ciscobrewers.com; 5 Bartlett Farm Rd., Nantucket, MA 02554) Nantucket's only microbrewery, this is the family operation of Randy and Wendy Hudson on the grounds of Nantucket Vineyard. You'll find their ale at Island cafés and bars, or you can stop, taste, and buy at the brewery. By the way, it's named for Cisco Beach, which is at the end of the road, and they have given names like Whale's Tale Pale Ale, Moor Porter, and Capt. Swain's Extra Stout to their brews.

Nantucket Vineyard (508-228-9235, fax 508-228-5154; www.nantucket.net/food/vineyard; 3 Bartlett Farm Rd., PO Box 2700, Nantucket, MA 02584) They planted the first grapevines in 1981 and tore them out in 1997 when they concluded it was more intelligent to bring grapes from the mainland than to try and coax growth on the Island. Dean and Melissa Long continue to make and bottle their own blends of whites and reds. No set tours, but you can come and taste afternoons in spring, summer, and fall. In winter, it's by chance or by appointment. The wines have names like Nantucket Sleighride, To the Wind, and Sailor's Delight. They also produce a very good hard cider called Shipwrecked and have fresh cider for sale in the fall.

Fahey & Formaggio (508-325-5644; www.faheywines.com, 49A Pleasant St., Nantucket, MA 02554) Wines, etc., to go with their gourmet food.

Hatch's Package Store (508-229-0131; 129 Orange St., Nantucket, MA 02554) Neighborhood store.

The Islander Package Store (508-228-5855; ped@nantucket.net; 3 Polpis Rd., Nantucket, MA 02554; after the rotary, take a left off Milestone Rd.) The largest selection on-Island, and they will deliver with minimum purchase. Plenty of parking.

Island Spirits (508-228-4484; www.islandspirits.com; 10 Washington St., Nantucket, MA 02554; off Lower Main) Delivers with a minimum purchase to your yacht, hotel, or home. This is a full-service liquor store with snack foods and — are you ready? — gas pumps.

Murray's Beverage Store (508-228-0071; murray23@nantucket.net; 23 Main St., Nantucket, MA 02554) Downtown's package store has everything you need, including a lightship basket for your hostess.

Nantucket Wine & Spirits (508-228-1136, www.21federal.net; Sparks Ave., Nantucket, MA 02554)

Siasconset Bookstore (508-257-6365; Main St., Siaconset, MA 02564) Books provide the decor, but it's a liquor store.

Via Provence (508-325-4800; 263 Polpis Road, Nantucket, MA 02554) A full stock of boutique wines.

CHAPTER SIX
Beyond the "Nantucket Sleigh Ride"
RECREATION

The proper response to the leg puller, "Do you want to sign up for a Nantucket Sleigh Ride?" is: "Sure, you bring the whale." The run of the harpooned whale pulling the whaleboat at twenty-five miles per hour may have been the only recreation afforded the whalers in those halcyon days of yore, but today it's a different story.

While recreation on Nantucket is inseparable from the natural

Rob Benchley

At least a dozen boat and sailboat charters are available for daytime excursions around the harbor and Nantucket Sound. Here the Christina *sails down the harbor channel.*

attributes of the Island, today whales get watched, not tailgated (much less ridden), and everything that is taken out of the sea or put into it is carefully monitored. Summer visitors polled on the Island's major attraction unanimously cried, "Beaches!" But boating, the second-place favorite, is basic, fishing is not only for supper but also for prizes, and releasing the catch is increasingly common. Golf and tennis are naturally considered better games when played aesthetically within view of the sea or a lighthouse.

Seasonal sports events from races to tournaments enliven the calendar. Organized bird walks and nature walks led by resident naturalists occur daily. There are classes and tours for all ages, sports-intensive day camps for the kids, tennis clinics, and saltwater fly-fishing schools. How about a session in dog obedience for the family canine? Or would you like a personal trainer to set up or pep up your own fitness program?

For those intent on getting away from organized *anything*, the Island is also the place for that. Nantucketers even have a name for it: "rantom scooting." The next step down is doing absolutely nothing. Considering the booming summer business of Nantucket Town's three bookstores and the public library, catching up on reading can be a winding-down end in itself.

Getting around the Island is both recreation and transportation if you go by bicycle, as nearly everyone does. "Hiking" can be anything from a casual stroll on a marked trail, a brisk walk along a bicycle path, or a half-day excursion to the outermost tip of Great Point. Jogging and running are especially healthful where the air is pure and constantly refreshed by sea breezes.

For more information about the Island's natural resources and ways to enjoy and appreciate them, see the next chapter, *Nature and the Environment*.

BEACHES AND BEACHCOMBING

Nantucket has 82 miles of beaches to choose from.

Rob Benchley

Beaches are the joy of Nantucket, and all eighty-two miles of them can be reached by foot, bike, or bus. The beaches are free and public or, if privately owned, have public access. Even in the heart of Town, a good beach is only a five-minute walk away. Seven are maintained by the Nantucket Parks and Recreation Commission and have lifeguards in July and August. In addition to their standard sun, swim, picnic, and play functions, certain beaches are also the sites of special events and performances as notable as the Fourth of July concert by the Boston Pops Orchestra.

All around the Island, beachcombing is an honorable pastime, just as visiting every beach one after another is considered a reasonable vacation itinerary for off-Islanders. (Islanders have already been there and done that.) For good shells, look especially in the tide pools, and follow the tides as listed in the local newspaper or any sporting goods store. Best pickings are when the tide is just going out. If you don't know a Waved Whelk from a Northern Moon Snail, the **Massachusetts Audubon Society** (508-228-9208, Lost Farm, 153 Hummock Pond Rd., Nantucket, MA 02554) has a nifty *Beachcombers Guide to the North Atlantic Seashore* to help you identify what you've found. You can also get checklists and information at the **Aquarium** (508-228-5387; 28 Washington St., Nantucket, MA 02554) and the **Maria Mitchell Science Library** (508-228-9219; 2 Vestal St., Nantucket, MA 02554).

If you intend to drive on the beach, note that only four-wheel vehicles are capable of it and these must have a valid sticker (Nantucket Police Department: 508-228-1212, fax 508-228-7246; 20 S. Water St., Nantucket, MA 02554), and the beaches on conservation land beyond the end of Wauwinet Road require further permits from the Trustees of Reservations (508-228-0006 or 508-228-3359). A word of caution: Tow truck operators say that their main business is pulling out cars stuck in the sand. Due to the fragile ecology of the Island, overnight camping is prohibited.

The following is a selection of Nantucket beaches and their joys, cautions, and treasures.

BEACHES ON THE SOUND AND SEA

Nantucket Town

In-Town beaches are all on the Sound and so have no surf; some are especially good for families with young children. To get there from Town, you can walk, bike, or hop on the shuttle. The best beaches for beachcombing are on the north side of the Island, facing the quiet Nantucket Sound.

Brant Point is at the end of Easton Street and overlooks the harbor channel, so you can see the boats rounding the point. The beach is better for boat watching than for swimming because of the strong current and sudden drop-offs under the water. It's a picturesque spot, however, especially in the evening when anglers cast from the rocks of Brant Point lighthouse. No lifeguard, food, or restrooms.

Treasure hunt on Children's Beach

Betty Lowry

Children's Beach on Harbor View Way just north of Steamboat Wharf was created in 1924 when the harbor was dredged. It has its own playground equipment, game tables, picnic tables, grassed area, and bandstand. This pleasant spot is the site of summer weekend band concerts as well as many children's events, such as an ecological treasure hunt and other environmental games. Supervised and educational programs are given almost daily, and there's a tie-dying session sponsored by the Nantucket Parks and Recreation Commission on Fridays at noon from mid-July through August. Food, showers, restrooms, and lifeguard.

Francis Street Beach is a five-minute walk from Main Street down Washington Street. The calm harbor is good for swimming and families, and the nearby aquarium has hands-on exhibits that children love. There's a jungle gym and kayak rentals; restrooms but no lifeguard.

Jetties Beach is a large family-friendly stretch of sand reached by foot or a short ride from Town along South Beach Street and continuing on North Beach Street. The great Sand Castle competition has been held here annually for quarter of a century and Fourth of July fireworks for much longer than that. As a matter of fact, all outdoor events that are likely to attract large numbers of people occur here. Jetties has everything from volleyball nets to public tennis courts. The skateboard park is open until dusk, and you can get the mandatory safety pads at the tennis courts. Windsurfing, sailboat, and kayak rentals are also right here. Swimming lessons for children ages six and up by the Nantucket Parks and Recreation Commission are offered July 4 through Labor Day, 9:30am to 12noon. Boardwalk, food, phones, changing rooms, showers, handicap-accessible restrooms, and lifeguard.

Dionis is beyond Jetties at the end of Eel Point Road on the north shore, three miles from Town. Since it, too, is on the Sound, the surf is mild. Families love it, and there are lots of shells. Climbing the sheltering dunes is not forbidden at present, but don't tread on the vegetation (see Chapter Seven, *Nature and the Environment*). If you want to have a cookout, you'll need a charcoal-fire permit from the Nantucket Fire Department (508-228-2324, fax 508-228-2430; 131 Pleasant St., Nantucket, MA 02554). Dionis Coffin was the wife of first purchaser Tristram Coffin, and her name was also given to the first railway train on Nantucket. In fact, you'll meet any number of women named Dionis on Nantucket even today. Her beach has restrooms and lifeguard.

Siasconset

There are actually three beaches on the eastern shore at Sconset — Lighthouse North, Lighthouse South, and Low Beach at Codfish Park — but they are generally considered as one very large beach. You can get here via the regular shuttle service or a seven-mile bike ride by paved bike path from Town. If you plan to swim here, note that seaweed can be a problem and so can the moderate to heavy surf. The name Siasconset means "near the great bone," and while this presumably harks back to some especially memorable whale skeleton of pre-colonial days, many a visiting child has found a bone on the beach to take back to show-and-tell in a mainland school in September.

This is a shore under constant attack from the Atlantic Ocean; after every major nor'easter — as the big storms are called in New England — the erosion is more pronounced. Despite all efforts to build sea walls and stabilize the sand, homes have been lost and others are endangered. "Enjoy it," said a woman walking on the beach recently. "We won't have it forever." Food and restrooms are available in the village but not on the beach. Lifeguard.

Everywhere Else

The South Shore is the Atlantic Ocean side of the Island, which means moderate to very heavy surf. These exciting beaches are favorites with the high-school and college-student crowd. Beachcombers will find shells usually broken, but other sea debris can be interesting.

Cisco is at the end of Hummock Pond Road, a four-mile bike ride (no bike path) from Town. Board and body surfing in heavy surf attract the young and fearless. Stopping at Bartlett's Farm on Bartlett Farm Road (508-228-9403; open daily 8am–6pm) to pick up dinner on the way back to Town is a local custom. Sometimes fast-food purveyors and a fish market are around on summer weekends. Not a good beach for small children. Lifeguard, no restrooms.

Surfside is a wide beach three miles from Town at the end of Surfside Road and the bike path. Surf is moderate to heavy (some days very heavy), and children need a lot of supervision. Good for playing beach games and surf casting. Kite flying is OK on the west but not the east (airport) side. The beach is especially popular with the teen and twenty-something crowd. The Star of the Sea Youth Hostel is in the 1874 Surfside Life Saving Station, now on the National Register of Historic Places, where once seven brave-hearted surfmen waited to rescue shipwreck victims. Parking, phones, showers, food, restrooms, and lifeguard.

Nobadeer is the large beach next to Surfside and closest to the airport. It's about four miles from Town, depending on your route. Moderate surf good for surf casting. Nobadeer attracts beach parties and pretty much the same crowd as Surfside. No parking, food, restrooms, or lifeguard.

Tom Nevers ("Pebble Beach") has very coarse sand and often heavy surf. Tom Nevers was a Wampanoag who kept watch for ships in distress from this spot. More recently it was the old navy base, where the Nantucket Parks and Recreation Commission now has a softball field. Plans are under way for other recreational venues. The county fair is held at Tom Nevers on the third weekend in September. No restrooms or lifeguard.

Madaket is at the westernmost end of the Island and five miles from Town. This is where Thomas Macy landed, the first purchaser to settle the Island, and it was the home of the legendary "Madaket Millie" (Mildred Jewett) who kept watch when the coast guard left and was named Warrant Officer of the Highest Rank by the coast guard for her efforts. Her ramshackle cottage is on the right just as you go over the bridge. In the early 1600s farmers on Martha's Vineyard raised cattle here, but in the Algonquin language, *Madaket* meant "bad land," presumably for its lack of fertility. This is a large beach with heavy surf and beautiful sunsets, a great place to picnic. To get there take the scenic bike path or the NRTA shuttle. Food is available nearby but not on the beach. Restrooms and lifeguard.

Miacomet Beach on the south shore has heavy, dangerous surf. No food, restrooms, or lifeguard.

FRESHWATER BEACH

Miacomet Pond is north of Miacomet Beach on the south side of the Island, and its western shore abuts conservation land. Good for young children, though snapping turtles may be encountered. Parking but no restrooms or lifeguard.

BICYCLING

Nantucket is a bike rider's dream come true. The only caution is that the winds can be very strong at times. Ride to Sconset from Town in an hour, to a beach in less; tour the Island in a day. The first bike path on the Island was made in 1896 (to Sconset), another in 1898 (between Madaket and Water Works Roads). Now wide, paved bicycle paths parallel the main roads and have restroom facilities at the ends. Milestone and Madaket have picnic areas and water fountains as well as rest stops. Naturally, you can also rest by the side of the path; just be wary of other riders, Rollerbladers, and joggers.

To get to the bike paths, look for signs with the bike icon on signposts: Sconset = red; Madaket = green; Surfside = black; Cliff = gray; Polpis = dark gray. Return to Steamboat Wharf and Town = blue. Mopeds are subject to all motorized vehicle laws and are not allowed on bike paths. (See Chapter Two, *Transportation*, "Nantucket on Two Wheels: Courtesies of the Path.") Always wear a helmet — helmets are required by law for children twelve and under. When you reach your destination, remove valuables from the rack or basket and lock your bike. (Report stolen bikes to police by calling 228-1212.) For a real bargain, bring your bike with you on the ferry for $5. For bike rentals and more information, see Chapter Two.

Cliff Road Bike Path: Approximately two and a half miles with rolling terrain. Begins near Derrymore Road and continues along Cliff Road to the Madaket Bike Path. A good place to pick up sandwiches, salads, and beverages to go is **Something Natural** (508-228-0504; 50 Cliff Rd., Nantucket, MA 02554).

Eel Point Rd. Bike Path: Approximately one mile long off Madaket Road near Cliff Road. Flat terrain to Dionis Beach — a great beach for families with small children because of low-to-no surf.

Madaket Bike Path: Approximately five miles with gentle hills and a winding terrain leads to Madaket Beach. Begins at intersection of Quaker and Madaket Roads and has rest areas and picnic areas.

Milestone Bike Path: Approximately seven miles with gentle hills. In late April, Milestone Road is lined with daffodils. Path begins at Milestone Rotary and leads to Sconset. Water fountain at the rotary.

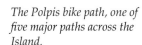

The Polpis bike path, one of five major paths across the Island.

Rob Benchley

Polpis Bike Path: Approximately eight miles with gentle hills and a winding terrain. Begins just beyond the intersection of Milestone Road and Polpis Road and continues along Polpis Road to just outside the village of Sconset. About halfway is the Life Saving Museum at Quaise, well worth a stop and a good place for your picnic. This bike path opened in 1997, with the governor of Massachusetts making the dedication.

Surfside Bike Path: Approximately three miles along flat terrain. Begins at Atlantic Avenue and Vesper Lane and ends at Surfside Beach. Water fountain and rest stop about halfway.

BIKE RACES

The Nantucket Cycling Club (508-228-6066, 228-1164; 211 Hummock Pond Rd., Nantucket, MA 02554) sponsors regular road races Saturday mornings in June, July, and August. The **Great Annual Hummock Pond Dirt and Mountain Bike Race** takes place July 5 on 5.3 miles of dirt and sand roads. The **Race Across Nantucket** is a twenty-eight-mile road race in August. For information call 508-228-6066/1164. The **Nantucket Challenge Series Triathlon** in late September includes an eighteen-mile biking section. For information call 508-285-4544.

BIRD WATCHING

*Sandpipers, among many
other shore birds, are seen at
every Island beach and pond.*

Rob Benchley

More than 350 species of birds consider Nantucket home, so bring along binoculars on your hiking and biking expeditions. A camera is also useful, especially to confirm sightings for the record. For more directed bird watching, join the group gathering at the high school parking lot on Atlantic Avenue at 6:30am Tuesdays, Thursdays, and Saturdays in the summer for bird walks led by an ornithologist from the Maria Mitchell Association. Or make arrangements with an individual birder for an escorted bird-watching expedition. (See Chapter Seven, *Nature and the Environment,* for more information about birding.)

Eco Guides: Strong Wings (508-228-1769; Nobadeer Farm Rd., PO Box 2884, Nantucket, MA 02584)
Maria Mitchell Association (508-228-9198, 508-228-0898; 4 Vestal St., Nantucket, MA 02554)
Massachusetts Audubon Society (508-228-9208; 153 Hummock Pond Rd., Nantucket, MA 02554)
Pure Privacy Farm (508-228-7563; 16 Miacomet Rd., Nantucket, MA 02554)

BOATING AND SAILING

Nantucket Harbor is ever more frequently designated as the foremost boating destination on the East Coast, which comes as no surprise to residents and boaters alike. One out of every four people on Nantucket owns a boat, and many families own two. As many as 2,500 boats shuttle in and out of Nantucket

*Large sailboats fill the boat
basin during the summer.*

Rob Benchley

Harbor on any given day in summer, leading to occasional traffic jams and gridlock. Feeding and supplying boating visitors is a growth industry, and nearly every purveyor on the Island makes many boat runs a day in season.

At present there are only two public boat ramps (in Nantucket Town and Madaket), but the marine superintendent is hoping for more. The town has a permit for 1,500 private moorings (there's a waiting list), which are often sold along with the boats. For information: Harbormaster/Marine Dept. Nantucket Town Pier (508-228-7260; 34 Washington St., Nantucket, MA 02554)

Yet boating is not limited to charters, renters, and owners. In summer you can board the *Wauwinet Lady* (a Fortier twenty-six) at Straight Wharf and go up-harbor on an hour cruise to lunch or dinner at Topper's, the celebrated restaurant at the Wauwinet Resort. Luncheon departure time is 11am with a 1:30pm return; dinner is 5pm with return (sunset cruise) at 8pm. Advance reservations are necessary (508-228-8768). The *Wauwinet Lady* can also be chartered.

BOAT CHARTERS

What's in a name? Usually a story that the skipper will be happy to tell you on your way to the fishing grounds. Fishing or adventuring or partying, the boats are ready. Just be sure to make arrangements well in advance. In addition to fishing and sailing expeditions, a private charter can take you to a secluded beach on Coatue. Stroll down Straight Wharf and look the boats over. If some look familiar, you may have seen them on one or more of the national morning television shows.

FISHING BOAT CHARTERS

Albacore (508-228-5074; albacore@nantucket.net; Slip #17 Straight Wharf, 22
   Sesapana Rd., Nantucket, MA 02554)

Boats galore.

Rob Benchley

Flicka (508-325-4000; Slip #1016 Straight Wharf, 101 Somerset Rd., Nantucket 02554)

Herbert T (508-228-6655; Slip #14 Straight Wharf, PO Box 2023, Nantucket, MA 02584) Nantucket, MA 02554)

Jacqueline C (508-228-4537; marcgenth@aol.com; 1 Chapel Way, Nantucket, MA 02554; at Madaket Public Landing)

Just Do It Too (508-228-7448; Slip #1013 Straight Wharf, Nantucket 02554)

Mon-Tucket Charters (508-228-6867; Slip #1018 Straight Wharf, Nantucket 02554)

Priscilla J /**Capt. Tom Mleczko** (508-228-4225, fax 508-228-0598; capttom@nan tucket.net; www.captaintomscharters.com; 3 Hinkley Ln., Nantucket, MA 02554; at Madaket Public Landing)

Topspin Charter Fishing (508-228-7724; topspin@nantucket.net; www.nan tucket.net/fishing/topspin; Slip #1010 Straight Wharf, PO Box 1444, Nantucket, MA 02554)

GENERAL BOAT CHARTERS

Endeavor (508-228-5585; endeavor@nantucket.net; www.endeavorsailing.com; Slip #1015 Straight Wharf, PO Box 64, Nantucket, MA 02554) Sloop with daily sails at 10am, 11:30am, 1pm, 4pm, and at sunset as well as private charters. U.S. Coast Guard-licensed captain. One-and-one-half-hour sails $22.50–$35 per person. Special one-hour sail at 11:30am is $15 per person. Theme sails with onboard entertainment are fun. Group and charter rates on request.

Harbor Cruises — *Anna W II* (508-228-1444; Slip #1012 Straight Wharf, PO Box 77, Nantucket, MA 02554) Cruises to see gray seals a specialty.

Jacqueline C (508-228-4537; 1 Chapel Way, Nantucket, MA 02554; at Madaket Public Landing) Fishing and pleasure cruises.

Monomoy Charters (508-228-6867; Slip #1018 Straight Wharf, Nantucket, MA 02554) Said to be "for serious fishermen."

The charter boat Endeavor *sets out for its sunset cruise.*

Rob Benchley

Nantucket Adventures, Inc. (508-325-5917; 41 Friendship Lane, Nantucket, MA 02554; at Town pier) Catamaran party boat can take fifty passengers; day sail with buffet lunch from Town pier daily; sunset sail with cash bar from Harbor Launch/Straight Wharf; special events, catering services, private charters.

Nantucket Sailing Charter, Inc. (508-228-3464; 152 Main St., Nantucket, MA 02554) Boats for all seasons and reasons.

Nantucket Sport Fishing (508-325-4000; flickadave@aol.com; Slip #1016 Straight Wharf, 101 Somerset Rd., Nantucket, MA 02554) Fishing and pleasure cruises on the *Flicka* and the *Christina*, a catboat that can accommodate large or small parties, including weddings.

Skip Willauer Sailing (508-325-2120; PO Box 1106, Nantucket, MA 02554) Setting sail is a Nantucket institution. Skip will take you where you want to go.

Sparrow (508-228-6029; Straight Wharf, Nantucket, MA 02554) Fishing and pleasure cruising

BOAT RENTALS

Force 5 Watersports (508-228-0700; info@force5watersports.com; www.force5watersports.com; 6 Union St., Nantucket, MA 02554; at) Small boats, lessons, Sunfish. May–Oct.

Nantucket Boat Rental (508-325-1001; ackboats@nantucket.net; nantucket.net/boating/boatrentals; Swain's Wharf, Nantucket, MA 02554) Twenty-foot center-console fishing/family boat, thirteen- and seventeen-foot powerboats for half day, day, week, and monthly rentals.

Nantucket Harbor Sail (508-228-0424; PO Box 3205, Nantucket, MA 02584; Petrel Landing on Swain's Wharf) Sail and outboard rentals from mid-June to late September.

Nantucket Island Community Sailing (508-228-6600; PO Box 2424, Nantucket, MA 02584) Dedicated to making boating an affordable activity on Nantucket, so check them out.

SEA KAYAKING

Quiet and ecologically sound, sea kayaking has gone way up as a popular sport on Nantucket. This is especially true in the shoulder season, when the number of boats in the water goes down. You can paddle to the jetties to visit the seals. You can explore harbors and ponds as well as ocean, even dig for shellfish at low tide right from the kayak. (Note: this requires a permit and knowledge of what can be taken and when. Contact Marine & Shellfish Dept. 508-228-7260; 34 Washington St., Nantucket, MA 02554.)

Nantucket Community Sailing (508-228-5358; PO Box 2424, Nantucket, MA 02584)
Nantucket Kayak Rentals (508-325-6900; PO Box 1378, Nantucket, MA 02554; Swain's Wharf at Petrel Landing)
Sea Nantucket Kayak Rentals (508-228-7499; Washington St. Ext., PO Box 225, Nantucket, MA 02554)

BOAT SUPPLIES AND MARINAS

Brant Point Marine (508-228-6244; 32 Washington St., Nantucket, MA 02554)
Glyn's Marine (508-228-0244; 8 Arrowhead Dr., Nantucket, MA 02554)
Grey Lady Marine (508-228-6525; 96 Washington St. Ext., PO Box 3216, Nantucket, MA 02584)
Madaket Marine (508-228-9086, 508-228-1163, 800-564-9086; 20 N. Cambridge St., Nantucket, MA 02554; at Madaket)
Nantucket Land & Sea Co. (508-228-4038; PO Box 1411, Nantucket, MA 02554; at Swain's Wharf;)
Nantucket Moorings (508-228-4472; 85 Bartlett Rd., Nantucket, MA 02554)
Nantucket Ship Chandlery Corp. (508-228-2300; PO Box 417, Nantucket, MA 02554; at Old South Wharf)

PRIVATE BOATS

Nantucket Boat Basin (508-228-1333; Swain's Wharf)
Nantucket Moorings (508-228-4472; 85 Bartlett Rd., Nantucket, MA 02554)
Town Pier (508-228-7260; 38 Washington St., Nantucket, MA 02554)

RACES AND REGATTAS

Annual Hurricane Cup Sailboat Regatta (800-626-2628) Held in early September.

Figawi Race (508-420-1400; Coming up on its thirtieth year, this sailboat race from Hyannis to Nantucket and back takes place Memorial Day weekend.

Opera House Cup (508-325-7755; Classic wooden-hulled sailboat regatta has been held in mid-August for more than quarter of a century and was named for its original sponsor, a Nantucket restaurant no longer in existence (and always referred to as the "late lamented").

SAILING LESSONS

Chris Fuller Sailing (508-228-7924; PO Box 2166, Nantucket, MA 02584)

Murphtime Sailing School of Nantucket (508-265-3910)

Nantucket Island Community Sailing Inc. N.I.C.S. (508-228-6600; 4 Winter St., PO Box 2424, Nantucket, MA 02584) More than 250 members, with a junior program at Polpis Harbor and adult program in Town. If you are a resident, a summer resident, or a regular visitor, give them a call.

Skip Willauer Sailing (508-325-2120; PO Box 1106, Nantucket, MA 02554) Private and small-group lessons.

DOG OBEDIENCE SCHOOLS

Since you must keep your dog under control at all times while on-Island, this may be the opportune moment to enroll him or her in a behavioral and obedience training program. Incidentally, the Commonwealth of Massachusetts requires vaccinations against the rabies virus for all dogs and cats visiting or residing in Massachusetts. (Also see the "Pets" section in Chapter Nine, *Information.*) The third week of September is the Annual Pets on Parade Pet Show organized by the MSPCA (508-228-1491) at the fairgrounds, where ribbons are awarded in such categories as Best Pet Trick and Best Kisser.

Canine Communications — (508-228-3246; PO Box 2802, Nantucket, MA 02584)

Shannon McIntyre — Dog Obedience (508-228-1800; PO Box 2181, Nantucket, MA 02584) Behavioral counseling and house training.

FAMILY FUN

Any place that has a beach named Children's Beach is thinking about families and how to keep them happy. Many Island residents and regular visitors started coming as youngsters — which may, in part, explain the emphasis on family fun and safety. Nevertheless, parental supervision is a good idea, for young children in particular, even if lifeguards are on duty. Children should be cautioned to stay on the marked trails in the heathlands, where bird nests and chicks are tucked in the grass, and told never, ever to uproot or trample anything, even on dunes. It's a perfect place to explain "how we behave" on a fragile island.

Family bicycle touring via the bike paths can be as long or as short as you like. Take along a picnic lunch, or stop for fast food at your destination. If you take the Polpis Road path, a good break is the **Nantucket Life Saving Museum** (508-228-1885; 158 Polpis Rd., Nantucket, MA 02554) where lifesaving boats, buoys, and the equipment used in rescue are displayed along with the story of the lightships that once marked the dangerous shoals. As far as anyone knows, this is the only lifesaving museum in the world. The building is a duplicate of the old Star of the Sea lifesaving station at Surfside Beach, now the AYH hostel. (For bike rentals see Chapter Two, *Transportation*.)

Family fishing expeditions are always popular, and most charters and guides provide equipment and training for children and adults alike. Whale- or seal-watching cruises are especially good family activities. **Harbor Cruises** has children's ice-cream cruises on the *Anna W II* (508-228-1444; Slip #1012 Straight Wharf). The **Friendship Sloop** *Endeavor* (508-228-5585; Slip #1015 Straight Wharf) sails into Nantucket Sound on a "Songs & Stories of the Sea" voyage featuring guitarist Steve Sheppard.

Watching the boats come and go out of the harbor is a favorite pastime at **Children's Beach.** Children also love to see the activity on the wharves, and the boatmen appear delighted with the young audience. **The Toy Boat** (508-228-4552; Straight Wharf), an old fishing shack turned toy store, inevitably has a project going every afternoon 2–4pm. It may be a bubble-blowing session or make-your-own sunglasses. The annual children's Pirates and Mermaids Parade is organized and led by a costumed pirate from this magical shop.

Mid-August's **Sandcastle & Sculpture Day** at **Jetties Beach** is also a family winner. Incidentally, playground equipment is available at these two beaches and the smaller **Francis Street Beach** in addition to the **Nantucket Elementary School** on Atlantic Avenue. Little children can feed the ducks at **Consue Springs,** a small pond just off Union Street about a fifteen-minute walk from Main St. You bring the bread.

Children old enough to swim can take lessons in windsurfing, kayaking, and sailing May through October at **Jetties Beach.** Pre-registration is preferred but walk-ins are welcome if space is available. Contact **Force 5 Watersports** (508-228-0700; 6 Union St., Nantucket, MA 02554;) or the **Nantucket Parks and Recreation Commission** (508-228-7213, fax 508-228-5347; parkrec@nantucket. net; 2 Bathing Beach Rd., Nantucket, MA 02554).

Whether your imagination is captured by the possibilities of those ocean breezes west of **Surfside Beach** or you're just looking for some wildly original decoration for the wall of a dorm, kites may be just the thing. **Nantucket Kiteman** (508-228-7089; 14 S. Water St., Nantucket, MA 02554) and **Sky's the Limit** (508-228-4633; Straight Wharf, at the Courtyard) have more kites than you thought existed. **Sport-Kite Fly Days** are often held on Sundays June through August. Call **Nantucket Kiteman** for locations.

Inside the Loines Observatory.

Frederick G. S. Clow /
The Inquirer and Mirror

Save an evening for a family visit to Open Night at **Loines Observatory** (508-228-8690) 59 Milk Street, Nantucket, MA 02554). **Maria Mitchell Association** astronomers are on hand at 9pm to show visitors how to use the telescopes. You'll need warm clothing and bug repellent. The MMA also has an aquarium, natural history museum, and library. Ask about its science classes for children. For more information: 508-228-9198.

For a change from family togetherness, the Island offers lots for children to do while their parents are doing boring adult stuff. The kids can even go to day camp or sports camp full time or join in special activities. **Murray Camp** (508-325-4600; 25-1/2 Bartlett Rd., PO Box 3437, Nantucket, MA 02584) organizes **"Kids' Night Out"** from 6–9pm three nights a week all summer long. One night it will be a "Sconset Ghost Walk" followed by ice cream at the Sconset Market (two groups ages 5 to 8 and 9 to 13); another, a beach Olympics or an exploration of the Island. **Nantucket Community School** (508-228-7257, ext. 1351; 10 Surfside Rd., Nantucket, MA 02554) has day and sports camp from all-star baseball to swimming lessons. **Nantucket Boys & Girls Club Sports Camp** (508-228-0158; 61 Sparks Ave., PO Box 269, Nantucket, MA 02554) has basketball, baseball, soccer, and football camp for age groups 7–18. **Strong Wings Adventure School** (508-228-1769; explore@strongwings.org; strongwings.org; 9 Nobadeer Farm Rd., PO Box 2884, Nantucket, MA 02584) offers "environmental and adventure-based education" through groups in July and August for ages 5–7, 8–11, and 11–14, including mountain biking, stunt-kite flying, and fort building. Programs run year-round plus three summer day camps for children from 5–14. **Force 5 Watersports** (508-228-0700; 6 Union St.,

---

Foggy Days

It comes on little cat feet — and lingers. Fog is the predictable of Island living, and you are going to have to bow to it. The planes won't fly. The mainland newspapers will be late. Lights will come on during the day. Traffic will slow. "So *now* what do we do?" the children demand as if expecting you to make it all go away. (Now you know why scheduled events always have "weather permitting" attached and nearly always provide indoor alternatives.)

Fortunately, being on Nantucket is more than going to the beach. In fact, you'll soon be wondering how you are going to get it all in. (If swimming is the only activity that will suffice, however, **Nantucket High School** has an indoor pool: 508-228-7262; 10 Surfside Rd., Nantucket, MA 02554)

In the local papers under *Island Calendar* are listings of concerts, lectures, demonstrations, and classes. Downtown the shops are open, and so are the museums. You can easily spend an afternoon at the **Whaling Museum** and the **Peter Foulger Museum** next door, a visit that will enhance your whole Nantucket experience. And the **Atheneum** has a spectacular new children's library wing.

These are perfect days for big bowls of chowder with the puffy New England crackers that are said to be like sailors' hardtack — but not so hard. Lobster bisque is another Nantucket restaurant standby, and there's always a soup of the day.

Unless it's a morning mist and expected to be gone by noon, the inns will have fires going in the main rooms. Off-season it's a certainty. Many serve four o'clock tea or wine and cheese. You may have missed these get-togethers because you've been out on the beach at that hour. Every lodging from the smallest guesthouse to the most posh resort has a shelf of board games and a supply of videos. On foggy days an expression of longing will probably result in popcorn freshly popped.

Nantucketers know how to treat fog. They deal with it.

Nantucket, MA 02554) has windsurfing, kayaking, and sailing lessons. Sailing lessons are also offered at **Nantucket Community Sailing** for ages 7–10, 10–13, and 13–16 (508-228-6600; 4 Winter St., PO Box 2424, Nantucket, MA 02584).

Children from four to twelve learn about the natural sciences, astronomy, and Nantucket history through a variety of field trips, demonstrations, and hands-on fun in July and August in **Maria Mitchell Children's Discovery Classes** Mon.–Fri. 9am–4pm (508-228-9198; 2 Vestal St., Nantucket, MA 02554).

The **InterNet Café** (508-228-6777; 2 Union St., Nantucket, MA 02554; upstairs) has a "Kids Night" during the summer for ages eight to twelve from 6–9pm where they spend three hours cruising the Net with a guide and playing interactive games. Light refreshments are included. For reservations: 508-228-6777. For ages seven to thirteen, **Dr. T1's Computer Club** (part of the Internet Café) has daily and weekend classes in reading, writing, math, music, history, and more as well as "The Awesome Club for Kids," a multifaceted program of summer enrichment for grades four through eight. Call for class schedules and more information: 508-257-6124.

The **Nantucket Atheneum** (508-228-1110; 1 India St., Nantucket, MA 02554) offers Story Hour in the new Children's Wing. For the schedule, call: 508-228-1110. **First Congregational Church** (62 Centre St., Nantucket, MA 02554) has Dial-a-Children's Story; call: 508-228-6050. There's a children's nook in the science library of the Maria Mitchell Association, too.

The **Nantucket Historical Association** sponsors "Living History for Children" in two-hour sessions, where they learn colonial life hands-on — maybe baking bread on the open hearth of the Oldest House or grinding corn at the Old Mill or how to get ready for a whaling voyage. For more information, contact: 508-228-1894.

The **Nantucket Parks and Recreation Commission** has a **Teen Center** (508-325-5340; First Way, Nantucket, MA 02554) and also holds tie-dying clinics on **Children's Beach** (check the Calendar in the newspaper) on Fridays from July 4 to Labor Day. Parents are expected to stay and supervise. For young artists on their own, the **Artists' Association of Nantucket** (508-228-0722; 19 Washington St., Nantucket, MA 02554), **Nantucket Island School of Design and the Arts** (508-228-9248; 23 Wauwinet Rd., Nantucket, MA 02554; Quaise), and **Shredder's Studio** (508-228-4487; 3 Salros Rd., Nantucket, MA 02554) offer classes for children and teenagers.

Family extends to neighbors and friends at **Generations Together,** a program of art projects, storytelling, and puppets Wednesday mornings in July and August at the Nantucket Island School of Design and the Arts (508-228-9348; 23 Wauwinet Rd., Quaise).

Pick up a copy of the Thursday newspaper, the *Inquirer and Mirror*, for a day-by-day list of events in the Island Calendar. The **Visitor Services Center** (508-228-0925; 25 Federal St., Nantucket, MA 02554) has free copies of Kid's Calendar, published by the paper in July and August.

For Rollerbladers, **Jetties Beach skateboard park** is open until dark but unattended. **Jetties Beach tennis courts** has the obligatory protective pads. **Nobadeer Mini-Golf** (508-228-8977; 12 Nobadeer Farm Rd., Nantucket, MA 02554) is made all the more convenient by a free shuttle from Town for groups of six or more. You can also take the NRTA shuttle. Indoor swimming can be a family affair at the **Nantucket Community School Pool** (508-228-7262; 10 Surfside Rd., Nantucket, MA 02554) Is it birthday party time? See **Balloons on Nantucket** (508-228-1916; 29 Main St., Nantucket, MA 02554; at Anderson's) and **The Party Pak** (508-228-3335, 90 Old South Rd., Nantucket, MA 02554).

Actors' Theatre of Nantucket (508-228-6325; United Methodist Church; 2 Centre St., Nantucket, MA 02554) has a Children's Theatre Program mid-July through August. The Community School's **Children's Summer Theatre** (508-228-7257;) has acting classes and puts on shows.

If you need child care, **Nantucket Babysitters' Service Inc.** (508-228-4970; babysit@nantucketbabysitters.com; www.nantucketbabysitters.com; 5 Windy Way, PO Box 842, Nantucket, MA 02554) is provided by the South Suburban Nurses Registry. Others sitting services include **All-Island Babysitting** (508-325-4031). In season, the Visitor Services Center (508-228-0925) registers babysitters.

For a nursery school, contact **St. Paul's Cooperative Nursery School** (508-228-0916; 20 Fair St., Nantucket, MA 02554); they will refer you to others.

FISHING AND SHELLFISHING

Rob Benchley

Fishing for (and catching) striped bass at Great Point.

Shellfishing limits are generous for noncommercial (recreational) and family takers. You can have a stupendous beach cookout with your day's gathering, though you'll need a permit for the fire. Fishing permits are also necessary: $25 for individuals over the age of fourteen includes scallops, crabs, mussels, eels, oysters, quahogs, and steamers.

Surf fishing and blue-water offshore angling are tops, especially on the south and east shores, and there's also freshwater fishing in the ponds. Spinning tackle may be rented at Island tackle shops, but fly-fishers must bring their own equipment. Popular brands of both types of gear are sold in local tackle shops, and while you're there, you can find out where the big ones are biting or even make arrangements to hire a beach guide. A guide will pick you up, take you there, supply the equipment, and instruct you as necessary.

Best beaches are **Great Point** and **Smith's Point** at the extreme opposite ends of the Island. No permit is required for striped bass (length is thirty-four inches), bluefish from boats and shore, May through November, or blue claw crabs. For information and permits: **Marine, Harbormaster, and Shellfish Department** (508-228-7260; 34 Washington St., Nantucket, MA 02554). The *Inquirer and Mirror* lists the harbor tides, or you can pick up a tide chart at the

Nantucket Ship Chandlery Corp. (508-228-2300; 1 Old South Wharf, Nantucket, MA 02554). Freshwater ponds — especially the north head of Hummock Pond off the Madaket Road and Sesachacha Pond (pronounced Sak-a-cha) off Polpis Road — have pickerel, white and yellow perch, crappie, sunfish, and occasionally a landlocked striped bass.

Mussels: Open season; permit required.

Bay scallops Closed season; recreational season Oct. 1–31; commercial season, Nov. 1–Mar. 31; permit required; limit one bushel per week. Scallops must have growth mark. Overscalloping has led to seeding by the Marine Department.

Eels: Open season; permit required. Eels are found in harbors and creeks during spring and fall.

Blue-claw crabs: Open season; no permit required. Return egg-bearing females.

Oysters: Closed season; recreational season Sept. 1–Apr. 30. Permit required; limit: half bushel per week. Oysters must be three inches in size.

Quahogs: Open season. Permit required; limit: half bushel per week. Quahog shell must be two inches in size.

Steamers: Closed season; recreational season Sept. 15–June 14. Permit required; limit: one ten-quart pail per week. Steamer shell must be 2.5 inches in size.

FISHING CHARTERS: SURF AND FLY-FISHING LESSONS

These charters come with tackle as well as lessons and as much guidance as necessary.

Albacore (508-228-5074; Slip #1017 Straight Wharf; 22 Sesapana Rd., Nantucket, MA 02554) Thirty-two-foot sportsfisherman with a large comfortable cockpit; for all ages, experienced and inexperienced. Fish guaranteed on five-hour trips.

Capt. Tom Mleczko (508-228-4225; capttom@nantucket.net; www.captaintoms charters.com; 3 Hinkley Ln., Nantucket, MA 02554) Three boats, two captains specialize in plugcasting and flycasting. Winner of the John Havlicek Fishing Tournament eleven out of fourteen years.

Herbert T (508-228-6655; Slip #1014 Straight Wharf; PO Box 2023, Nantucket, MA 02554) Up to six people to fish at one time. Four two-and-a-half-hour trips a day, $50 per person. Plugcasting. Private charters also available.

Whitney Mitchell Surf Fishing (508-228-2331; 15 Masaquet Ave., Nantucket, MA 02554) Experienced guide with four-door Jeep wagon takes you to many beaches wherever the fish are. "Fishing gear and local chatter included."

FLY-FISHING SCHOOL

A one-day fly fishing school in June for beginner to advanced fly fishermen includes casting, knots equipment, and more at **Cross Rip Outfitters** (508-228-4900; 24 Easy St., Nantucket, MA 02554).

FISHING TACKLE AND GEAR

Catch of the day: a prized striped bass.

Rob Benchley

Beginners to advanced anglers will find in these purveyors not only rods and reels but also repairs, rentals, gifts, guide service, and information on charters, along with supplies and support systems for deep-sea, surfcasting, and freshwater fishing as well as shellfishing.

Barry Thurston's Tackle Shop (508-228-9595; Thurston@nantucket.net; PO Box 652, Nantucket, MA 02554; at Candle and Salem Sts.)
Bill Fisher Tackle (508-228-2261; fisherst@nantucket.net; 14 New Ln., PO Box 975, Nantucket, MA 02554)
Brant Point Marine (508-228-6244; 32 Washington St., Nantucket, MA 02554)
Cross Rip Outfitters (508-228-4900; www.crossrip.com; 24 Easy St., PO Box 55, Nantucket, MA 02554)
Nantucket Tackle Center (508-228-4081; 41 Sparks Ave., Nantucket, MA 02554; at D&B Auto, behind Stop & Shop)

FISHING TOURNAMENTS

John Havlicek Celebrity Fishing Tournament (508-228-1500) An annual June sports celebrity benefit event since 1981. It raises money for the John Havlicek Child Development Clinic.
Hooked on Nantucket Bluefish Tournament (508-228-4081) "Nantucket Blues" means neither a special shade of denim nor a state of despondency caused by having to depart the Island. These blues are bluefish, and the Bluefish Tournament is held in late May.
Nantucket Billfish Tournament (508-228-2299; The Nantucket Anglers Club) First week in August. For thirty years, sharks, marlin, yellowfin tuna, and

the like have been game in the literal sense for five days. Anglers accumulate points for boating (catching), tagging, and releasing to win awards and titles. For example, the High Hook Award is for the top angler in offshore catch and release. In addition to the top five individual anglers and crews, there's a Captain's Cup, a White Marlin Release Trophy, awards for First Eligible Billfish, Last Eligible Billfish, Heaviest Mako Shark, and the top five Yellowfin/Albacore Tuna.

FITNESS

Whether you want a place to work out or have a pampering massage in your own quarters, Nantucket provides. Personal trainers and classes will put or keep you in shape. You may even graduate to participate in the **Coed Volleyball Tournament** held on Jetties Beach in late July.

Lynn Tucker Body Treatments (508-228-5981; 36 Vesper Ln., Nantucket, MA 02554) Complete spa body treatments; steam bath; massage therapy; pedicures; sports-injury treatment. Appointment only.

Spa to Go (508-228-5574) The facilities of a spa can come to you, including massage, facials, manicures, and pedicures. Available seven days a week; seasonal.

Tresses & The Day Spa (508-228-0024, 800-540-0524; tresses@nantucket.net; 117 Pleasant St., Nantucket, MA 02554) Hair and skin care salon. Body treatments include mood and aromatherapy, herbal body wraps, sports massage, Swedish massage, reflexology, lymphosage, and even a fifteen-minute stress break. Spa morning and evening gift packages.

Personal trainers are available from **Andrea Lee's Fitness Focus** (508-228-0220; 3 Fair St., Nantucket, MA 02554); **Dave & Sandy Schulz** (508-228-9448; 7 Macy's Ln., Nantucket, MA 02554); **Kimberly Layman** (508-228-1679; 218 Cliff Rd., PO Box 2551, Nantucket, MA 02584); **Great Expeditions** (508-228-8982; www.great-expeditions.com; 98A Madaket Rd., PO Box 2091, Nantucket, MA 02554).

GOLF

Island golf is casual rather than compulsive — or as one golfer explained it: "On Nantucket, golf is fun."

Miacomet Golf Club (508-325-0335, clubhouse; 12 W. Miacomet Rd., PO Box 2479, Nantucket, MA 02584; off Somerset Rd.) Public. Nine-hole Bent grass course. Built in 1964. Designed by Ralph Marbel. Terrain is flat, so the course is easy to walk. Beginners will enjoy playing here because of the wide fairways and large greens. Weekday green fees for nonmembers are $29 for nine holes *during peak season;* $55 for eighteen. Clubhouse, restaurant, bar, and pro shop.

Tees	Yardage	Rating	Slope	Par
Yards (MGA)	6674	72.4	118	74
Yards/women	6004	73.5	118	74

Classification: Public.
Dress Code: No tank tops or cutoffs.
Season: Open all year, weather permitting.
Tee Times: Accepted 4 days in advance.
Earliest Time to Call: 7am in-season.
Pro Shop Phone: 508-325-0333.
Pro Shop Opens: 7am in-season.
Golf Carts: Gas carts available; $38 per cart (18 holes); $20 per cart (9 holes).
Rental Clubs Available: Yes.
Caddies Available: No.
Walking: Yes.
Driving Range: No.
Additional Training Facilities: Putting green, sand, chipping area.
Pro on Site: Yes.

The Sankaty Head lighthouse watches over players at the Sankaty Head Golf Club.

Frederick G. S. Clow

Sankaty Head Golf Club (508-257-6391; PO Box 293, Siasconset, MA 02564; at Sankaty Rd. and Polpis Rd.) Private. Open to the public in the fall only. Guests must be accompanied by a member. Bar, snack bar, and restaurant. Eighteen-hole Bent grass course with water in play. Built in 1922. Designed by Phil Wogan. This beautiful course by the Sankaty Head lighthouse offers a view of the Atlantic Ocean from fourteen holes. Fairways are wide open, and there are a lot of hills that can cause uneven lies.

Tees	Yardage	Rating	Slope	Par
Back Tees	6623	72.5	129	72
Middle Tees	6372	71.2	127	72
Forward Tees	5563	72.8	120	75

Ranking:
No. 4 by *Golf Digest:* America's Top State Golf Courses 1997–98.
No. 84 by *GolfWeek:* America's 100 Best Classical Courses 1997.
Classification: Private.
Dress Code: No denim. Collared shirt and Bermuda shorts required.
Season: May 15 to Oct. 15.
Tee Times: Accepted 3 days in advance.
Earliest Time to Call: 7:45am.
Pro Shop Phone: 508-257-6391.
Pro Shop Open: 7:45am.
Golf Carts: Electric golf carts available $15 per person (18 holes); pull carts $7.50 per person (9 holes).
Caddies: Available.
Pro: On site.
Rental Clubs: Available.
Additional Training Facilities: Driving range, putting green, sand, chipping area.

Siasconset Golf Club (508-257-6596; PO Box 613, Siasconset, MA 01564; at Milestone Rd.) Nine-hole Bent grass course with water in play. Historic course built 1894. Snack bar only.

Tees	Yardage	Rating	Slope	Par
Men's	5086	68.1	113	70
Women's	5086	0.0		70

Ranking: 83 by *Golf* magazine: the First 100 Clubs in America 1995.
Classification: Public.
Dress Code: Shirt and shoes required.
Season: June 1–Oct. 15.
Pro Shop Phone: 508-257-6596.
Pro Shop Opens: 8am.
Pro: On site.
Rental Carts: Pull carts only ($2).
Rental Clubs: Available.

Caddies: Not available.
Driving Range: No.

Miniature Golf

Major fun for all ages, Nantucket's very popular miniature golf course is in a garden setting complete with flower beds, ponds, and a waterfall. **Nobadeer Mini-Golf** (508-228-8977; PO Box 1500, Nantucket, MA 02554; at Nobadeer Farm and Sun Island Rd. between Sconset bike path and airport road) offers nineteen holes and practice green, parking, light food, and is near a NRTA shuttle stop. Open daily seasonally, 9am–11pm. Free bus from Town for groups of six or more by reservation.

GOLF TOURNAMENTS

The **Annual Pro-Am Golf Tournament** at Sankaty in early June is a celebrity and golf pro tournament for the benefit of the Nantucket Boys and Girls Club (508-228-0158; Sparks Ave., Nantucket, MA 02554). This has been called the number one fun event of the summer.

The **Nantucket Cottage Hospital Annual Golf Benefit** at Sankaty Head Golf Club is a golf scramble in September (508-228-1200 or 508-257-6391) and includes a steak dinner after the game.

The **Annual Harlan Davis Golf Tournament** is a benefit at Miacomet Golf Club in October (508-325-0333).

For information on additional tournaments, contact the Miacomet Golf Club (508-228-0334).

The Exiles
God bless the sea-beat island!
And grant for evermore
That charity and freedom dwell,
As now, upon her shore.

—John Greenleaf Whittier, 1850

HIKING

The protected public lands of Nantucket are open to hikers and are connected by dirt and sand walking paths and mowed roadways that lead to viewpoints and beaches. The trails meander over hilltops with sweeping views of Nantucket Sound, Nantucket Harbor, and the Atlantic Ocean. They go past ket-

---

Microscopic Bad Guys: Ticks

Lyme disease (named after a town in Connecticut) and babesiosis have both been reported on Nantucket. Both diseases are spread by the bite of the pinhead-size deer tick, not to be confused with the big fat eastern wood ticks your pet brings in from any outing. The trouble is, you may never see the deer tick. If you do see any evidence that you may have been bitten, get to a physician at once. These diseases are treatable but must be diagnosed early to avoid serious complications. Be sure to inform your doctor that you (or your pet) have been in grass and woodland areas where deer ticks are known to be around.

Precautions: Those who are pregnant, lack a spleen, or are otherwise immunologically unresponsive should avoid the woodlands altogether. Use insect repellent. Walkers should wear shoes, socks, and long light-colored pants tucked into the socks. Watch for dark-brown dots that won't brush off, and check your children frequently if they've been playing in grassy or woodland areas. If the tick is embedded, remove by gently tugging with small tweezers; then wipe the spot with rubbing alcohol. Save the tick in a labeled container, making note of the date and where on the body the bite occurred.

If the site looks red and feels warm a few days to a week later or if you experience flulike symptoms, see a doctor and bring along the tick.

Lyme disease manifests itself with an expanding ringlike rash and mild flulike symptoms (fatigue, fever, chills, aches and pains, sore throat or headache). If not treated it can involve the heart, joints, brain, or nervous system.

Babesiosis is far less common than Lyme disease. It is caused by a microscopic parasite in the deer tick and creates a malarialike infection by bursting red blood cells in the victim's bloodstream. Symptoms may include fever alternating with chills, enlarged liver and spleen, and an extremely low red-blood-cell count.

If you need a doctor: Nantucket has a fully staffed hospital on Island, Nantucket Cottage Hospital (508-228-1200; 57 Prospect St., Nantucket, MA 02554)

---

tlehole ponds and hidden forests of tupelo, maple, beech, and oak trees. They cross the middle moors south from Squam and Polpis to the outwash valleys and beaches from Madequecham to Tom Nevers, past meadows and wetlands full of heathland plants. Around Squam Swamp off the Wauwinet Road is a wooded path that takes you on a round trip of slightly more than a mile past fern and beech groves, small ponds, and one of the Island's few flowing streams. Also at the eastern end: the Windswept Cranberry Bog and the Masequetuck Reservation in Quaise. A favorite hike is to Altar Rock, the Island's second highest point at ninety-seven feet (Folger Hill is 109 feet) and conceivably a site of ancient ceremonies. Take the Altar Rock Road off Polpis Road.

Other good short hikes are around Gibbs Pond in the east and Eel Point in the west. The 6.6 miles of walking trails on the Sanford Farm, Ram Pasture, and Woods between Madaket Road and the Atlantic Ocean are very popular, especially a six-mile trail that goes around and alongside Hummock Pond. You access the farm from a parking area off Madaket Road near the Cliff Road intersection.

Watch for the roadside maroon posts topped by the gull-and-wave logo of the Nantucket Conservation Foundation.

HUNTING

Many of Nantucket's game animals were imported in the 1920s by groups like the Nantucket Sportsmen's Club, who visualized a running to the hounds. These days hunters' quarry includes waterfowl, game birds, rabbit, and deer in season. (A deer population explosion has increased the limit and supply.) The Island's western black-tailed jackrabbit can dash thirty-five miles an hour in short bursts and its normal hop of five to ten feet can reach up to twenty feet when it's frightened.These very large critters have black-tipped ears to match their tails.

Hunting permits are available at the town clerk's office (508-228-7216, fax 508-325-5313; twnclerk@nantucket.net; 16 Broad St., Nantucket, MA 02554).

To the Lighthouses

Storm clouds roll in over Great Point lighthouse.

Rob Benchley

Nantucket's three lighthouses just may be the most photographed or otherwise artistically depicted beacons on earth. You will see them rendered on canvas, paper, and needlepoint; on book covers, T-shirts, and Christmas cards. None is open to the public, but all are worth visiting, if only to take a picture.

Brant Point Light, 1902, was originally built in 1746, sixty-four years before the United States Lighthouse Department was established. Brant Point Light is second only to Boston's Beacon Light as oldest in the nation. However, the white wooden lighthouse you see today as you enter the harbor is the tenth to occupy this vital spot. It is twenty-six feet high and has a ten-mile range. It oscillates for four seconds, with a one-second eclipse.

It's a great place to pose the kids for Christmas card pictures, and you get there by crossing a footbridge from the end of Easton Street. You can read about one family's life near the light in the entertaining autobiographies *Cheaper by the Dozen* and *Belles on Their Toes* by Frank Gilbreth and Ernestine Gilbreth Carey. On Daffodil Weekend coast guard personnel hang a ring of daffs on the side and at Christmas Stroll, a wreath decorated with crossed oars.

Great Point Light, 1765, was erected to guide whaling ships around the outer limit of Nantucket and used 1,600 to 1,800 gallons of high-grade strained spermaceti oil annually. The first accurate American chart of the entire New England coast showing Nantucket Shoals and Georges Banks was prepared here by the lighthouse keeper in 1790. By 1890 more than forty-three shipwrecks had occurred in Great Point's jurisdiction, some caused by navigational confusion with beams from the two lightships stationed nearby. Finally a red sector was installed to the flashing beams, making the difference between lighthouse and lightship clear to navigators. The present light, a white tower with solar panels, was raised in 1984 and stands seventy feet above sea level. It was built to withstand high tides and fifteen-foot waves, and its white light flashes every five seconds. The paved road ends at Wauwinet, but it's a challenging hike to the end of the point.

Great Point Light figured in the famous Nantucket Bank Robbery of 1795, when the thieves escaped in the lighthouse's rescue boat. It was the setting for murder in Jane Langton's mystery novel *Dark Nantucket Noon,* and at various times mermaids have been reported cavorting in the waters nearby.

Sankaty Head Light, 1850, white with a red midstripe, is on the National Register of Historic Places. It stands seventy feet tall atop a ninety-foot bluff overlooking both the sea and the golf course. Visible for more than twenty-four miles, it enabled ships to save a day's time by using an otherwise dangerous but deep channel inside South Shoal. In 1854 the platform around the lantern was widened to accommodate ladies wearing hoopskirts. Electric light was not installed until 1945, and today the light flashes every 7.5 seconds.

You can reach Sankaty Head Light by taking Polpis Road past Sankaty Golf Course and turning east at the lighthouse sign just before entering Siasconset, but the road is closed at the present time due to erosion. To see the former lens in operation, visit the Whaling Museum in Nantucket Town.

Massachusetts licenses are valid on Nantucket. Hunting areas include the following recreational sites: **Coskata Coatue Wildlife** (963 acres), **Middle Moors Reserve** (723 acres), **Larsen Acres** (513 acres), and **Sanford-Fowlkes Reserve** (415 acres). For more information contact Nantucket Parks and Recreation Commission (508-228-7213, fax 508-228-5347; parkrec@nantucket.net; 2 Bathing Beach Rd., Nantucket, MA 02554). Hunting supplies are generally available at the gear and tackle shops listed in the section on "Fishing" above.

Deer ticks are carriers of Lyme disease and babesiosis; hunters should watch for tiny dots that won't brush off and take precautions (see "Microscopic Bad Guys: Ticks" above).

ICE SKATING

Nantucket Ice (508-228-2516; iceskate@nantucket.net; 26 First Way, PO Box 3155, Nantucket, MA 02584) scheduled to debut in 2001 is mid-Island, between the elementary and high schools, and open to all. Fundraising boomed when Nantucket's own Allison Jaime (A. J.) Mieckko won an Olympic gold medal as a member of the U.S. Women's Hockey Team in 1998.

"RANTOM SCOOTING"

This is Nantucket's own word for just going around without a fixed itinerary, a sort of serendipity on the move. We assume "rantom" is derived from "random," but "scooting"? Whatever, it can be accomplished by bike, foot, boat, or car. Given the size of the Island, it's likely you won't get too lost. While a picnic lunch that you bring along is a bonus, you can always pick up a bite to eat somewhere along the way.

The opposite of rantom scooting is "squantum," which means a picnic or outing with a specific location in mind. Scooting may logically precede squantum, as in stumbling on the perfect place and returning to it regularly.

RUNNING AND RUNNING EVENTS

Island marathons are good training for the Big One in Boston

Rob Benchley

If an infinite number of running enthusiasts convened for the sole purpose of envisioning the perfect combination of elements for their activity, they might very well come up with Nantucket. The Island has variety of terrain from flat to gently rolling. Generously wide bike paths keep runners out of the street, and there's no stopping for traffic lights. The paths bend and twist, preventing the mesmerizing "straightaway syndrome." The head winds may be considered challenging. The air is fresh and pollution-free. Marathoners to meanderers: Go ahead, breathe deeply. It isn't going to kill you.

Those five wide paths going to all points of the Island may have been made for biking, but they are even better for running. The views are spectacular: moors (Polpis), wildflowers (Madaket), the sea (Cliff Road), cranberry bogs (Milestone). Surfside Path is even lit at night. Polpis, Madaket, and Milestone are for the long-distance runners; Surfside beckons to those who would like to end their run with a dip in the Atlantic. Too tired to make the return run? Ride back on the NRTA shuttle.

Walking and running races begin in March with the Nantucket Marathon (26 miles) and the half-marathon (13.1 miles) (508-228-7218) and continue in May with the ten-kilometer **Annual Cranberry Classic** (508-228-6873) followed by the classic relay **Nantucket Iron Man Race** in mid-June (508-228-6873). On the Fourth of July, there's the **Annual Firecracker 5K Race** (508-228-4750), and in August comes the **Annual Rock Run** (508-228-5817), a fifty-mile marathon over rocks, sand, and everything else that circles Nantucket, rain or shine. The run begins at 5am, and the winner comes home when it's over. Funds raised go to the Special Needs Advisory Council and the Nantucket Special Olympics.

SCENIC FLIGHTS

Especially popular on special event weekends, scenic flights are available on clear days year-round. Taking one of the small planes from the mainland is a scenic flight in itself (see Chapter Two, *Transportation*, for information). However, **Ocean Wings Air Charter** (508-325-5548, 800-253-5039; wings@nantucket.net; www.oceanwings.com; 26 Macy's Ln., Nantucket, MA 02554; at Nantucket Memorial Airport) does sightseeing tours and also operates a flight school and regular charter service.

SWIMMING

Sea swimming is, of course, all around the Island (see the section above on "Beaches" for choosing surf or calm), and freshwater swimming is at Miacomet Pond. An indoor public swimming pool with lessons and family swims is the **Nantucket Community School Pool** (508-228-7262; Nantucket High School, 10 Surfside Rd., Nantucket, MA 02554).

TENNIS

Two-week tennis clinics are sponsored by the Nantucket Parks and Recreation Commission late June through the end of August. For information: 508-325-5334. Tennis courts at clubs and at the beach:

Brant Point Racquet Club (508-228-3700; 48 North Beach St., Nantucket, MA 02554) Nine clay courts; the site of the Nantucket Tennis Classic in late July.
Jetties Beach public tennis courts (508-325-5334)
Tristram's Landing Tennis Club (508-228-4588; 440 Arkansas Ave., Nantucket, MA 02554; in Madaket)

For tennis courts at hotels see Chapter Three, *Lodging*. While the tennis courts of the Casino in Sconset are private, the tennis pro shop is open to the public, and you might even wangle a court if no one else is playing and you're staying in Sconset.

TOURS

Touring the Island on your own by foot or by bicycle is easy in most places, thanks to the bike paths and a little help from the NRTA shuttle if needed (described in Chapter Two, *Transportation*). Suggested itineraries for self-guided tours are described below. (The more rugged of them may require a four-wheel-drive vehicle or boat in some places.)

Many visitors who are day-trippers from Cape Cod via the ferry bring bikes or rent them on arrival for a day of touring. (No advance ferry reservations are necessary for bicycles.)

Packing along lunch for your day's outing is always an option, since the Island offers endless picturesque spots for picnics. If you undertake the treks to Great Point or Coatue, you will need to bring water, as well. (See "To the Lighthouses," above.)

Another suggestion is to take an introductory tour by van or bus. It's an inexpensive way to get an overview of the Island in just an hour and a half or so, and will give you ideas for leisurely returns to various sites on your own. (See Chapter Nine, *Information*, and Chapter Two, *Transportation*, for listings.)

NORTH

From Capaum to Hummock Pond is the site of **Old Sherborn,** the Island's center from 1660 to 1720. Capaum was Cappamet Harbor before it silted up. The first pumping station was built at Washing Pond in 1878. The Nantucket Conservation Foundation owns the **Tupancy Property** on Cliff Road and has suggestions for a self-guided tour.

SOUTH

It's no surprise that on this Atlantic front, all roads lead eventually to beaches and the sea. The **Indian Burial Ground** is on Surfside Road. **Surfside Beach** itself was once the epicenter of a land boom that fizzled. The 1874 Life Saving Station is now the **Star of the Sea Youth Hostel** operated by American Youth Hostels.

Follow Hummock Pond Road to **Cisco Beach,** and do as the Town residents do: Shop at **Bartlett's Farm** and the **fish vendor** at Cisco Beach. **Nantucket Vineyard** (wines and ciders) and **Cisco Brewers** (a year-round microbrewery) are on Bartlett Farm Road off Hummock Pond Road and offer informal unscheduled tours of their operations as well as selling their own products.

EAST

Coatue may translate to "at the pine tree place," but the name is obviously from the distant past. Today Coatue is approximately 500 acres of barrier beach extending from the east jetty in Nantucket Harbor northeast to **Coskata Pond,** the saltwater pond and marsh system between **Wauwinet** and **Great Point.** It is one of the most undisturbed in the Northeast for the simple reason that it is difficult (many say impossible) to get there. The pavement ends at Wauwinet, and after that it takes a jeep to make the hour's jouncy drive mostly through soft sand to reach the beginning. A boat is the preferred vehicle for touring this remote spot, by sailing to the head of the harbor and through the narrow mouth of the pond.

Coatue's natural function is to protect Nantucket Harbor by holding back the restless water of Nantucket Sound and providing a safe haven. Its scalloped southern edge has six points named First Point, Second Point, Third Point, Five-fingered Point, Bass Point, and Wyers Point. First Point to Bass Point is maintained by the Nantucket Conservation Foundation as a wildlife refuge. On the inner harbor side eel grass, fish, and shellfish flourish. Severe storms breach between First and Second Points and across the harbor at the "Haulover," a thin stretch of sand at Wauwinet where boatmen once dragged their boats across as a shortcut to avoid the sail around Great Point. Off-road vehicles are permitted, but at high tide the south shore is considered impassable, and in summer it's closed to traffic so that boaters can pull their craft up on the beach.

Like Coatue, getting to **Great Point** requires four-wheel drive beyond the end of the pavement in Wauwinet. The lighthouse at Great Point is the northernmost point of Nantucket and has prevented as well as overseen many shipwrecks in its long history. This is not the 1818 original, by the way, but a rubblestone replica erected in 1986 to replace the one demolished by storm in 1984. Seabirds by the hundreds congregate on the conservation land, and there are also miles of beaches ideal for surfcasting as well as bird watching. Just for fun, read Jane Langton's murder mystery *Dark Nantucket Noon* with its Great Point setting.

For **Coskata-Coatue Wildlife Refuge** and the **Great Point National Wildlife Refuge,** pick up a map and regulations at the Larson-Sanford Center, 118 Cliff Road in Town (508-228-2884) or seasonally at the Gatehouse, Wauwinet Road (508-228-0006).

Siasconset village is always worth a special trip, but the loop of Milestone and Polpis Roads make it the midpoint in a scenic tour of about fifteen miles. This tour is all by good roads, by the way, and can be taken by car, bike (on the two bike paths), shuttle, or a combination — going one way by foot or bike and the other by shuttle bus. The **Milestone Cranberry Bog** is off Milestone Road.

Along Polpis Road is the **Old Polpis Burial Ground** and off the road at Quaise is the **Nantucket Life Saving Museum.** The museum has picnic tables. In Sconset village you will see spacious sea-cliff homes as well as the famous gentrified fishing shanties wearing their dress of pink roses from late June to September. Sconset's days as an actors' colony are not eclipsed, either. The Casino, built in 1899–1900, still looks much as it did when high-profile summer residents like Lillian Russell and Joseph Jefferson held their own theatricals, and a street named Broadway became an inside joke. The Manhattan wits loved to say they were spending the summer "just off-Broadway."

Further back in history, the **Sconset Pump** at the corner of Shell and New Streets dates from 1776, and the cottage "**Auld Lang Syne**" (1676) is arguably even older than "The Oldest House" on Sunset Hill in Nantucket Town. **Sankaty Head Light** (1850) on Baxter Road is picturesque but not open to the public — the area around the light is closed as well as the light itself.

WEST

As you head west, notice the **Abiah Folger Franklin Fountain** on Madaket Road. Abiah was the daughter of Peter Foulger (the original spelling of Folger), the half-share man who was conceded to be the intellectual of the initial group. Abiah married Josiah Franklin and moved to Boston, where she became the mother of seventeen children, including Benjamin Franklin who was number fifteen and the youngest son. It's said she was visiting her family here while she was carrying Ben and that he missed being a Nantucketer by a scant two months. As a boy and young man, Ben visited the Island but apparently thought his cousins a bit peculiar. He told about one occasion when some of them called on him in Philadelphia. He invited them to lunch later in the week, but they demurred, saying they were waiting for a better offer from someone else. He said he never heard from them again so assumed the better offer prevailed. The **Peter Foulger homestead** is on Wannacomet Road, and the **Forefathers Burial Ground** is west of Wannacomet Road.

Madaket at the western end of the Island may be reached by bike or shuttle as well as by car, and the round-trip from Town is only about ten miles. The bike path is five miles long with appealing views, gentle hills, and bends. There are rest stops and picnic places along the way as well as at the end. At Madaket you'll find conservation areas as well as beach. **Smith Point** on the southern end of the harbor is considered especially fragile wetland, so proceed with caution and acute environmental awareness. **Eel Point** on the northern end of the crescent is part of a larger wildlife reservation and good for a leisurely stroll but also requires raised eco-consciousness. Seeing the sunset from Madaket is a time-honored Nantucket tradition, so you may want to time your tour to take in this nature-made spectacular.

CENTER

In addition to the many things to see in **Nantucket Town** — from the wharves to the museums to the shops, historical sites, and mansions — you can also create a tour just beyond the historic downtown. Walk or ride out South Beach Road to **Easton,** then north to **Brant Point Lighthouse.** On the way you pass the **Coast Guard Station** (no visitors). Then go west on Hulbert Avenue to Jetties Beach, with its range of recreational facilities, sweep of sand, and calm waters. (See "Beaches and Beachcombing," above.) Return on **Cliff Road,** where the rich summer people built their sumptuous homes in the 1920s and 1930s.

WATER SPORTS

A surfer rides a Nantucket wave.

Rob Benchley

Nantucket is no Hawaii, but "Surf's up!" is still a cry at Cisco Beach on the Atlantic shore, while on the other side of the Island, the harbor is literally alive with watercraft on any summer's day. Despite the traffic, the large protected harbor with its coves and points retains its sense of remoteness, and a sail to the head of the harbor is as mandatory to the Nantucket experience as lunching on quahog chowder. You can rent gear, take group or private lessons, go by sail, powerboat, waverunner, windsurfer, or pontoon. If you're going to brave the Atlantic side of the Island, check the **Surf Report:** 508-228-SURF.

Force 5 Watersports (508-228-0700; 6 Union St., Nantucket, MA 02554) Lessons, kayaks, sailboats.

Nantucket Boat Rentals (508-325-1001; Straight Wharf,) Powerboats.

Nantucket Harbor Sail (508-228-0424; Petrel Landing on Swain's Wharf) Sail and outboard mid-June to late Sept.

Sea Nantucket Kayak Rentals (508-228-7499; Washington St. Ext., Nantucket, MA 02554) Kayak rentals.

Skip Willauer Sailing (508-325-2120; PO Box 1106, Nantucket, MA 02554) Private lessons, cruises.

The Sunken Ship (508-228-9226; 12 Broad St., Nantucket, MA 02554) Scuba diving.

Upper Deck (508-228-36332; 6 Broad St., Nantucket, MA 02554) Windsurfer equipment and rentals.

WHALE WATCHING

Incredible as it would have seemed to those early Nantucketers, the whales they knew are no longer an unending resource. Right whales (so called because they were the "right whales to catch" since they floated rather than sank after death) are so endangered that there may be as few as thirty remaining in the Atlantic. The worldwide moratorium on whaling has resulted in the proliferation of other kinds of whales, but rights may well be doomed. Whale-watching boats as well as private seagoing craft operate under strict rules to protect the great creatures.

Bestowing names upon whales goes way back before *Moby-Dick*. There was a wily customer called Old Crooked Jaw, for example, who was on every whaler's want-list in the early 19th century, and recently off Nantucket a mammoth has been dubbed Dracula for reasons that are not entirely clear.

If you go whale watching, bring along a windbreaker. The wind can be sharp and cool out on the water. If you are prone to be seasick, check with the captain about the condition of the seas where he will be sailing. If it sounds rough, you might want to take an antimotion pill an hour before sailing.

Nantucket Whale Watch (978-283-0313, in Massachusetts 800-322-0013, nationwide 800-942-5464; Straight Wharf) Narrated by experienced naturalists from the nonprofit Center for Oceanic Research and Education. Cruises are Tuesdays mid-July to mid-Sept. 9:30am–4:30pm. The boat M.V. *Yankee Freedom* is air-conditioned and serves food. Cruises leave from the Hy-Line Dock, Straight Wharf, to the feeding grounds of whales, dolphins, and marine birds. The **Gloucester-Nantucket Overnight Express Service** is a basic bunk-aboard trip departing Monday nights from Gloucester, Massachusetts, and arriving on Nantucket Tuesday mornings.

Harbor Cruises (508-228-1444; PO Box 77, Nantucket, MA 02554; Slip #1012 Straight Wharf) Seal cruises aboard the *Anna W II* in winter. Look especially for the gray seal, until recently thought to be extinct in New England; it has now reappeared on Nantucket.

The Essex of Nantucket

The tremendous power the whale is able to put forth when enraged is illustrated by the tale of a collision with one that resulted in the loss of the ship *Essex* of Nantucket. On the 13th of November, 1820, the ship was among whales, and three boats were lowered. A young whale was taken. Shortly after, another of great size, supposed to have been the dam of the one just killed, came against the ship with such violence as to tear away part of the false keel. It then remained some time alongside, endeavoring to grip the ship in its jaws; but, failing to make any impression, swam off about a quarter of a mile, when, suddenly turning about, it came with tremendous velocity toward the *Essex*. The concussion not only stopped the vessel's way, but actually forced her astern. Every man on deck was knocked down. The bows were completely stove. In a few minutes the vessel filled and went on her beam ends.

— Samuel Adams Drake, *Nooks and Corners of the New England Coast*, 1876

(The story of the *Essex* was an inspiration for Herman Melville's "*Moby-Dick*" and is covered historically by Nat Philbrick's *In the Heart of the Sea: The Tragedy of the Whaleship Essex.*)

CHAPTER SEVEN
The Fragile Island
NATURE AND THE ENVIRONMENT

Nantucket has long been blessed with people who care about its future. However foresighted in escaping the restrictions of Puritan Massachusetts, those first purchasers were not adventurers in search of El Dorado but settlers who had committed themselves to building a world in a very small place. Unlike a frontier, an island is finite. Contrary to the impulses that won the West, moving on was not considered an option.

So they and those who came after them

Rob Benchley

Reflections on Sesachacha Pond, on the Island's east end.

worked within the constraints of their Island. They quickly put limits on how much wood could be taken from the patches of forest here. When their ships crossed the Atlantic, they brought back not only merchandise but also living recollections of that other island, Great Britain, in the form of cuttings taken from favorite shrubs. In this simple way the broom and heather of Scottish highlands were introduced to Nantucket moors. Seeds gathered in English gardens were planted and tended beside Nantucket doorsteps. When the whalers set off for South America, the Pacific Islands, and Asia, the horticulture of Nantucket was also expanded. The hibiscus of Tahiti failed, but the *rosa rugosa* of Japan thrived.

On the mainland of Massachusetts Bay Colony, deer and rabbits were captured, transported, and released a few at a time in the hopes that propagation would eventually result in a supply of game. (This was repeated in the 1920s by the Nantucket Sportsmen's Club.) Foxes were brought in, too, probably for the wrong reasons. What may well have been a passing desire for a Boxing Day fox hunt in the style of the English countryside ended up balancing the ecosystem — at least for a while. (There are no longer any foxes on the Island.) In other parts of the world these well-intended transfers of flora and fauna often had unhappy results. The very same animals multiplied until they became pests; these very plants spread and choked out native species. But that didn't happen here. The rigid climate and sandy soil of the Island accepted or rejected, but the struggle for survival prevented any descent into nuisance.

Today's Nantucketers — seasonal as well as year-round residents — see the quality of their lives as inextricable from the natural world around them; it's a special place, to be sure, but also a fragile place. Furthermore, as custodians of the Island they love, they expect to work and pay for the privileges they enjoy and to help preserve them. So now there is no helter-skelter building to satisfy real-estate-market demand. Nearly 40 percent of the total land (80 percent of what is currently uninhabited) is owned by the Nantucket Conservation Foundation (mainly through private bequests) and the Land Bank, a publicly operated land acquisition program trust, funded by taxes and bond issues. The Island's registered voters may have numbered only 5,273 in 1983, but they began with an $11.5 million Land Bank bond financed with land transaction fees. In 1997 Nantucketers agreed to a further $25 million Land Bank bond that raised the residential property tax bill higher still. In 2000 the permanent population headed toward 10,000, but the commitment continues apace.

Nantucket 150 Years Ago

Nantucket! Take out your map and look at it. See what a real corner of the world it occupies; how it stands there, away off shore, more lonely than the Eddystone lighthouse. Look at it — a mere hillock, and elbow of sand; all beach, without a background. There is more sand there than you would use in twenty years as a substitute for blotting paper. Some gamesome wights will tell you that they have to plant weeds there, they don't grow naturally; that they import Canada thistles; that they have to send beyond seas for a spile to stop a leak in an oil cask; that pieces of wood in Nantucket are carried about like bits of the true cross in Rome; that people there plant toadstools before their houses, to get under the shade in summer time; that one blade of grass makes an oasis, three blades in a day's walk a prairie; that they wear quicksand shoes, something like Laplander snowshoes; that they are so shut up, belted about, every way inclosed, surrounded, and made an utter island of by the ocean, that to their very chairs and tables small clams will sometimes be found adhering, as to the backs of sea turtles. But these extravaganzas only show that Nantucket is no Illinois.

— From *Moby-Dick*, by Herman Melville

Nonprofit groups organized to protect and preserve the Island's natural resources have multiplied. Even the business community has rallied with a program that is attracting nationwide attention and inquiries from much larger places: Members of the chamber of commerce–backed Green Fund annually gave a portion of their profits — totaling more than $250,000 over

Jetties protect the harbor.

Rob Benchley

five years — to Island conservation groups, solely for the acquisition of open spaces to be held in perpetuity for public benefit. Nantucket's environment is its key to prosperity.

Protecting beaches, dunes, marshes, ponds, bogs, grasslands, moors, and forests also means teaching respect for the environment. Nantucket has working museums where scholars come to learn and where the public is invited to see work in progress as well as specimens. Nationally known experts speak regularly at the Coffin School, the Atheneum, Mitchell House, and the Whaling Museum on topics as diverse as shifting shorelines and the cautionary tales of a novice sea captain. Bird walks and nature walks led by experts alternate on summer days. Loines Observatory is open two nights a week to give visitors a look through the telescopes.

Not only educational programs but also explicit rules and penalties extend to off-Islanders as well as Islanders. Permits are required for acts taken for granted elsewhere, such as driving on the beach or even using a barbecue grill. No camping or sleeping out is permitted on the beaches or anywhere else on-Island. Restrictions are posted and enforced by the regular police force and the special environmental police. (For example, the fine for driving over beach grass or coastal dunes is $50; the fine for sleeping on the beach is $200.) When the population goes from around 10,000 to more than 50,000, as happens every summer, the demands on limited energy resources are staggering. Nantucket keeps its waste on-Island in a limited landfill, and barges in fuel and gasoline. Until recently it generated its own electrical power. The Island has only one fire department.

The dedicated ecotourist who wants to explore Nantucket will need binoculars, sunglasses, hat, long-sleeved shirt, long trousers in a light color (to make deer ticks visible), and shoes with socks for forays into the brush. But even the casual visitor who never leaves sidewalk, beach, or bike path will benefit from a visit to the Maria Mitchell complex of science museum, library, and observatory in the heart of Nantucket Town. Ongoing natural history as much as the visible dream of a romantic past is what Nantucket is all about.

BEACHES, SHORES, AND DUNES

Nothing can stop the ravaging sea, and after every severe storm, people go down to the beach at Sconset and stand silent for a minute or two, surveying the loss. The optimists among them will note that on the other side of the Island or just around the headland, a beach has grown by a few yards of new sand, but most will shake their heads. Nature doesn't use a tape measure, and the Island always loses.

Fiddler crabs, whelks, and hermit crabs live in the intertidal flats. Jellyfish are around in late summer. Insects are common — and voracious — on the dunes and especially near dune wetlands. Dune vegetation shelters small birds and animals as well as holding the sand in check. American beach grass (marram grass) is the primary stabilizer of the dunes. It has a dense interconnected system of fibrous roots that binds the dunes together, while wind-blown sand accumulating at the base of the plant promotes the dune growth. It sounds like a foolproof natural system, but foot traffic and off-road vehicles destroy beach grass as well as other delicate plants growing near the shore.

Tides change twice a day (two highs and two lows). Times for high and low tides are in the newspaper, and you can also pick up a chart in any of the marine-supply stores. On the beach the tideline is indicated by a row of sea debris.

Nantucket offers a great variety in its eighty-eight miles of seashore. There are marine cliffs (scarps) at Squam Head and Sankaty Head. The Outer Beach curves towards spits of land and sand. There are thirty-three sand beaches around the Island, with minor dunes at Waquoit on the south side and sheltering dunes at Dionis Beach on the north. Eel Point Reserve overlooking Madaket Harbor has extensive dunes as well as marshlands.

The barrier beach complex of Coskata-Coatue forming the northeast hook of the Island comprises more than 1,100 acres of sandy beaches, dunes, salt marsh, oak forest, and windblown moors across these two interlocked barrier beaches. Coatue, a 500-acre barrier beach, extends from the east jetty of Nantucket Harbor northeast to Coskata Pond, a saltwater pond and marsh system between Wauwinet and Great Point. It has an undulating southern shoreline with six distinct points that look like melting candle wax from the air. Coatue is one of the least disturbed barrier beaches left in the northeast, probably because it is so difficult to reach. Opposing winds that caused sand buildup and erosion in opposite directions created the points. This barrier may be low and narrow, but without it Nantucket Harbor would be less safe and calm, and the low-lying streets of Town would flood.

All Nantucketers have a special relationship with the sea.

Rob Benchley

Just beyond Wauwinet is the "Haulover," a thin stretch of sand where boats were literally dragged from sea to harbor to save the hours it would take to sail around Great Point. Two-thirds of Coatue is owned by the Nantucket Conservation Foundation, and The Trustees of Reservations (TTOR) owns the other third.

Flying over Coatue, you see what appears to be a barren landscape. Yet there is a century-old red-cedar forest down there, and when you hike it, you see lady's slipper orchid, sea lavender, American holly, horn poppy, salt-meadow grass, beach heather, bayberry, beach pea, salt-spray rose, eastern red cedar, and prickly pear cactus. Cactus? On Nantucket? Yes, prickly pear, which flowers in late June and early July, is the only cactus growing in the eastern United States.

The 1,127-acre Coskata-Coatue Wildlife Refuge and the five-acre Medouie Creek area at Wauwinet are protected by the Trustees of Reservations. The refuge, home to the imported western black-tailed jackrabbits and deer, but mostly a breeding ground for migratory and local birds, is open all year. The paving ends at Wauwinet, and while there is no fee for pedestrians, over-sand vehicles must have permits to go farther. Access is subject to occasional closure during shorebird nesting season.

From June to October, TTOR offers three-hour tours of the refuge led by a naturalist, which includes a climb to the top of the lighthouse otherwise closed to visitors. Tours in a nine-passenger (air-conditioned) Ford Expedition leave the parking lot of the Wauwinet Inn Gatehouse at 9:30am and 1:30pm and are limited to eight with a minimum of four. The fee is $30 for adults and $15 for children fifteen and under. Bring your own snacks and beverages (no alcohol), and don't forget sunglasses, sunscreen, hat, camera, and binoculars. By registration only: 508-228-6799. Members of TTOR get discounts on vehicle permits and passes. (See also Chapter Six, *Recreation*.)

BIRDING

Smith's Point, Madaket, is a good site for bird watching.

Betty Lowry

On the Coskata salt marsh, snowy egrets, great blue herons, whimbrels, ospreys, least terns, roseate terns, and piping plovers are the inhabitants and visitors, the avian version of Islanders and off-Islanders. If you have been to the Galapagos Islands of South America, you will recognize the same bird attitude: protective of their young, cautious, but by and large unafraid of humans.

Almost every issue of the weekly *Inquirer and Mirror* contains a report on what's flying, nesting, and generally residing on the Island. KEEP YOUR EYES PEELED FOR A RARE BOAT-TAILED GRACKLE, the headline commands. Furthermore, a flight of ten American oystercatchers was seen flying over from Tuckernuck; the rare and endangered sparrow-size piping plover was observed foraging in the mud flat; a killdeer first seen at the landfill has nested and the chicks are running around. Note that there was a great egret, a night heron, an unusual sharp-shinned hawk . . . You get the picture.

Nantucket is on the flyway for more than 340 species of land and shore birds, and summer storms often direct skimmers and exotic terns to the Island for rare sightings. Open ponds and mud flats are attractions. The Bartlett Farm area is a favorite of migrating shorebirds, and Polpis Pines looks like home to summer nesting birds. The Harbor Flats at the end of Washington St. at low tide is a good place to see water birds. Short-eared owls and northern harriers nest in the Nantucket grassland, though they are rare on the mainland.

Other good viewing sites are Great Point north of Wauwinet, Nantucket Town Harbor, Sconset meadows and beaches, east side of the Island, Long Pond, Madaket Beach, Madaket Bay, and Eel Point. Herring gulls raise their families in spring and, in winter, seabirds are best seen at Sankaty Head, Dionis

Beach, Tom Nevers Head, Cisco Beach, and Surfside Beach. Nesting sites monitored by the Coastal Waterbird Program of the Massachusetts Audubon Society are Smith's Point at the western tip and Low Beach at the eastern heel. Wetlands (salt marshes, freshwater marshes, wet meadows, swamps, bogs, and pond shores) offer food, nesting sites, and protection. Piping plovers and the also-endangered least terns are seen at the Haulover, Great Point, Coatue, Smith's Point, Surfside, and Sconset Beach. Look for diving ducks offshore. You might even see the courtship of the marsh hawk, whereby the male drops his prey so that the female can catch it in her talons midair.

Strong Winds/Eco Guides (508-228-1769; PO Box 2770, Nantucket, MA 02584) John K. Simms, author and birder, leads groups of up to six.

Maria Mitchell Association (508-228-9198; 2 Vestal St., Nantucket, MA 02554) Bird walks organized by the Maria Mitchell Association and led by ornithologists are every Tuesday, Thursday, and Saturday morning in summer starting at 6:30am. Departure point is the high school parking lot on Atlantic Avenue. For a recorded message or to contribute your own bird report, the **Maria Mitchell/Massachusetts Audubon Bird Hotline** is 888-224-6444. Look for *Birding Nantucket* by Kenneth Blackshaw and Edith Andrews in the MMA gift shop.

Massachusetts Audubon Society (508-228-9208, 800-AUDUBON; 153 Hummock Pond Rd., Nantucket, MA 02554) Summer field research projects and general birding information.

Nantucket Conservation Foundation, Inc. (508-228-2884; The Larsen-Sanford Center, 118 Cliff Rd., Nantucket, MA 02554) Map of the properties owned by the corporation.

The Trustees of Reservations (508-228-0006; www.thetrustees.org; 111 Wauwinet Rd., Nantucket, MA 02554) Information about over-sand vehicle permits for the Coskata-Coatue Wildlife Refuge.

The Nantucketer at Sea at Night

With the landless gull, that at sunset folds her wings and is rocked to sleep between billows; so at nightfall, the Nantucketer, out of sight of land, furls his sails, and lays him to his rest, while under his very pillow rush herds of walruses and whales.

— Herman Melville, *Moby-Dick*, 1851

ENDANGERED SPECIES

The list of endangered species is ever changing and subject to fluctuations within a long-term trend. The Gulf Stream flowing two hundred miles away

Rare Flora and Fauna on Nantucket

The Nantucket's Coskata-Coatue Refuge has a pine-oak forest with rare Nantucket holly trees, and off Wauwinet Road at Polpis in a hollow protected from the wind is a grove of old beech trees known as the Hidden Forest. Elm trees fallen to disease elsewhere throughout Massachusetts are still going strong on Main Street, Nantucket Town.

Broom crowberry, a low-branching shrub, and St. Andrews Cross, a sprawling plant of the St.-John's-wort family, are found in the moors. You'll see bushy frostweed or rockrose with yellow flowers that open only in sunlight and only last a day. Eastern silvery aster with its lilac flowers, purple New England aster, and white-flowered New England blazing star bloom here. The only place in the United States where bell heather grows is Nantucket. Thanks to the Gulf Stream, the Island growing season is longer than the mainland, and its autumn show of red highbush blueberries and golden wildflowers lasts well into November. Today Nantucket has the greatest variety of plant life of any place its size in the Western Hemisphere.

The Muskeget mouse, a large, pale-colored vole with a long narrow skull and coarse fur, lives on the isle of Muskeget west of Tuckernuck. The likelihood of your seeing one is very rare, indeed. But neither will you see some animals common on the mainland: Skunks, raccoons, and chipmunks don't live on the Island.

tempers Nantucket's climate, while the Island's location between the Atlantic Ocean and the Nantucket Sound makes it both a natural landfall for migrating birds and a habitat for flora and fauna of all types. Grasslands and marshlands lost to development or pollution on the mainland are still healthy wildlife refuges on Nantucket. Recently, gray seals have been discovered breeding on sandspits of the Nantucket coast and have appeared on the beaches of Coskata-Coatue and on the islets off Madaket. Muskeget, a remote isle halfway between Nantucket and Martha's Vineyard that is also a National Natural Landmark, is home to the Muskeget mouse (a vole) as well as to a colony of gray seals. The seals were thought to be all but extinct in New England.

Birds on the endangered list include the children's favorite, the piping plover (which has its own Island protection society), roseate tern, common tern, arctic tern, bobolink, American black duck, common moorhen, American bittern, northern harrier, whippoorwill, cooper's hawk, red-shouldered hawk, upland sandpiper, grasshopper sparrow, king rail, olive-sided flycatcher, pied-billed grebe, gray-cheeked thrush, golden-winged warbler, northern parula, vesper sparrow, eastern meadowlark, eastern bluebird, and short-eared owl.

The spade-footed toad was thought to have been extinct after DDT was used to control mosquitoes post-WWII, and there was great excitement when one was discovered in 1997 — although, unfortunately, as roadkill. The possibility of regenerating a species is cause for general celebration and headlines hereabouts.

When a dead loggerhead sea turtle of great size washed up on Coatue, it rated two pages of press coverage and a necropsy, although the species is not unusual on the East Coast and is considered "threatened," not "endangered." Three critically endangered sea turtles that live in Nantucket waters are the leatherback, Atlantic Ridley, and the green turtle. Leatherbacks are most common in the rips between Nantucket and Monomoy, where they find plenty of jellyfish to eat. All sea turtles are federally protected.

Nantucket as a Status Symbol

To be a true Nantucketer you must have been born here. And nothing short of reincarnation can change your status. . . . My status is that of a summer visitor who decided to settle down. Nantucket is my home, but I'm not "a Nantucketer." I'm a reformed tourist.

— Robert Benchley

GRASSLANDS, HEATHLANDS, AND MOORS

The vista of Folger's Marsh as seen from the Polpis bike path.

Rob Benchley

Nantucket has one-third of all the moors in North America and a heathland comparable to medieval England — startling statistics for an Island of its modest size and a heritage Islanders embrace. Nantucket is the only place in the western hemisphere where Scottish heather is completely naturalized. In late summer it carpets the moors of Coskata. Lowbush blueberry, bearberry, and huckleberry thrive on the central heath.

When thirty-five patches of wetlands were destroyed by the construction of the Polpis Road bike path, a wetland replication process was used to reclaim an equivalent area. The wetland created is a coastal-plain pond and expected to contribute to the biological diversity of the island by nurturing rare forms of vegetation. Island wetlands range from salt- and freshwater marshes to wet

Nantucket Wildflowers

From plantain-leafed pussytoes and downy swamp milkweed through skydrop aster, sea rocket, nodding bur marigold, little mouse-ear chickweed, bastard toad-flax, rough boneset, and poor-man's-pepper, the names alone are enough to hook you on Nantucket wildflowers. Or how about lady's thumb, nodding ladies'-tresses, mad-dog skullcap, and bird's-foot violet?

Whether you are biking along the peaceful roads, climbing the dunes, or just gazing across the moors, you will see wild blossoms. Not the great sheets of color as in Texas bluebonnets or California poppies, but what appears to be an infinite, if somewhat subtle, variety. If "infinite" is too grand a word, consider 1,265 — the number of flowering plants recorded in the comprehensive study *The Vascular and Non-Vascular Flora of Nantucket, Tuckernuck, and Muskeget Islands,* by Bruce A. Sorrie and Peter W. Dunwiddie, jointly published in 1966 by four conservation-minded organizations and available in the Maria Mitchell Science Library on Nantucket.

A checklist of the 284 you are most likely to encounter is a little less daunting and has the common as well as the scientific name for each species. Pick up a free folder at the Maria Mitchell Association, 2 Vestal St. (508-228-9198). No pictures, alas, so you'll also need a field guide (suggested: *Newcomb's Wildflower Guide*, Little, Brown & Co.)

In brief, the annual wildflower show begins modestly in spring with broom crowberry, then gains momentum as wild roses crest in midsummer, and progresses to Scotch broom in September. October is cranberry harvest, huckleberry bush, and autumn foliage. It's a tapestry, not a patchwork, and it spreads over a landscape, not a garden. The maritime climate of the Island, warmer in winter and cooler in summer than the mainland, extends the wildflower growing season.

Nantucket's settlers and each wave of newcomers brought with them memories of home and souvenirs of travel in the form of plant slips and seeds. Azaleas, arborvitae, and buttonbush were right at home in cool, damp seaside gardens already flourishing with such native plants as swamp rose mallow, Joe-pye weed, milkweed, swamp aster, blue and yellow flag iris, high- and lowbush blueberry, winterberry, elderberry, pussy willow, groundsel bush, reeds, rushes, sedges, ferns, sassafras, tupelo, maple, inkberry, and swamp azalea.

Nantucket wildflowers from native seed stock — including swamp rose mallow, cardinal flower, Joe-pye weed, blue flag iris, and blazing star — are for sale on-Island. Ask in the flower shops, or make an appointment with Peter H. Boynton: 508-228-1757.

An organization for those interested in conserving native plants throughout New England is the New England Wild Flower Society (617-237-4924, 508-877-7630; Hemenway Rd., Framingham MA 01701-2699). The NEWF does not have a sanctuary on Nantucket.

meadows, swamps, bogs, and pond shores. They supply food, nesting sites, and protection to hundreds of species of birds and animals.

Wetlands are essential to water quality since they are natural filters. They also serve as nurseries for fish and shellfish. The value of ecosystem services from providing pure water to holding soil is well appreciated on Nantucket, where resident and visiting scholars are quick to cite the dollar costs of substituting artificial for natural controls.

Grasslands are more than beautiful silvery seas rippled by the winds. They also sequester carbon, and so carbon dioxide is not released to warm the planet and heighten climate change.

Cranberries grow in the wet meadowland claimed by some to be the largest contiguous bog on the continent if not the world. Not only are the cranberry bogs a colorful attraction that culminates in the annual October Cranberry Harvest Weekend beloved by tourists, but they are also a profitable enterprise, since the bogs are leased to Northland Cranberries, Inc., a major agribusiness.

The Sanford Farm, Ram Pasture, and **The Woods** in southwest Island is 767 acres of wetland, grassland, and forest with a view of the south shore from the Ram Pasture barn. Wildflowers and wildlife can be spotted along the six-mile round-trip trail that travels alongside Hummock Pond to the sea. You can reach the Nantucket Conservation property from a parking area off Madaket Road near the Cliff Road intersection.

Eel Point Reserve, the 109-acre hook of land overlooking Madaket Harbor, has extensive dunes and marshlands with wildflowers, wild grapes, bayberries, and more. Take Eel Point Road off Cliff Road and park on the dirt road, or if you're coming by bike path, take a right off the Madaket path onto Eel Point Road.

Long Pond is a 64-acre reserve owned by the Land Bank. A one-mile path runs on the shore of the pond past a natural cranberry bog. Take the Madaket Road to a dirt road across from the sign to Hither Creek. Cross the bridge to reach a parking area and the trail entrance.

Other natural areas well worth exploring are **Larsen Acres**, a 513-acre moorland on the south side of Milestone Rd., and the 189-acre **Pocomo Meadows** and **Medoule Marsh** off Wauwinet Road. Specimens of heathland wildflowers grow in the **Reference & Study Garden** next to **Maria Mitchell Birthplace**, 1 Vestal St., Nantucket, MA 02554

MUSEUMS

Egan Institute of Maritime Studies (508-228-2505, fax 508-228-7069; eganinst @nantucket.net; www.marinehomecenter.com/eganinstitute; 4 Winter St., Nantucket, MA 02554; at the Coffin School; June–Oct.) Under the direction of historian Nat Philbrick, the institute brings experts in the field of maritime science to the Island and sponsors a series of lectures on associated topics.

The Maria Mitchell Association (508-228-9198; www.mmo.org; 4 Vestal St., Nantucket, MA 02554) Named for Nantucket's famous woman astronomer who not only discovered a comet, using a telescope set up on the top of the Pacific Bank, she also became the nation's first woman professor of astronomy, at Vassar College, Poughkeepsie, New York. The association sponsors field trips, bird walks, nature walks, and marine ecology walks for all ages plus a special children's program. It operates the following sites open to the public in season:

The **Aquarium** (508-228-5387; 28 Washington St., Nantucket, MA 02554; Tues.–Sat. 10am–4pm, early June–Aug.) contains local marine life. Night openings are scheduled to show the nocturnal behavior of Nantucket sea creatures. It sponsors marine ecology trips, as well.

The **Hinchman House** (508-228-0898; 7 Milk St., Nantucket, MA 02554) contains the **Museum of Nantucket Natural History** and the association's gift shop. Children's nature classes are held here, and bird and nature walks are conducted by Hinchman House staff members.

The **Maria Mitchell Observatory** (508-228-9273; 3 Vestal St., Nantucket, MA 02554) and **Loines Observatory** (508-228-8690; 59 Milk St., Nantucket, MA 02554) are research facilities for astronomers and interns and are not open to the public except for Public Viewing Nights during the summer. A pass covering admission to all but the observatories is available. Lectures on navigation, astronomy, and history are offered during the summer at the Mitchell House headquarters. The **Maria Mitchell Science Library** (508-228-9219; 2 Vestal St., Nantucket, MA 02554) has a prized collection of books, journals, and historical documents on natural science and astronomy, including Maria Mitchell's own papers. Library privileges are free, and it's open year-round, with computer and Internet access available for patrons. Summer hours are Tues.–Sat. 10am–4pm; Wed.–Fri. 2–5pm and Sat. 9am–noon for the rest of the year.

Maria Mitchell Children's Discovery Classes teach children ages four through twelve about the natural sciences, astronomy, and Nantucket history through a variety of field trips, demonstrations, and hands-on fun. Mon.–Fri. 9am–4pm, June 30–Aug. 22. More information and reservations: 508-228-9198. Children also have their own corner in the **Maria Mitchell Science Library** at 2 Vestal St.

Nantucket Historical Association (508-228-1894; nhainfo@nha.org; www.nha.org; 15 Broad St., PO Box 1016, Nantucket, MA 02554) Through its properties, exhibits, and lectures, this organization has maintained and preserved Nantucket history for more than a century. Admission fees, visitor's passes, and NHA membership give access to the Town's primary historical sites: Quaker Meeting House, Fire Hose Cart House, Hadwen House, Macy-Christian House, Old Gaol (Old Jail), Old Mill, Oldest House, Peter Foulger Museum, Whaling Museum, Fair Street Library and Research Facility. (See Chapter Four, *Culture,* "Museums.")

The Whaling Museum (508-228-1736; 15 Broad St., Nantucket, MA 02554) Extensive public education programs about whales, dolphins, and seals on

Tues. at 8pm mid-July to late August sponsored by the **Marine Mammal Conservation Program** (508-223-0390) The Nantucket Historical Association's **Living History for Children** series (10am and 2pm Tuesdays in July and August) includes ecological history as well as social history in hands-on experiences.

NATURE, ENVIRONMENTAL, AND PRESERVATION ORGANIZATIONS

Visitors who will be on-Island for a season may want to contact these organizations for volunteer opportunities as well as to find out more about their ongoing programs. Memberships in the organizations, where available, provide access to properties and publications as well as tangible support and tax deductions.

The Angry Plover Society (508-228-6782) Public education about protecting this endangered small bird. The society is affiliated with the Nantucket Shorebird Protection Program.

Egan Institute of Maritime Studies (508-228-2505, fax 508-228-7069; eganoinst @nantucket.net; www.marinehomecenter.com/eganinstitute; 4 Winter St, Nantucket, MA 02554; at the Coffin School) Sponsors scientists and a lecture series with speakers who are professionals in the field.

The Environmental Studies Program introduces secondary school students to Island crafts and occupations as well as historic preservation, resource conservation, and coastal ecology. Working with other agencies and institutions, the foundation is aiding in the development of critical data relating to water supply and shoreland erosion. A map of the properties is available at the Larsen-Sanford Center, 118 Cliff Rd., Nantucket, MA 02554.

Madaket Land Trust (508-228-0841; 47 Starbuck Rd., Nantucket, MA 02554) The trust owns acres in the Madaket area, including beaches and dunes from the southerly end of Long Pond westward to Madaket Road and most of the open land in the Tristram's Landing area. Its mission is to acquire, maintain, preserve, and protect open land in the Madaket area.

Maria Mitchell Association (508-228-9198; www.mmo.org; 4 Vestal St., Nantucket, MA 02554) An eminent scientific and educational organization. In addition to its nature library, aquarium, natural history museum, and two observatories, the association sponsors bird walks and nature walks on alternating days all summer, fall field trips that combine birds and nature, a children's program, and holds open evenings at the Aquarium and Loines Observatory.

Marine Mammal Conservation Program (508-228-7283) Volunteer whale spotters work with the sixth-grade science class at Cyrus Pierce Jr. Middle School. They report any live whale sighted from beach, boat, or plane; count

Whales and Water Life

A beached sperm whale — here a forty-six footer on Low Beach in Siasconset — is a rare occurance.

Frederick G. S. Clow

No one knows what makes whales beach themselves, but the settlers followed the example of the Wampanoag and were quick to take deadly advantage of the huge creatures stranded on the shore. Pilot whales seem especially prone to what people interpret as suicide, and so are the most frequently in need of rescue. While right whales now seem to be heading for extinction, the small (at twenty-eight feet long) minkes appear to be flourishing worldwide. Humpbacks (thirty to sixty feet) are the variety now most frequently encountered by the whale-watching boats (see Chapter Six, *Recreation*, "Whale Watching"). *Note: If you see a stranded marine mammal, stay away from it and call the police (508-228-1212), who will alert the Marine Mammal Stranding Team.*

At the other end of the scale, the intertidal flats and the wetlands are havens for young fish and shellfish. Eelgrass is a crucial component of scallop growth because it provides habitat and protection for scallop larvae. Eelgrass in turn depends on light and water chemistry. It's one big ecosystem.

and note their location. Whale ID charts and observation instruction available year round.

Marine Mammal Stranding Team (508-228-1693) Volunteers help with the rescue of sick or injured seals or sea turtles and with whales or porpoises caught on a sandbar or beach. Training is provided. The team also answers questions about common marine mammals in and around Nantucket waters and distributes informational materials to beach users. (To report a stranding, call the police department at 508-228-1212.)

Massachusetts Audubon Society (508-228-9208, 800-AUDUBON; 153 Hummock Pond Rd., Nantucket, MA 02554) The Society's Coastal Waterbird Program protects nesting sites on Massachusetts beaches. Smith Beach and Low Beach are of special attention at this time.

Rules Off the Roads

Protect is the operative word on Nantucket. Protect the plants on the dunes, the grasslands, and heathlands. Protect the shrubs and the forest and the birds, insects, butterflies, and wildlife on land and sea. Protect the beaches. Here are rules to follow on land and sea to help protect this all-too-fragile island:

In general . . .

Keep vehicles and bikes on well-established roads and paths.
Don't pick wildflowers.
Keep your pet on a leash.
Take your litter back with you. (Also, litter attracts predators, especially crows and gulls.)
Respect private property.
If you are walking across a dune, avoid trampling beachgrass or other plants.
Stay out of areas where snow fencing has been installed to encourage the accumulation of blowing sand.
Do not pick or uproot any beach vegetation — living or dead.
Discourage children from climbing on, jumping from, or digging holes in bluffs.
If you must drive on the beach, stay clear of vegetated areas while driving or parking off-road vehicles.

For the birds . . .

Read and respect posted regulations and beach closings — portions of beaches used by nesting endangered birds are closed to vehicular and/or pedestrian traffic.
Don't fly kites or leave fishing line near bird nesting areas.
Respect signs that mark nesting areas, and stay outside of fencing that has been installed to protect them.
If you spot a nest, especially when you are outside a vehicle, don't linger. Adult birds get jittery and will leave their nests, exposing eggs or chicks to excessive heat and predators.
Be cautious when you walk through dune grasses that adjoin nesting areas. Frightened chicks will often seek refuge there and are easily crushed.

Marine manners . . .

Keep your boat at least one hundred feet away from marine animals, five hundred feet from right whales.
Stand clear of light-green bubble patches that may indicate feeding whales below.
Do not feed the mammals, and toss no garbage overboard.
Diving on whales is a violation of federal laws.

Nantucket Civic League (508-257-4447; PO Box 181, Nantucket, MA 02554) Composed of representatives from twenty-one Island-area associations, comprising over 21,000 members, including those concerned with preservation to benefit residents, seasonal residents, and visitors.

Nantucket Conservation Foundation, Inc. (508-228-2884; 118 Cliff Rd., PO Box 13, Nantucket, MA 02554) This umbrella environmental organization is a locally based nonprofit established in 1963 to protect the land by owning it. It is professionally staffed, and membership is nearly 3,000. At present it is Nantucket's largest landowner, protecting and managing beaches, hardwood forests, dunes, shrub lands, bogs, heathlands, marshes, grasslands, and ponds. Two rangers live on the Coatue and Middle Moors properties from spring through fall, and a part-time ranger patrols the additional lands. **The Nantucket Heathlands Partnership** is under the NCF.

Nantucket Historical Association (508-228-1894; nhainfo@nha.org; www.nha.org; 15 Broad St., PO Box 1016, Nantucket, MA 02554) Owns, protects, and preserves more than twenty historical structures.

Nantucket Land Bank (508-228-7240; 22 Broad St., Nantucket, MA 02554) First approved in 1983 by a town meeting vote, the land bank was created by the state legislature to raise revenue for the purchase of conservation land by a 2 percent tax on land transactions. Now widely copied as a vehicle for holding undeveloped land, the Nantucket Land Bank was first in the nation.

Nantucket Land Council (508-228-2818; 6 Ash Ln., PO Box 502, Nantucket, MA 02554) This private nonprofit local environmental group promotes sustainable landscapes, watches conservation proposals, and takes legal action when necessary to protect land under conservation restrictions.

First Light

. . . there's a squabble between Massachusetts and Maine over dibs to the first ray of light. Astronomers at Nantucket's Maria Mitchell Observatory say the eastern town of Sconset could see the sun a full minute before any place on Maine, barring fog banks and other factors. But the United States Naval Observatory claims that Acadia National Park's Cadillac Mountain in Maine is better positioned for the sunrise.

— C. J. Hughes, *National Geographic Traveler*, December 1999

Nantucket Parks and Recreation Department (508-228-7213; 2 Bathing Beach Rd., Nantucket, MA 02554; at Jetties Beach) In addition to overseeing the beaches and operating the diverse recreation facilities of the Island, the department sponsors children's programs. Many of these involve nature walks along the beach and constant reinforcement of environmental awareness and care.

Nantucket Tree Fund (508-228-1823;) A project of the Nantucket Garden Club (PO Box 627, Nantucket, MA 02554), the fund provides seeds and seedlings on request.

Preservation Institute: Nantucket (508-228-2429; 11 Centre St., Nantucket, MA 02554) Summer program of the University of Florida College of Architecture focuses on documentation of historic structures, planning and design in historic context, and preservation technology. Students earn nine graduate or undergraduate credits for course work completed during the seven-week session.

Sconset Beach Preservation Fund (508-325-0048; 18 Sesapana Rd., Siasconset, MA 02564) Promotes study and action to control erosion on Sconset's beaches.

The Trustees of Reservations (508-228-3359; 111 Wauwinet Rd., PO Box 172, Nantucket MA 02554-0172; 508-228-0006; at Wauwinet Inn Gatehouse) Founded in 1891, the world's oldest land trust is a nonprofit statewide organization "dedicated to preserving properties of exceptional scenic, historic, and ecological value." On Nantucket, TTOR owns the Coskata-Coatue Wildlife Refuge with its ten miles of shoreline, Coskata Pond, and Great Point lighthouse (the lantern is maintained and operated by the U.S. Coast Guard).

University of Massachusetts Nantucket Field Station (508-228-5268, fax 508-228-7834; 180 Polpis Rd., Nantucket, MA 02554) A year-round campus of the University of Massachusetts supporting research into Nantucket's plant and animal ecology in aquatic, terrestrial, and marine habitats and into the Island's geology, archaeology, history, and literature. The station hosts field trips, short courses, and conferences. Call or e-mail wtiffany@aol.com for summer course schedule.

Betty Lowry

Dunes on the Atlantic need all the protection they can get.

CHAPTER EIGHT

A Tisket, a Tasket, More Than a Lightship Basket

SHOPPING

Nantucket has been a trading hub since the early 19th century, dealing not only in whale oil and its byproducts such as candles and corset bone but also in goods from around the world. Local shopkeepers were equally prepared to meet the demands of those who returned from multiyear voyages with money in their pockets. Today, the affluent off-Islanders who love to shop find merchants still more

Courtesy of the Nantucket Historical Association

Shopping on Main Street c.1897.

than ready to oblige. In summer, when the population increases fivefold, the downtown seems as popular as the beach. In December, the **Christmas Stroll** (see Chapter Four, *Culture*, "Special Events") brings huge crowds from the mainland to shop in a Christmas-card setting.

Maintaining that 19th-century ambiance has been a challenge. It helps that today's prime shopping area is concentrated within the registered Old Historic District, so crass commercialism can be controlled. Blatant signs are outlawed, and if shop windows tend to be a trifle cluttered, that, too, is authentic to the period. For special events, such as the **Daffodil Weekend,** store windows are judged for the attractiveness and appropriateness of their displays, with ribbons awarded for the best. Walking around to view the windows and second-guess the judges is part of the entertainment.

Today upscale shops and galleries interspersed with cafés line Main Street and its tributaries from the harbor to Centre Street. Artists show and sell in the replicated fishermen's shanties on South Wharf. You can buy antiques, gifts, and jewelry on Centre, the Petticoat Row of the days when whalers' wives were the shopkeepers of the Island. Benches provide drop-down rest for the

Cobblestones, used originally as ships' ballast, now pave Main Street.

Rob Benchley

weary, and in summer flowers bloom cheerfully in tubs and window boxes. Historic plaques inform you that this was the corner where stood the store of Rowland Hussey Macy (1822–1877), who went on to establish a certain noted New York emporium named R. H. Macy's, or that here lived George Pollard, captain of the *Essex*, whose ship was attacked by a whale and became the basis for Herman Melville's classic *Moby-Dick*.

Oddly, there are no agreed-upon hours of opening and closing for the merchants. Though some open earlier and some stay open later, especially in summer, 10am to 7pm is reasonable Monday through Saturday, 10am to 6pm on Sunday year-around. (In the winter, stores that cater especially to tourists may open only on weekends or not at all.) While shopping is very much concentrated in Nantucket Town, general stores like the Sconset Market on Post Office Square in Siasconset and Peter Piper's Market off the Surfside road carry a few souvenirs, T-shirts, toys, cards, and prints as well as gift-worthy Nantucket specialty foods (see Chapter Five, *Restaurants and Food Purveyors*). Handcrafted jewelry is sold in art, home, and clothing shops as well as jewelry stores.

Nowhere on the Island will you find anything approaching a mall. On Nantucket the closest thing to a chain store is a discreet sign that tells you the artist also maintains a gallery in Palm Beach, Florida, Carmel, California, Aspen, Colorado, or a similar oasis.

NANTUCKET PARTICULARS

Nantucket has style, and its name plainly printed on a sweatshirt gives that ordinary garment instant cachet. Yet the most readily identified article associated with Nantucket is not visibly labeled at all. The lightship basket, useful and durable, appears not only as an over-the-arm handbag but is also replicated in everything from tiny gold earrings to Wedgwood fine china dinnerware. Other motifs from whaling days — ships' knots and sailor's valentines, for example — are incorporated into jewelry, gifts, and fabrics. You'll find old and new scrimshaw-decorated objects galore, along with authentic marine antiques and old wooden cranberry-gathering scoops. Nantucket lighthouses and rose-covered Siasconset cottages are reproduced on everything from T-shirts to needlepoint canvases, from Christmas tree ornaments to English enamel pillboxes.

Nantucket's own flag is designed in the burgee style used to identify ships. The image is a sperm whale (representing Nantucket) superimposed over a cordage circle (the globe) and the compass rose. A harpoon indicates the north and south points. Colors are blue and white, as in sky, sea, and beach. You can hang it over your doorway or fireplace at home if not on your yacht. On the Island it flies on flagpoles, too.

Hand-carved boats are a specialty of The Toy Boat shop on Straight Wharf.

Rob Benchley

Toy whaling boats and handmade replicas of Nantucket's colorful catboat Rainbow Fleet are for the young as intricate ship models are for adult collectors. Kitchen and food shops stock a one-handed peppermill called the Nantucket Peppergun. You can buy a Nantucket lounge chair for your patio. It's easy to get hooked on cranberry-chocolate confections — not to mention beach plum jelly, wild blueberry preserves, and cranberry-blossom honey. Then there's a Nantucket-ground (if not grown) coffee.

Perfume-shop-blended fragrances have names like Nantucket Dunes, Nantucket Rose, Nantucket Summer, and Nantucket Woods. Candle scents promise to recall not only the endangered *rosa rugosa* but also the moors and mists. Folk and fine handcrafts with practical and decorative purposes have been made on the Island for centuries. In fact, it is difficult to imagine a Nantucketer with idle hands.

ANTIQUES AND AUCTIONS

As you might expect in a place that reveres its past, Nantucket is a mecca for antiques lovers. Three major weekend antiques shows every summer bring exhibitors from all over the country, while proceeds from admissions and benefit previews support Island good works and projects. Two shows are usually held in the high school auditorium and one at The Boathouse — Island Marina. You are urged to get to them by shuttle since parking is very limited. On the other hand, downtown you can walk to the American Legion Hall, site of auctions every week in summer and once a month off-season, and to the Point Breeze Hotel, where Friday-night auctions occur with some regularity.

Not every antiques dealer stays open year-round, though some have limited hours in winter. The rule of "open by chance or by appointment" works, too. Dealers post their home phone numbers on the doors of their shops.

ANTIQUES

Artifacts from days of yore await antiquers outside Fleur-de-Lis on Easy Street.

Frederick G. S. Clow.

With some thirty antiques shops in Nantucket Town, it is best just to wander. Pick up the annual *Guide to Nantucket Antique Shops* in any one of them for a full list and summaries of what you can expect to find. You can also look over the Internet Antiques Network (508-228-7751, 888-266-4799; www.nantucket mall.com; service@nantucketmall.com). Here are a few shops that specialize in Nantucket, New England, and American antiques and are open all year:

The Antiques Depot (508-228-1287; 14 Easy St., PO Box 3080, Nantucket, MA 02584; open May–Oct.) The collection changes often, and prices are reasonable. Old decoys are a specialty.

David L. Place Antiques & Estate Jewelry (508-228-6000; lumina@nantucket.net, 17 Correia Ln., Nantucket, MA 02554; open Apr.–Dec. 21) Country and formal small furniture, paintings, scrimshaw, fine porcelain, sterling.

Fleur-de-Lis (508-325-0700; www.fleurdelis-nantucket.com; fleur@nantucket. net; 27 Easy St., Nantucket, MA 02554) Americana.

Forager House Collection (508-228-5977, 877-936-7243; forager@nantucket.net; 20 Centre St., Nantucket, MA 02554; Jan.–Apr., weekends only) Folk art, Americana, whirligigs, toys, marine items, rugs, painted furniture, accessories, Nantucketiana, old lightship baskets, master prints.

The J. Butler Collection (508-228-8429; 36 Centre St.; Nantucket, MA 02554; year-round) The Old Guard type of antiques.

Leonards Antiques (508-228-0620, 888-336-8585; oldbeds@aol.com; www. Leonardsdirect.com; 31 Washington St.; Nantucket, MA 02554) Beds a specialty. Reproductions, too. Call for hours.

Lynda Willauer Antiques (508-228-3631; 2 India St., Nantucket, MA 02554; late May–late Sept.) American and English fine antique furniture; Chinese export porcelain; samplers; quilts.

Manor House Antiques Coop (508-228-4335; 31-1/2 Centre St., Nantucket, MA 02554) Collectibles of all sorts in a group shop.

Nantucket Country (508-228-8868; 888-411-8868; gsdutton@msn.com; www. ackisland.com/nantucketcountry; 38 Centre St., PO Box 1046, Nantucket, MA02554) 19th- and 20th-century country furniture and antiques, folk art, primitive paintings, kitchenware, and period quilts, among other things. Murals by Islander Kolene Speier make you wish you could take home the walls of this 18th-century house.

Nina Hellman Marine Antiques (508-228-4677, fax 508-228-1934; marantqs @nantucket.net; www.nauticalnantucket.com; 48 Centre St., Nantucket, MA 02554; daily May–Dec.; weekends Jan–Apr.) Marine antiques, including scrimshaw, nautical books and instruments, ship models, whaling material, paintings, and prints; folk art, silver, ephemera, and maps. A contemporary scrimshander often gives demonstrations during high season.

Paul LaPaglia Gallery (508-228-8760; 38 Centre St., Nantucket, MA 02554) Framed prints are the specialty; also, other Nantucket memorabilia, rare graphics, and old postcards at affordable prices.

John Rugge Shop (508-325-7920; 5 India St., Nantucket, MA 02554; year-round) Antiques and collectibles in a well-known shop.

Sylvia Antiques (508-228-0960; sales@sylviaantiques.com; www.sylviaantiques.com; 6 Ray's Court, PO Box 1049, Nantucket, MA 02554) Furniture, glassware, porcelains, scrimshaw, ship models, and marine and decorative arts shown to advantage in an old barn. Also lightship baskets old and new.

Tonkin of Nantucket (508-228-9697; tonkin@capecod.net; www.tonkin-of-nantucket.com; 33 Main St., PO Box 996, Nantucket, MA02554) 18th- and 19th-century furniture silver, china; scrimshaw; marine paintings.

Val Maitino Antiques (508-228-2747; valmai@nantucket.net; www.valmaitinoantiques.com; 31 North Liberty St., PO Box 1570, Nantucket, MA 02554) Furniture, marine items, hooked rugs, weather vanes, lighting fixtures, lightship baskets, and more.

Vis-à-vis Ltd. (508-228-5527; visavis@nantucket.net; www.internationalbou
tiques.com; 34 Main St., Nantucket, MA 02554; daily, Mar.–Dec.; weekends
Jan.–Feb.) Quilts, hooked rugs, furniture, accessories and antique jewelry.

AUCTIONS

Auctions are a time-tested fund-raiser and are sponsored by churches, charities, and fraternal organizations throughout the year. While you may find
great bargains or even a real treasure at these events (especially if you know
your antiques), the best-authenticated pieces — especially Island art such as
scrimshaw and lightship baskets — will probably be offered at the two permanent auction houses. As a rule for any auction, go to the previews first, and
examine the objects up close. It's easy to get swept away in auction fever and
overbid, even those who consider themselves to be calm, cool, and rational by
nature. In addition to the off-Islanders just having fun, there will be serious
antiques dealers from the mainland in the audience around you.

Nantucket Town

Raphael Osona Auctions (508-228-3942; 21 Washington St., PO Box 2607,
Nantucket, MA 02584) Estate auctions with two-day previews: furniture, silver, paintings, jewelry, decoys, folk art, marine items, scrimshaw, lightship
baskets, memorabilia. Sale times 9:30am Saturdays; weekly in summer and
once a month in May, June, October, November, December. Catalogs available and absentee bids accepted.

Everywhere Else

Mark J. Enik Island Antiques & Island Auction House (508-332-5852; 5
Miacomet Ave., PO Box 661, Nantucket, MA 02554; off Surfside Rd.) Mark J.
Enik holds year-round auctions with Thursday and Friday previews.
Appraisals and sales. The shop is open daily.

ART GALLERIES AND STUDIOS

You see them setting up easels at the wharf and by the cranberry bogs or
hauling canvases and portfolios on and off the ferry. Their work hangs in
banks, restaurants, museums, schools, and dress shops as well as galleries. At
times it seems that being a recognized artist is a qualification for Island citizen-
ship. For art lovers, just keeping up with the shows opening and continuing is
a major undertaking. Most helpful in that regard is the **Artists' Association of
Nantucket** (508-228-0294; 19 Washington St., Nantucket, MA 02554), an organization with members all over the world. On the Island, the association advo-

Artists capturing the cranberry harvest on canvas.

Betty Lowry

cates for artists and artisans, offers workshops and classes, and supports community events such as the **Nantucket Arts Festival** in October.

Shows, events, openings, and demonstrations throughout the year are listed in the newspaper. Note that some galleries are closed from November to May, since their owners are likely to be teaching on the mainland or working in the studios they maintain in warmer climes. Your gallery and studio browsing could begin at Old South Wharf but should not stop there. Here are a few of the many that specialize in Nantucket scenes and themes:

Nantucket Town

Arsenault Gallery (508-228-1052; 10 Old North Wharf, Nantucket, MA 02554)
Artists' Association of Nantucket Gallery (508-228-0294; aan@nantucket.net; www.nantucketarts.org; 19 Washington St., Nantucket, MA 02554) Open all year.

No one misses an opening at The Artists' Association Little Gallery.

Betty Lowry

Sailor's Valentines

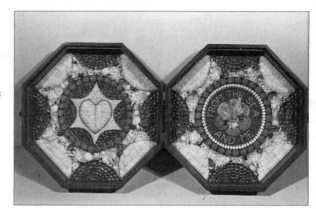

A sailor's valentine crafted by Sandi Blanda is exhibited at the Sailor's Valentine Gallery in the old Macy Warehouse.

Frederick G. S. Clow

Picture the lonesome sailor in the South Pacific on a four-year whaling voyage thinking of his sweetheart back on Nantucket. He wants to bring her a sure-enough symbol of his love, but what to do? He looks about, sees a zillion seashells, and he has a great idea. He gathers them and in his spare time composes them into a picture with the words he wants to say spelled out in the center. How can she resist this labor of love that he has so painstakingly crafted just for her?

The time is 1830 to 1880, and the scenario actually went more like this: The sailor is on his way home at last, and the ship stops in Barbados or maybe Trinidad. He and his mates go ashore, and here are all the locals selling shell jewelry, shell-covered boxes — shell everything, including shell mosaics in symmetrical patterns of flowers complete with romantic messages and all. BE MINE, they entreat; REMEMBER ME, BE TRUE. Furthermore, they are neatly mounted in eight-sided glazed wooden cases. What a perfect gift for Elizabeth, Lydia, Dionis, or what's-her-name!

Forget the Hallmark card. These sailor's valentines are prime collectibles today as authentic West Indian commercial folk-art handcraft, if not genuine shipboard-made stuff. Originals are often in excellent condition, probably because they were treasured by the recipients. **Peter Foulger Museum** has a permanent collection and so does the art gallery called **The Sailor's Valentine** on Lower Main Street. The **Whaling Museum** even has a somewhat crude example that appears actually to have been made by a sailor using Pacific shells, perhaps in imitation of the flashy West Indian pieces he had seen but couldn't afford. Sailor's valentines also show up at auctions and in antique stores, and they are replicated in miniature by Island goldsmiths. Now and then throughout the summer, children are encouraged to make them in craft workshops.

One clue to the generally West Indies origin of these pieces — as opposed to the notion of the lovelorn sailor-craftsman — may have been the frames all made in the same way and of Spanish cedar wood at that. A researcher in the 1960s also noted that the shells were native to the West Indies, not the South Pacific. The real clincher was when some of these creations turned out to have MADE IN BARBADOS or MADE IN TRINIDAD on the back or even spelled out in tiny shells.

Oh, well, it's the thought that counts.

William J. Dickson Studio-Gallery (508-228-2304; wjnd@aol.com; www.nan tucket.net/art/dickson; 1 Francis St., Nantucket, MA 02554) Nantucket photographs.

G. S. Hill Gallery (508-228-1353, fax 508-325-4714; gshill@nantucket.net; www. gshill.com; 40 Straight Wharf, Nantucket, MA 02554)

Made on Nantucket (508-228-0110; www.madeonnantucket.com; 44 Main St., Nantucket, MA 02554; upstairs)

Mielko Gallery (508-228-0014; info@nantucketfinearts.com; www.nantucket love.com; 4 Old South Wharf, Nantucket, MA 02554)

Nantucket Glassworks (508-228-7779; www.nantucket.net/art/glasswork; 28 Centre St., Nantucket, MA 02554)

Sailor's Valentine Gallery (508-228-2011; 12 Straight Wharf, Nantucket, MA 02554; at the Macy Warehouse, Lower Main Street)

South Wharf Gallery (508-228-0406; 21 Old South Wharf, PO Box 1461, Nantucket, MA 02554)

Stephen Huneck Gallery (508-228-9977; 32 Centre St., Nantucket, MA 02554)

William H. Welch Gallery (508-228-0687, 800-900-9779; www.williamwelch gallery.com; 14 Easy St., PO Box 2847, Nantucket, MA 02584)

The (X) Gallery (508-325-4858; 12 Orange St., PO Box 1234, Nantucket, MA 02554)

Siasconset and *Everywhere Else*

Many artists live outside Nantucket Town, so if you're looking for one in particular, scan the yellow pages of Anderson's *Nantucket Phone Book* (not Verizon or the *Nantucket Directory*). You'll find these useful books at your inn or the Visitor Services Center, 25 Federal Street.

Barbara Kauffmann Locke Studio Gallery (508-257-9842; One New St., Siasconset, MA 02564)

S. Warren Krebs Studio (508-228-4655; krebsway@nantucket.net; www.nan tucket.net/art/krebs; 57 Union St., Nantucket, MA 02554; south of Town)

BOOKS, CARDS, AND MUSIC

B ooks and cards are sold in boutiques, antiques stores, galleries, gift shops, and museums as well as these more or less specialty places.

Nantucket Town

Anderson's (508-228-4187; 29 Main St., Nantucket, MA 02554)

The Camera Shop (508-228-0101; posters@nantucket.net; www.nantucket posters.com; 32 Main St., PO Box 731, Nantucket, MA 02554; upstairs)

Coffin's Gift Store (508-228-4662, 800-896-4662; www.coffingiftstore.com; Zero India St., Nantucket, MA 02554)

The Hub (508-228-3868; www.thehubofnantucket.com; 31 Main St., PO Box 986, Nantucket, MA 02554)

Logos Book Store (508-228-8582; 15 Washington St., Nantucket, MA 02554) Judeo-Christian emphasis.

Mitchell's Book Corner (508-228-1080; www.mitchellsbookcorner.com; 54 Main St., Nantucket, MA 02554) A separate room dedicated to Nantucket books including many not available elsewhere.

The Museum Shop (508-228-5785; nhainfo@nha.org; www.nha.org; 11 Broad St., Nantucket, MA 02554; at the Whaling Museum) Nantucket, decor, and art books.

Musicall (508-228-9306; 4 East Chestnut St.) New and used CDs, books on tape, instruments.

Nantucket Bookworks (508-228-4000; 25 Broad St., Nantucket, MA 02554)

Nantucket Pharmacy (508-228-0180; 45 Main St., PO Box 1056, Nantucket, MA 02554)

Paper'tucket (508-228-2110; 4A South Water St., Nantucket, MA 02554)

Everywhere Else

Island Pharmacy (508-228-6400; islpharm@nantucket.net; www.islandrx.com; 122 Pleasant St., Nantucket, MA 02554; mid-Island)

CLOTHING

Nantucket style tends to be classic and understated. The sweatshirts emblazoned with NANTUCKET come in all colors and are stocked in every general store and marine supply shop on the Island as well as in sportswear stores in Town. The orangey-red cottons faded to rosy pink (trademark: "Nantucket Reds") were the accidental invention of **Murray's Toggery Shop** and have become an Island fashion statement. Shopping for clothing, like just about everything on Nantucket, is a low-stress activity. Markdowns are taken even in midsummer, and off-season is clearance time. (See also Chapter Nine, *Information*, for a list of bargains.) Except for the thrift shops and outlets, prices generally begin in midrange and go up.

Nantucket Town

Annakajan's (508-228-2723; 1 North Beach St., Nantucket, MA 02554) Whimsical, sophisticated clothing for women.

Annie & The Tees, Inc. (508-228-9107; 46 Main St., Nantucket, MA 02554) Not the only T-shirt purveyor, by any means, but if your time is limited and

One way to let everyone know where you've been: a Nantucket sweatshirt.

Betty Lowry

you want reasonably priced shirts and hats that scream NANTUCKET, Annie's has them in all sizes.

Beautiful People (508-228-2001; 13 Centre St., Nantucket, MA 02554) You don't have to be a waif-thin fashion model to find wearable clothes here.

Best & Co. (508-228-8073; 40 Centre St., Nantucket, MA 02554) Subtitled "the Children's Department Store," this shop for the privileged child has a parallel in Greenwich.

Bramhall & Dunn (508-228-4688; 16 Federal St., Nantucket, MA 02554) All kinds of nice wear for men and women and gift items, too.

Cashmere Nantucket (508-228-7611; 32 Centre St., Nantucket, MA 02554) Look for sweaters in Nantucket colors: cranberry red, marine blue, cottage gray.

Force 5 Watersports (508-228-0700; 6 Union St., Nantucket, MA 02554) Just what the name implies, for those who take their water sports seriously.

Hepburn (508-228-1458; 3 Salem St., Nantucket, MA 02554) For women, this is as elegant as the Island gets.

Island Breeze (508-325-4622; 48 Main St., Nantucket, MA 02554) Breezin' Up clothing for adults and children in good colors and prices.

Island Pursuit (508-228-5117; 2 Straight Wharf, Nantucket, MA 02554) Clothes for any fashion-conscious harbor resort in the western hemisphere.

Joan Vass Nantucket (508-228-7118; 23 Centre St., Nantucket, MA 02554) Designer clothes, Island-style for women.

Kidding Around (508-228-7952; 2 Broad St., Nantucket, MA 02554) Children's wear, toys, and accessories.

Kiwi John's (508-228-5507; www.kiwijohns.com; 19 South Water St., Nantucket, MA 02554) Good sweatshirts, T-shirts, shorts, and prices.

The Marina Clothing Co. (508-228-6868; 5 Old South Wharf, PO Box 2697, Nantucket, MA 02584) Menswear and interesting accessories you won't find anyplace else.

Miss Wear (509-228-1241; 3 Old South Wharf, PO Box 2697, Nantucket, MA 02584) Simple elegance in basic clothes.

Murray's Toggery Shop (508-228-0437, 800-368-2134; reds@nantucket.net; www.nantucketreds.com; 62–68 Main St., PO Box 839, Nantucket, MA 02554) This Nantucket standby since 1913 has men's, women's, and children's sportswear and shoes and is the place to get original "Nantucket Reds." (Part of the building was the original Macy's before Roland H. Macy went on to New York to found the department store in 1858.) **Murray's Warehouse** (228-3584; 7 New St., Nantucket, MA 02554) is the bargain outlet.

Nantucket Sports Locker (508-228-5669; 30 Main St., PO Box 1467, Nantucket, MA 02554) Popular men's and women's fashions, reasonably priced.

Nobby Clothes Shop (508-228-1030; 17 Main St., PO Box 538, Nantucket, MA 02554) Useful clothes for active children and adults.

The Peanut Gallery (508-228-2010; 8 India St., Nantucket, MA 02554) Unusual children's clothing for infants to preteen.

Peter Beaton Hat Studio (508-228-8456; www.peterbeaton.com; 16-1/2 Federal St., Nantucket, MA 02554) Not what you would expect to find on Nantucket, these hats are creations for off-Island occasions as well. Designer Darcy Creech lists Hillary Rodham Clinton, Barbara Bush, and Martha Stewart among her patrons and fans. Hillary wore a Creech design at the inaugural festivities in January 1993.

Pinwheels (508-228-1238; 7 South Beach St., Nantucket, MA 02554) Children's clothes and toys, including pinwheels.

Rose Garden (508-325-5877; 9B South Beach St., Nantucket, MA 02554; opposite Harbor House Hotel) Custom-made designer clothes for women.

The Sunken Ship (508-228-9226; 12 Broad St., Nantucket, MA 02554) Sportswear for all ages.

Sweaters Ltd. (508-228-3204; 42 Centre St., Nantucket, MA 02554) Sweaters has just what the name implies and lots of them.

Together (508-228-3181; 19 Main St., Nantucket, MA 02554) Variety in wearable fashions.

Wolfhound Imports (508-228-3552; 21 Main St., Nantucket, MA 02554) Great sweaters and classic sportswear for men, women, and children. Also pure wool blankets with an Island map logo.

Zero Main (508-228-4401; Zero Main St., PO Box 517, Nantucket, MA 02554) Women's clothing and shoes.

Everywhere Else

Bayberry Classics Fashion Shop at Marine Home Center (508-228-0900; 6 Bayberry Court, Nantucket, MA 02554; in Freedom Square) Wearable sportswear to fill any gap in your outdoor wardrobe.

Murray's Warehouse (508-228-3584; 7 New St., Nantucket, MA 02554; south of Town) Bargain clothing for the whole family.

Rob Benchley

Shopping for gifts at Nantucket Looms on Main Street.

CRAFTS SHOPS

The annual **Nantucket Folk Art and Craft Show** the first weekend in August is an invitational show and sale featuring about seventy traditional artisans from all over the country. Pottery, jewelry, carving, textiles, woodwork, handcrafted furniture, and more are showcased in a benefit production at Nantucket High School and preceded by a charity fund-raiser "Meet the Artists" preview Thursday night. Ticket information: 508-325-4974.

Although crafts are a staple of every gift shop, here are a few that rate special attention:

Nantucket Town

The Design Guild (508-228-4634; 18 Broad St., Nantucket, MA 02554) Hand-carved wooden shorebirds were the accessories of choice on a recent visit, but you never know what new pieces of creative art for the home will be on display.

Four Winds Craft Guild, Inc. (508-228-9623; www.sylviaantiques.com; 6 Ray's Court, Nantucket, MA 02554) Contemporary work by Island artisans as well as antiques, Nantucket memorabilia, and decorative art. Lightship baskets.

Leslie Linsley Nantucket (508-325-4900; 15 Old South Wharf, Nantucket, MA 02554) Handcrafted home accessories by Island artisans. Linsley's own decoupage plates and platters are imaginative.

Made on Nantucket (508-228-0110; 44 Main St., Nantucket, MA 02554) Interesting work in arts and crafts for fair prices make this upstairs gallery a worthwhile stop. Most items are one-of-a-kind, and the turnover is rapid. On Sundays, June 1 through August 31, artists demonstrate their craft.

Nantucket Looms (508-228-1908; www.nanttucketlooms.com; 16 Main St., PO Box 1510, Nantucket, MA 02554) Hand-weaving plus handcrafted gifts, foods, art, and specialty items.

No Strings Attached (508-228-6060; 29 Centre St., Nantucket, MA 02554) Beads, bangles, buttons, and bows for you to compose into your own wearable art.

The Spectrum Galleries (508-228-4606; 26 Main St., Nantucket, MA 02554) The work of American artists and craftsmen from far and near.

Vis-à-vis (508-228-5527; www.internationalboutiques.com; 34 Main St., PO Box 1438, Nantucket, MA 02554) Handmade jewelry with semiprecious stones, women's apparel, painted shirts.

GIFTS

Regardless of its designation, nearly every shop on Nantucket also sells gifts. If you're shopping for Christmas in July, be assured you will find that Nantucket merchants have anticipated your wish. You'll find gifts for all ages and interests, including your house sitter, your pet sitter, even your pet. Here is a sample of many. (Also see Chapter Five, *Restaurants and Food Purveyors*).

Anderson's of Nantucket (508-228-4187; anderson@nantucketonline.com; www. nantucketonline.com/Andersons; 29 Main St., PO Box 1018, Nantucket, MA 02554) English enamel boxes with Nantucket designs are exclusive here; also gold Christmas tree ornaments in Island motifs.

Coffin's Gift Store (508-228-4662, 1-800-896-4662; www.coffinsgiftstore.com; Zero India St., Nantucket, MA 02554) This little corner store behind the post office has a zillion gift and collectible items.

Cold Noses (508-228-5477; www.coldnoses.net; Straight Wharf, Nantucket, MA 02554; in the Courtyard) Gifts for your pets and thank-you cards for your pet sitter.

Craftmasters of Nantucket (508-228-0322; www.craftmastersnantucket.com; 7 India St., Nantucket, MA 02554) Jewelry and leather gifts. Fine contemporary scrimshaw on piano-key ivory and prehistoric-mammoth ivory.

Expressions of Don Freedman (508-228-3291; 6 Old South Wharf, Nantucket, MA 02554) The gift for couples you won't find duplicated is the Nantucket Beach Bag Blanket. It's all cotton, handloomed, and opens to a two-person blanket.

Geronimo's (508-228-3731; 800-738-7297, fax 508-228-5389; www.geronimos.com; 119 Pleasant St., Nantucket, MA 02554) Accessories for the plain and pampered pet as well as pet-theme gifts for owners. There are even soft toys shaped like the Island for dogs and ultrasuede mice for cats who have everything.

Hill's of Nantucket (508-228-1353; www.gshill.com; 14 Straight Wharf, Nantucket, MA 02554) Full of gifts, including suncatchers, wind chimes, and even afghans in Nantucket themes. A porcelain dinner service and accent pieces are hand decorated with pictures of flower-filled lightship baskets. The paintings and prints of G. S. Hill that formerly hung in a separate gallery on South Wharf are now shown here.

The Lion's Paw (508-228-3837; lionspaw@nantucket.net; Zero Main St., Nantucket, MA 02554) Nice things, many hand painted. Expensive — but not for Nantucket.

Jewel of the Isle (508-228-2448, 800-927-2148; jewel@nantucket.net; www.jewel oftheisle.com; 6 Straight Wharf, Nantucket, MA 02554) Limited-edition posters left over from the Nantucket Film Festival are bargains here and make great gifts for college students as well as collectors.

The Museum Shop N.H.A. (508-228-5785; nhainfo@nha.org; www.nha.org; 13 Broad St., PO Box 1016, Nantucket, MA 02554; at the Whaling Museum) Top-quality items, including collectibles, decorative pieces, books, and authentic reproductions of museum objects.

Nantucket Glass Works (508-228-7779; fax 508-228-7770; www.nantucket.net/art/glasswork; 28 Centre St., Nantucket, MA 02554) Glass art, jewelry, and perfume bottles by New England artists. Hand-blown champagne glasses engraved with wedding date and the names of the bride and groom are the work of glassblower owner Robert Dane.

The Nantucket Sleigh Ride (508-325-4980; www.nantucketsleighride.com; 3 India St., PO Box 1223, Nantucket, MA 02554) Collectibles, folk art, and Christmas tree ornaments, many with Nantucket subject matter.

Olde Nantucket Candle (508-325-7906, 877-653-3225; www.oldenantucketcan dle.com; 12 Oak St., PO Box 3369, Nantucket, MA 02584) Handmade aromatic candles named for Nantucket scents as well as appropriate candleholders.

Seldom Scene (508-325-0577; 35 Old South Rd., Nantucket, MA 02554) "Eclectic extras" is the slogan, and it's true. Unusual antiques, reproductions, and whimsical crafts make this a fun place to poke around.

Stephanie's Nantucket (508-228-0624; www.stephaniesnantucket.com; 74 Centre St., Nantucket, MA 02554) Many facets to this new shop but especially unusual and mostly handmade gifts and children's clothing.

HOUSE AND GARDEN

Nantucket's eclectic style extends to its homes. Those fog-gray shingles are a cover for rooms as warm and bright as a summer day, but you won't find a lot of contemporary. Some especially tempting shops:

A bloom-bedecked path leads to Flowers at the Boarding House, a garden accessory shop on Federal Street.

Betty Lowry

Nantucket Town

Blooms in the Belfry (508-257-6533; 5 New South Rd., Nantucket, MA 02554) Garden ornaments.

Bramhall & Dunn (508-228-4688; 16 Federal St., Nantucket, MA 02554) Handmade rugs and kilims, some on consignment.

Claire Murray (508-228-1913, 800-252-4733, fax 508-228-1964; www.clairemur ray.com; 11 S. Water St., Nantucket, MA 02554; at India St.) Hand-hooked rugs famous all over the country started here in Nantucket when Claire Murray moved to Nantucket from New York, opened a B&B, and needed something to do during the winter. Her rug kits — complementary lessons included — can save two-thirds off the price of the finished item. Also in the shop: woven throws, home accessories, and Nantucket Wildflowers toiletries.

The Complete Kitchen (508-228-2665, 800-824-6660, fax 508-228-2605; tckack @nantucket.net; www.completekitchen.com; 25 Centre St., Nantucket, MA 02554) Practical and decorative things for the kitchen you didn't know you needed in a delightful jumble of a shop. The products of more than four hundred vendors include gourmet foods.

The Design Guild (508-228-4634; 18 Broad St., Nantucket, MA 02554) Island-made and -inspired accessories.

Erica Wilson Needle Works (508-228-9881; 25 Main St., Nantucket, MA 02554) Needlepoint for you to do and already done, plus hand-painted china and sweaters, toys, and rugs.

Handblock (508-228-4500; fax 508-228-5643; court@nantucket.net; www.hand block.com; 42 Main St., Nantucket, MA 02554) Things for the home, especially linens.

Island Trader Galleries (508-228-1179; www.islandtradergalleries.com; 16 Macy's Ln., Nantucket, MA 02554; off Surfside Rd.) Linens, wicker, and interior accessories.

Leslie Linsley Nantucket (508-325-4900; 15 Old South Wharf, Nantucket, MA

02554) Handcrafted home accessories by Island artisans, especially crib quilts and wall hangings for the nursery.

Nantucket Chintz (508-228-3348; 39 Washington St., Nantucket, MA 02554) Designer fabrics.

The Salon at Sailor's Valentine Gallery (508-228-2011; 12 Straight Wharf, Nantucket, MA 02554; at the Macy Warehouse) From antique furniture to tramp art and kilims, lots of things you never thought you would find on Nantucket.

Weeds (508-228-5200, fax 508-228-5202; www.weeds-nantucket.com; 14 Centre St., PO Box 1403, Nantucket, MA 02554) Exclusive here are lightship baskets replicated in Bennington porcelain and fine-bone china in Wedgwood's "Nantucket" pattern. Both lines are designed by artist George P. Davis. Weeds also has marine and garden items, 19th-century English furniture, and collectibles.

Everywhere Else

Ensembles (508-325-4400; 17 North Beach St., Nantucket, MA 02554) Bed and bath are the stars of the show.

Marine Home Center (508-228-0900; info@marinehomecenter.com; www.marine homecenter.com; Lower Orange St., Nantucket, MA 02554) Where Islanders go for practical items is a good place to browse.

Nantucket Pottery Works (508-228-0026; 49 Sparks Ave., Nantucket, MA 02554; in the Sanford Boat Building) Everything, including powder-room sinks, painted by a local artist.

The Nantucket Trading Emporium (508-325-0714/4800, 800-863-2771, fax 508-325-0702; 6–8 Amelia Dr., Nantucket, MA 02554) Everything for the home, including gourmet delicacies to put on the table.

JEWELRY

R emember the fairy tale about the promise to turn straw into gold? Well, lightship baskets aren't made of straw (rattan, actually), but they've been turned into gold. The jewelers of Nantucket are artists as well as merchants and will design and create dreamy pieces for special occasions. Engagement and wedding rings are big sellers, too. Auction houses and antiques stores frequently have selections of estate jewelry.

Bill Rowe Nantucket (508-228-7171; 19 Centre St., Nantucket, MA 02554) Miniature oil pendants; gold and gem-set jewelry to remind you forever of Nantucket (as if you could forget!).

The Cutting Edge (508-228-3737; 20 Federal St., Nantucket, MA 02554) Fine jewelry and glassware but also miniature 1846 fire-brigade buckets in 14-karat gold and sterling silver. Full-size wooden buckets, too.

Diana Kim England, Goldsmith (508-228-3766, 800-342-1468; www.dianakim england.com; 56 Main St., Nantucket, MA 02554) Limited editions of miniature lightship baskets with tiny scrimshawed lids.

The Golden Basket (508-228-4344, 800-453-2758; thegoldenbasket@thegolden basket.com; www.thegoldenbasket.com; 44 Main St., PO Box 397, Nantucket, MA 02554) Lightship baskets, of course, as jewelry handcrafted in gold, platinum, and sterling silver.

The Golden Nugget (508-228-1019, 800-582-8205; 39 Straight Wharf, PO Box 397, Nantucket, MA 02554)

Jewel of the Isle (508-228-2448, 800-927-2148; jewel@nantucket.net; www.jewel oftheisle.com; 6 Straight Wharf, Nantucket, MA 02554) Custom designs of Nantucket themes in gold.

Jewelers' Gallery of Nantucket (508-228-0229, 800-550-0229; www.jewelers gallerynant.com; 21 Centre St., Nantucket, MA 02554) Antique, estate, and handcrafted jewelry. The Lillian H. Waine collection of sailor's valentines pendants in 14K gold is memorable.

Parham's Gems of the Sea (508-325-5899; 9A S. Beach St., Nantucket, MA 02554) Pearls.

S.J. Patten Jewelers (508-228-4882, 800-649-1818; 35 Main St.,) Gold lightship baskets and other Nantucket themes.

Girl Talk, 1876

The average conversation is still interlarded with such sea phrases as "cruising about," "short allowance," "rigged out," etc. I heard one woman ask for the "bight" of a clothes-line. I had it from credible authority that a Cape Cod girl, when kissed, always presented the other cheek, saying, "You darsent do that again." A Nantucket lass would say, "Sheer off, or I'll split your mainsail with a typhoon."

— Samuel Adams Drake, *Nooks and Corners of the New England Coast*, 1876

LIGHTSHIP BASKETS

It sometimes seems every shop on the Island has new lightship baskets or their scrimshaw decorations to sell, and old baskets turn up at auction or in the antique stores. You can also buy direct from the basket maker, either ready-made or custom crafted. They also give lessons in basket making, and they repair baskets, in case you find a damaged treasure. (See "The Story of the Lightship Basket" below for more details.) It's wise to telephone first both to be sure the basket maker is there and to get directions. Here are the major lightship-basket purveyors:

Making a lightship basket.

Betty Lowry

Nantucket Town

Anderson's of Nantucket (508-228-4187; 29 Main St., Nantucket, MA 02554)

Four Winds Craft Guild (508-228-9623; www.sylvaiaantiques.com; 6 Ray's Court, Nantucket, MA 02554)

Nantucket Basket Works (508-228-2518; 14 Dave St., Nantucket, MA 02554)

Nantucket Lightship Baskets (508-228-2326; 13 Deer Run Rd., Nantucket, MA 02554)

The Packet Shop (508-228-4872; 1 Old South Wharf, Nantucket, MA 02554)

Salt Meadows (508-228-0230; 78 Union St., Nantucket, MA 02554)

The Spectrum Art Galleries(508-228-4606; 26 Main St., Nantucket, MA 02554)

Susan & Karl Ottison (508-228-9345; 170 Orange St.)

Terry Sylvia Studio (508-228-2926; Zero Washington St., Nantucket, MA 02554; at Sylvia Antiques)

Val Maitino Antiques (508-228-2747; valmai@nantucket.net; www.valmai tinoantiques.com; 31 North Liberty St., PO Box 1570, Nantucket, MA 02554)

Everywhere Else

Manny Dias Basket Shop (508-228-1889; 52 Surfside Rd., Nantucket, MA 02554) A multigeneration family production line.

Michael Kane's (508-228-1548; 18A Sparks Ave., Nantucket, MA 02554)

John Kittila III (508-325-5875; 3 Washington Ave., Nantucket, MA 02554; in Madaket.

Karol Lindquist (508-257-6727; PO Box 1370, Nantucket, MA 02554) Classes in basket making are booked by off-Islanders who center their visits around them. Year-round.

The Lightship Shop (508-228-4164; 20 Miacomet Ave., PO Box 312, Nantucket,

The Story of the Lightship Basket

Today it's the ultimate status symbol of Nantucket, this collectible handbag passed down from mother to daughter, and — like precious antiques — the older the better. Perhaps lightship baskets satisfy the Yankee requirements of long lasting, all-purpose, and handmade, but they also affirm both the owner's Island connection and affluence. A top example of a present-day lightship basket can cost more than $1,000, not including the scrimshaw decoration on top.

For this, the maker signs and dates the basket on its wood bottom, and the owner gets a Certificate of Authenticity from the Nantucket Basket Makers & Merchants Association (NBMA) assuring that the basket has been made on the Island. Not that anyone can tell the difference just by looking, but there is talk of denying the Nantucket-made mark even to baskets produced by born-and-bred Islanders who make them while they are off-Island (for example, while wintering in Florida).

Not all lightship baskets are women's handbags, and they did not begin that way. As sturdy farm and kitchen baskets, they were designed to fit in nests of seven or eight, and you can still buy them in all sizes and for diverse purposes. While the traditional over-the-arm handbag basket with a fitted lid is what the name implies today, the same materials and techniques are used to build baskets around ice buckets, glass vases, and lamp bases. Small open baskets for nuts or trinkets cost about $100.

Lightship baskets are made not only by recognized artisans but also by any number of Islanders with a little (or a lot of) time to spare. They are sold through shops or directly from their maker's home and are often custom-made. The decoration on the top is usually priced separately and ranges from a simple cut-out bone or ivory whale with a scrimshaw eye to a full scrimshaw scene, a stand-up sculpture, artfully arranged shells, or even a Nantucket theme hand-painted on the skeletal remains of an ancient mastodon. Baskets are also reproduced as gold and silver jewelry, in porcelain, and in a line of English Wedgwood bone china called simply "Nantucket."

Basically, the lightship basket is made of narrow staves fitted into a hardwood disc base, then built around a mold and woven from the bottom up with fine rattan. Rims are fitted, nailed, and then laced. Handles are usually attached with bone or ivory pegs. The lids are woven curved, fit evenly all around, and are topped with a hardwood oval to bear the decoration. Well made, the baskets are said to last indefinitely; the natural darkening of time only enhances their value.

The first baskets in this style (though without lids) began to appear in Nantucket about 1820, shortly after whalers rounded the Horn and were introduced to the long stringy rattan of the Pacific Islands. While basket-weaving techniques were roughly the same as those of the Algonquins, the construction followed the methods shipboard coopers used making oil casks, buckets, and tubs. Materials varied, depending on what was at hand — wood, or even whale baleen, the stringy keratinous material that hangs from the roof of a toothless whale's mouth and acts as a strainer.

Why "lightship" baskets? They took their name from the ships anchored off the coast to aid navigation around the shoals. Lightship crew members, with little to do but clean the lamps and stand long watches, passed the time by making utilitarian baskets for their families on shore. Nantucket lightship baskets are often traced, specifically, to ten men of the Nantucket South Shoal Lightship situated twenty-four miles south of Sankaty Head lighthouse in 1856.

In 1946, after the end of World War II, Jose Formoso Reyes brought his family from the Philippines to Nantucket, where his wife had relatives. Despite his Harvard graduate degree and university teaching experience, Reyes could find no openings in the schools. To provide for his family, he did odd jobs such as mending cane and rush chairs using techniques he had learned as a boy. One of his Nantucket friends, basket maker Mitchell ("Mitchy") Ray, whose family had been making traditional lightship baskets for three generations, urged Reyes to try his hand at this craft.

Using many of Mitchy Ray's molds, Reyes experimented with a basket design that could be used as a woman's purse. He fashioned simple closures for its woven lid and decorated the top with an ebony whale. This creation he called a "Friendship Basket," first in honor of the friendship between his original home and his adopted one and affirming the name later when he heard the baskets were conversation starters between women carrying like baskets all over the country.

The samples he made for sale were such an instant and unanticipated success, they stimulated new interest in the craft throughout the Island. Reyes became a full-time basket maker, signed his work, and in the next twenty years personally made more than five thousand baskets.

Materials used making baskets today are not indigenous to Nantucket, and copies are coming in from all over the globe. While selling a spurious handbag is not likely to happen on the Island, the quality of craftsmanship varies, and there is ongoing experimentation with shapes, styles, and the designs on top. At one time teaching lightship basket making was clandestine in an attempt to limit production, but now even off-Islanders can buy a kit or take a class — most makers are also teachers. It's time-consuming work and hard on the fingers.

The story of both the lightships and the baskets is shown and told at the new **Nantucket Lightship Basket Museum** (508-228-1117; 49 Union St., Nantucket, MA 02554). This is the place to check authenticity before investing in an antique basket. Open Wednesday through Sunday 10am–5pm.

MA 02554; halfway between Town and Surfside) A very large collection as well as lightship-basket kits and classes.

Sayle's Lightship Baskets (508-228-9876; 112 Washington St. Ext., PO Box 1233, Nantucket, MA 02554) Carvings and custom scrimshaw as well as more than sixty styles and sizes of baskets.

Timothy D. Parsons (508-228-8714; 80 Old South Rd., Nantucket, MA 02554)

MARINE SUPPLY

Nantucket Town

Brant Point Marine (508-228-6244; www.brantpointmarine.com; 32 Washington St., Nantucket, MA 02554)

Nantucket Marine (508-228-5510; www.nantucketmarine.com; 85 Pleasant St., Nantucket, MA 02554)

Nantucket Ship Chandlery Corp. (508-228-2300; shipchan@nantucket.net; www.nantucket.net/boating/chandlery; 1 Old South Wharf, Nantucket, MA 02554)

Everywhere Else

Glyn's Marine Inc. (508-228-0244; 8 Arrowhead Dr., Nantucket, MA 02554; off Old South Rd.)

Grey Lady Marine (508-228-6525; 96 Washington St., Nantucket, MA 02554)

Madaket Marine (508-228-1163, 800-564-9086; 20 N. Cambridge St., Nantucket, MA 02554; Madaket)

Nantucket Land & Sea Co. (508-228-4038; 16 Margaret's Way, PO Box 1411, Nantucket, MA 02554)

Nantucket Moorings (508-228-4472; 85 Bartlett Rd., Nantucket, MA 02554)

SCULPTURE AND CARVINGS

Scrimshaw is the primary sculpture and carving art of Nantucket, though you will also see some nice wood carvings, especially of marine objects. (See "The Story of Scrimshaw" below.) In addition to the scrimshanders listed here, lightship-basket stores also carry scrimshaw decorative pieces to be mounted on basket lids. Collections of old scrimshaw appear frequently on auction house lists, so check with these to see what they have coming up.

Ivory carving and scrimshaw have long been associated with Nantucket. Here, artist Nancy Chase works on a miniature striped bass in her studio.

Rob Benchley

The Story of Scrimshaw

Long, idle hours faced everyone aboard a whaling ship, from captain to cabin boy. During a voyage of two to four years, boredom was an occupational hazard. Crew members needed something to occupy their hands, so they practiced an ancient handcraft, raising it to skill and eventually to naïve art. Scrimshaw, the craft of carving or engraving on bone or ivory, was not invented by American whalemen, but it is probably safe to say it reached its zenith in their hands. They had the basic material, and they had the tools. Fresh, soft bone, baleen, and teeth from the whales were byproducts of the whaling business. Jack knives for carving and strong canvas needles (normally used for sewing sails) for engraving (the eye end was embedded in a piece of wood) were the sailor-craftsman's implements. Some ships had foot-powered turning lathes for carpenters and coopers that could also be used to trim large pieces of raw material. All had files for smoothing the rough edges of bone or tooth, and lamp black or soot from the blubber tryworks rubbed in the scratches brought out the incised designs.

Most of all, the men had time. We know from their logs and letters that "scrimshanding" occupied most of their free hours, becoming for some a creative passion. They drew pictures of their ships, the whales, the action, and the places they visited. They drew dreams and fantasies or meticulously copied the illustrations of books and magazines as unlikely as *Godey's Ladies Book*. A piece of scrimshaw in the author's collection shows a furious whale tossing a whaleboat and its crew into the air, its mouth open to catch an unlucky sailor. Undoubtedly copied from a 19th-century woodcut, it's an amazing example of concentrated detail in two inches of space on a four-inch whale tooth.

With this method the whalers decorated useful items as gifts for their women at home: tatting shuttles, crochet hooks, bodkins, and corset busks. They made elaborate handles for walking sticks and carved dolls and toy whales and ships for children. They whittled tools and tool handles for shipboard use, and made plaques and lids for boxes. These pieces were rarely signed or dated, even by those with great talent.

They worked under the worst possible conditions, more often than not in the fo'c'sle of the ship where they had their bunks. This triangle inside the bow took the greatest bounce on the ship and was airless and dark, as well. A steady hand and perfect vision must have been prime requirements.

Scrimshaw artists today have strong magnifiers, fine tools, and good lighting, and they work with true inks, often in color, on polymer plastic, recycled ivory piano keys, and sometimes on tusk and bone (not freshly harvested, however). You'll see their work in galleries and on the lids of Nantucket lightship baskets, and it is not cheap.

Authentic 19th-century pieces demand high prices and so have attracted forgers. Authenticating a scrimshaw work involves analysis of the original materials and the wear of years and neglect. Value is based on the complexities of art, condition, size, and, inevitably, demand. Before you buy, study the examples in Nantucket's Whaling Museum, and talk to the Island specialists in maritime art and antiques.

Nantucket Town

Craftmasters of Nantucket (508-228-0322; www.craftmastersnantucket.com; 7 India St., Nantucket, MA 02554)

Charles A. Manghis (508-325-8815; 48 Centre St., Nantucket, MA 02584) at Nina Hellman Antiques.

Hostetler Gallery (508-228-5152; hostetler@eureka.net; www.davidhostetler.com; 2 Old South Wharf, Nantucket, MA 02554) Rare woods from far shores become folk goddesses.

Lee Ann Papale (508-228-9504; 170 Lower Orange St., PO Box 2337, Nantucket, MA 02554) Scrimshaw, including mini-miniatures.

Nantucket Woodcarving (508-325-7010; woodcarver@nantucket.net; www.nan tucketwoodcarving.com; 110 Orange St., Nantucket, MA 02554) The motto is "If it can be drawn, it can be carved," but the art of wood sculpture here goes far beyond commercial signs and quarterboards. By appointment only.

The Scrimshander Gallery (508-228-1004; 19 Old South Wharf, Nantucket, MA 02584) Custom scrimshaw for your lightship basket plus old and new examples of the art. Ship models, too.

Tobias Gallery (508-228-9497; 16 Old South Wharf, Nantucket, MA 02554) The sculptor himself may be outside carving alabaster as you pass by.

Whitlock Gallery (508-325-7900; 13 Old South Wharf, Nantucket, MA 02554) Wood carvings and bronze castings of wood originals. Abstractions of sea themes ("Surf Cast," "Back Cast," and "False Cast" were the titles of a recent series inspired by fishing) are all carved with chisel and mallet.

Everywhere Else

Anastasia Toombs Fusaro (508-228-3120; PO Box 3327, Nantucket, MA 02484) Scrimshaw only.

SPECIALTY

Nantucket Town

The Camera Shop & Nantucket Video (508-228-0101, fax 508-228-6897; info@ nantucketposters.com; www.nantucketposters.com; 32 Main St., Nantucket, MA 02554) Film, batteries, processing, posters, prints, notecards, and post-cards. Open seven days a week.

Cross Rip Outfitters (508-228-4900; crossrip@nantucket.net; www.crossrip.com; 24 Easy St., PO Box 55, Nantucket, MA 02554) The complete saltwater fly-fishing outfitter has equipment, gifts, clothing, and art. Lessons, guide service, and rentals will put you in the briny before you can say, "Moby who?"

The Fragrance Bar (508-325-4740, 800-223-8660; perfume@nantucket.net; www.

nantucketnaturaloils.com; 5 Centre St., Nantucket, MA 02554) More than five hundred essential oils give you a lot of choice in finding the perfect blend. Nantucket-named scents are a specialty, but the shop also stocks healing herbs, creams, and aromatherapy items. The collectible hand-blown glass perfume bottles make good gifts.

Nantucket Ship Chandlery Corp. (508-228-2300; shipchan@nantucket.net; www.nantucket.net/boat/chandlery; 1 Old South Wharf, PO Box 417, Nantucket, MA 02554) Marine hardware, supplies, Nantucket burgee flags, gifts, and real gear for real boaters.

Stitches of Nantucket (508-325-7244; 14 MacLean Ln., Nantucket, MA 02554) Custom embroidery and monogramming includes translating your own art into threads.

TOYS

S ome toys, like youth, are wasted on the young. Or maybe it's just that they can bring out the child in each of us. Nantucket toy stores have vast selections, from handmade wonders to supplies for model builders to plastic buckets for small beachcombers.

Nantucket Town

Nantucket Kiteman (508-228-7089; kiteman@capecod.net; www.nantucket kiteman.com; 14 S. Water St., Nantucket, MA 02554) More than four hundred flags and banners in stock; also bright, flamboyant, and unusual kites. They're not just for kids anymore.

The Peanut Gallery (508-228-2010; 8 India St., Nantucket, MA 02554) Handmade doll clothes, among other things.

The Sunken Ship (508-228-9226; 12 Broad St., Nantucket, MA 02554) Lots of kid stuff still afloat here.

The Toy Boat (508-228-4552, fax 508-228-7781; thetoyboat@nantucket.net; www. thetoyboat.com; 41 Straight Wharf, PO Box 2297, Nantucket, MA 02554) This shop looks tiny, but it has everything — including Nantucket exclusives such as a handmade Rainbow Fleet. Whenever there's a child-centered event on the Island, the Toy Boat is actively involved in carrying it off. They show movies and have daily craft programs for kids, too. Owner-designer is the multitalented Loren Brock.

CHAPTER NINE

Needs to Know

INFORMATION

Here are the safety pins for your trip to Nantucket, holding together the bits and pieces that ease planning and make anticipation connect with reality. In this chapter you will find the following topics:

Betty Lowry

Nantucket wants you to know where you're going.

AMBULANCE, FIRE, EMERGENCY, AND POLICE

The general twenty-four-hour emergency number anywhere on Nantucket is **911**. Other numbers you may need to know:

Coast Guard	**508-228-0388**
Environmental Police	508-228-5262
Fire (non-emergency)	508-228-2323
Hospital	508-228-1200
Poison Control	800-682-5211
Police (non-emergency)	508-228-1212
Sheriff	508-228-7263
State Police	508-228-0706

TTD/TTY (Telecommunication Device for the Deaf/Tele-typewriter)
Emergency (direct relay)	**911**
Emergency	800-249-9949

AREA CODES AND ZIP CODES

AREA CODES

The area code for Nantucket is **508**. The area code for Boston is **617**. Directory Assistance for local numbers is **411**.

ZIP CODES

02554: All Nantucket street addresses and PO boxes numbers 10-1999
02584: All PO boxes 2000 and higher
02564: All Siasconset boxes

BANKS AND ATMS

Fleet: 508-228-1917, PO Box 1850, 61 Main St.; and 508-228-0645, 21 Sparks Ave., Stop & Shop Plaza
Nantucket Bank: 508-228-0580; 104 Pleasant St.; and 508-228-0580, 2 Orange St.

ATMs are located in the following: Bank lobbies; Nantucket Memorial Airport; Steamship Authority, Steamboat Wharf; A&P, Whale St.; Stop & Shop, Pleasant St.; 44 Atlantic Ave.

BARGAINS

While the Island by and large deserves its reputation as a pricey destination, there are moderately priced rooms in all but a few of the lodgings (see Chapter Three, *Lodging*), and breakfast is usually included. You can't camp or sleep out on the beach on Nantucket, but there's a youth hostel. Off-season, room rates fall dramatically, and package plans may include dine-around meals, passes to museums, and transportation to and from the Island.

Since nearly all food must be shipped in, dining is higher than on the mainland, and there are no cheap fast-food chains. There are restaurants in the moderate class, however, as well as sandwich, pizza, ethnic, and take-out places that are inexpensive (see Chapter Five, *Restaurants and Food Purveyors*). And with two competitive supermarkets as well as specialty markets and reasonable gourmet deli, putting together a beach picnic is an affordable snap.

Good shoppers will find good bargains on Nantucket, too. There are a couple of factory outlets, thrift shops everyone checks out, a bin of sweatshirts and a rack of sale items in just about every store you pass. As soon as summer is officially over — that is, after Labor Day —storewide clearance sales begin. In December markdowns of 50 percent enable you to do your Christmas shopping with affordable flair (See Chapter Eight, *Shopping*). Massachusetts's sales tax is 5 percent, with no sales tax on clothing priced below $175.

There are no charges to use Nantucket's gorgeous beaches or to walk the paths through the moors. While parking is impossible in summer, and over-times are closely monitored at any time of year, at least you don't need to hunt around for coins to feed the meters — there *are* no meters. A violation of Nantucket's many regulations, however, can bring on a large and immediate fine.

Bargains all year around include the NRTA shuttle (50¢ to $1 and free for those six and under or sixty-five and over) and the $10 museum pass that admits you to all the properties and museums of the Nantucket Historical Association. If you go for the tax-deductible family membership, you'll get membership cards that provide admissions for two adults (accompanying children under eighteeen free), 10 percent discount at the museum shop, and the quarterly magazine *Historic Nantucket*.

BOOK LIST

Nantucket is a bookish place. (After all, how many tourist offices listing activities for visiting youngsters include "Reading" among them?) The **Atheneum** — the public library (508-228-1110; 1 India St., Nantucket, MA 02554) — has been the agreed-upon center of culture since 1834. When the

The Atheneum is more than a public library, it's a community center.

Rob Benchley

Great Fire of 1846 destroyed the building and its total collection, the library had such high priority that it was rebuilt, restocked, and reopened within six months. Ralph Waldo Emerson gave the dedication along with copies of his own works. Recently renovated, the Atheneum continues to be a community center. The **Maria Mitchell Science Library** (508-228-9219; 2 Vestal St., Nantucket, MA 02554) is a little gem. Both it and the Atheneum have special spaces for children. Serious researchers can also use the facilities of the **Nantucket Historical Association Research Center Library** (508-228-1655; 17 Broad St., Nantucket, MA 02554) for a daily fee (or free to NHA members).

In addition to the Town's four always-crowded bookstores, many general merchandise and gift shops also carry books. The **Museum Shop** of the **Nantucket Historical Association** (508-228-1894; 17 Broad St., Nantucket, MA 02554) has a good selection of Nantucket books, including some you won't find anyplace else. **Mitchell's Book Corner** (508-228-1080; www.mitchells bookcorner.com; 54 Main St., Nantucket, MA 02554) has a separate room for Nantucket books and publishes a free annual Nantucket book list that is especially useful for mail orders.

Even aboard whaling ships, reading for pleasure was common. During all those months and years at sea, the whalers had time for it. Books circulated among the entire crew; by the end of the voyage, book covers were frayed and pages tattered. At home the waiting women wrote letters, kept journals, and read.

The Island has forever attracted writers, and there is a constant flow of limited-edition books by descendants of early settlers expanding upon their genealogies and adding more footnotes to history. Nantucket's repositories are comparable to the Library of Congress — everything written must be kept and catalogued — the silly with the scholarly. Books long out of print or privately printed are here waiting for the researcher to find them in the Atheneum, the **Edouard A. Stackpole Library and Research Center** of the Nantucket

Historical Association (second floor of the **Peter Foulger Museum**), and the Maria Mitchell Library. Higginson Book Company reprints of Nantucket genealogy and history are available through Mitchell's Book Corner.

If you're just looking for a good summer read, you'll find that thrillers with local settings go well with lemonade on Nantucket beaches. It can be especially entertaining to catch the writers in their goofs of Island peculiarities (one character fears being delayed by a nonexistent stoplight; another writer puts Tuckernuck Island at the wrong end of Nantucket). Children can follow the adventures of peers and pets on-Island. Outsized books of photography are worthy souvenirs. So read before you go, while you're there, and after you return. It's one of the secrets of great travel experience. The following lists are choices from a voluminous selection.

Books You Can Buy

ABOUT WHALES AND WHALING:

Cary, William S. *Wrecked on the Feejees.* Fairfield, Wash.: Ye Galleon Press, 1987. $14.95. Logbook of the sole survivor of a Nantucket whaler shipwreck.

Chase, Owen, et. al. *Narratives of the Wreck of the Whale Ship Essex.* Mineola, N.Y.: Dover Publications, 1989. $5.95 paper. Reprint of the classic account of the sinking of the Essex by a whale that became the tale of Moby Dick.

Dow, George F. *Whaleships and Whaling.* Portland, Me.: Southwest Press, 1925. $10.95 paper. History of the great old days in pictures.

Garner, Stanton, ed. *Captain's Best Mate. Hanover, NH: University Press of New England, 1984.* $19.95 paper. The journal of Mary Chipman Lawrence, who accompanied her husband on a four-year whaleship journey.

Heffernan, Thomas. *Stove By a Whale.* Middletown, Conn.: Wesleyan University Press. $15.95 paper. Original complete account of the sinking of the Essex plus information on the subsequent lives of some of the Nantucketers on board.

Melville, Herman. *Moby-Dick or The Whale.* First edition: New York, 1851. Many editions, including paperbacks, are currently available. For an enthusiastic portrait of Nantucket Town, see Chapter Fourteen.

Naslund, Sena Jeter, *Ahab's Wife or the Star-Gazer*, Illustrated by Christopher Wormell, New York: William Morrow, 1999. $28.00. Nineteenth-century Nantucket as seen through the eyes of Una, the wife of Ahab before the day of Moby Dick. Historical characters take their natural places in a novel that rings with literary truth.

Philbrick, Nathaniel, *In the Heart of the Sea*, Illustrated. New York: Viking, 2000. $24.95. The sinking of the whaleship *Essex* in 1820 was reality not morality play (as it became in *Moby-Dick*), yet the tragedy of its survivors tells much about the human spirit. Nantucketer Philbrick, a fine writer as well as maritime historian, follows the whalers for three months at sea through terror, death, cannibalism, and the aftermath. Won the National Book Award for Non fiction 2000.

Poe, Edgar Allan. *The Narrative of Arthur Gordon Pym of Nantucket*. London: Wiley & Putnam, 1838. Various editions can be found of this macabre and classic story of mutiny on a whaleship.

Severin, Tim, *In Search of Moby Dick: Quest for the White Whale*, New York: Basic Books, 2000. $24.00. Sea legends from the day aboard the *Essex* to the late 20th century in all the Pacific waters. Southeast Asian fishermen know his like, and the spiritual aspects of the creature are continued beyond Melville.

ARCHITECTURE, GARDENS AND DECORATIVE ARTS

Duprey, Kenneth, *Old Houses on Nantucket, 2nd edition*. Illustrated. New York: Hastings House, 2000. $18.95 paper. A popular and useful book returns better than ever.

Forman, Henry Chandlee. *Early Nantucket and Its Whale Houses*. New York: Hastings House, 1966. $30. Reprint of a classic on early Nantucket architecture. Much of it still stands.

Garland, Catherine A. *Nantucket Journeys, Exploring the Island, Its Architecture, Its Past*. The evolution of the Island and its architecture presented with architectural drawings.

Gott, Peter. *Sconset Summer Windows*. 2000. $18.95 paper. A book that shows — not tells — why Sconset is a place of endless fascination for visitors and residents alike.

Linsley, Leslie. *Nantucket Style*. New York: Rizzoli, 1990. $29.95 paper. The interiors of more than twenty-five Nantucket houses. Some of these are occasionally open to the public.

Simon, Laura, *Dear Mr. Jefferson: Letters from a Nantucket Gardener*, New York: Crown, 1998. $23.00. A real garden in a real place (Squam woods off the Wauwinet Road) described in detail for an imaginary pen pal. Simon starts everything, including onions, from seed with a spare bedroom converted to birthing room. You don't have to be an avid gardener to enjoy this book.

Stackpole, Edouard, and Melvin B. Summerfield. *Nantucket Doorways*. New York: William Morrow, 1992. $12.95, paper reprint. A tour worth taking on foot as well as by book.

CHILDREN'S BOOKS

Aiken, Joan. *Nightbirds on Nantucket*. Illustrated, New York: Dell, 1969. $5.95 paper. A fast-talking young stowaway and a cabin boy have adventures aboard a whaling ship and afterward on Nantucket when mysteries follow them ashore.

Barnes, Peter W., and Cheryl Shaw. *Nat, Nat, The Nantucket Cat*. Illustrated by Susan Arciero. Vacation Spot Publishing. $15.95. Adventures of a cute, nosy cat just right for little kids.

Brett, Jan. *Comet's Nine Lives*. Illustrated by author. New York: Putnam, 1996.

$15.95. Comet uses eight of those lives, then faces a hurricane. Ages 4 and up.

Gormley, Beatrice. *Maria Mitchell, The Soul of an Astronomer*. Grand Rapids, Mich.: Wm. B. Eerdmans, 1995. $8.00 paper. The newest biography of a famous Nantucket scientist. Ages 8–12.

Melville, Herman. *Moby Dick Or The White Whale*. Adapted by Geraldine McCoughrean, and illustrated by Victor G. Ambrus. New York: Oxford University Press, 1998. $19.95. The tale is shortened, and there is more allegory than psychology, but much of the original Melville is retained. Combine this book with a visit to the Whaling Museum. Ages 10 and up.

Miles, Mary. *What's So Special About Nantucket?* Illustrated by Barbara Kauffmann-Locke. Nantucket: Faraway Publishing, 1998. $17.00. Tuck tries to find out by going place to place. A good catalyst to getting your children to write their own book, *How I Spent My Summer Vacation.*

Miller, Jean. *The Island of Greasy Luck*. $10.00 paper. An eight-year-old goes on a whaling voyage along with other adventures in 19th-century Nantucket. Ages 7–11. (Out of print but still available in book stores on Nantucket.

Murphy, Jim. *Gone A-Whaling: The Lure of the Sea and the Hunt for the Great Whale*, Illustrated. Clarion 1998. Ages 8 and up) The diaries of boys and young men who signed on as cabin boys or common seamen were the basis for this thrilling book.

Tausig, Jared and Eva Maria. *Escape from the Chanticleer*. Illustrated by Barbara van Winkelen. Nantucket: Winds & Dragons, 1995. $17.95. A carousel horse who lives in the garden of a famous restaurant takes off through the lanes and along the shore of Sconset.

Turkle, Brinton. *Thy Friend Obadiah* and *Rachel and Obadiah*. New York: Penguin Books, 1982. $5.95 paper. These are the only two titles available of a classic Nantucket children's series. You may be inspired to ask your hometown rare book dealer to put through a search for others.

Weller, Frances Ward, *Madaket Millie*. Illustrated by Marcia Sewall. New York: Philomel Books, 1997. $15.95. You won't doubt for a minute that Millie Jewett was the real person who took over the work of the Nantucket Coast Guard station when it was closed and patrolled the beaches year round. You can still see her place at Madaket, and there are memorable photographs of her craggy face in the art galleries. Ages 5–9.

Wolfe, Liz, *The Best of Nantucket for Kids: Creative Projects for Children*. Map & Legend. $9.95 paper. Things to make and do "the Nantucket way" from the pages of *Nantucket Map & Legend*. The author wrote the columns and before coming to the Island, ran a preschool in Michigan.

COOKBOOKS

The Nantucket Chamber of Commerce (508-228-1700; 48 Main St., Nantucket, MA 02554) is where you are sure to find the collections of recipes from Daffodil Weekend, Cranberry Harvest, and Nantucket Noel. A history of the event opens each book followed by the recipes of amateur and professional Island cooks. Most of the dishes have won acclaim and ribbons in the various annual cookery competitions, but the recipes are uncomplicated. For example, the Yellow-Fin Tuna Marinade is half a cup of cranberry honey and half a cup of teriyaki mixed in a jar. The books are spiral-bound, about 75 pages long, and cost under $10.00.

These other cookbooks are also Nantucket flavored.

Bartlett, Dorothy. *Bartlett's Ocean View Farm Cookbook.* $14.95 paper. Recipes by Island cooks compiled by the owner of Nantucket's premium supplier of farm-fresh vegetables, berries, and fruits using native ingredients to make dips to desserts.

Chase, Sarah Leah. *Cold Weather Cooking.* New York: Workman, 1985. $22.95 cloth, $15.95 paper; and *The Nantucket Open House Cookbook,* $12.95 paper, by the founder of the former Nantucket gourmet shop Que Sera.

Dawson, Mark & Anne Blake. *Nantucket Recipes from the Fog Island Café.* Sandwich Mass.: Chapman Billies, 1996. $14.95. The proprietors of the Fog Island Café are graduates of the Culinary Institute of America, Hyde Park, New York, and their restaurant across the street from the Atheneum has become a regular stop for the health-and-flavor conscious Nantucketer. Most cooks would guard these recipes, so it's gratifying to see them shared.

Ivas, Nancy. *Healthy Home Cooking from Nantucket.* Illustrations by Lee Papale. Hanover, Mass.: Christopher Publishing House 1995. $17.95. Cooking tips as well as healthful recipes by a Nantucket nutritionist.

Simon, Susan, *The Nantucket Table*, Illustrated. San Francisco: Chronicle Books, 1998. $29.95. Nantucket recipes and lore by a professional New York caterer. Also *The Nantucket Holiday Table*, a sequel with even more about the way people live and dine as well as easy-to-follow recipes.

CRAFTS

Many books have been written about Nantucket's chief crafts: scrimshaw carving and lightship basket making. Here are a few that have proven to be instructive.

Carpenter, Charles H., Jr., and Mary Grace Carpenter. *The Decorative Arts and Crafts of Nantucket.* Photographs by Arthur d'Arazien. New York: Dodd, Mead & Co., 1987. 257 pp. $29.95. A sumptuous book that goes beyond show-and-tell to mini-biographies of people whose lives and life-styles touched on these cultural aspects of Nantucket from 1700 to the present. Included are souvenirs from faraway places and a useful glossary.

Lawrence, Martha R. *Lightship Baskets of Nantucket.* Text and photography by Martha R. Lawrence. Atglen, Penn.: Schiffer Publishing, 1990. $24.95 paper. The author makes her own baskets so writes as artisan as well as historian and explainer of the craft.

Lawrence, Martha. *Scrimshaw, The Whaler's Legacy.* Text and photography by

Martha Lawrence. Atglen, Penn.: Schiffer Publishing, 1993. $69.95. A well-illustrated history and survey of the scrimshander's art that goes beyond the whale-tooth engraving we usually think of as scrimshaw.

McGuire, John E., *Basketry: The Nantucket Tradition*. Photographs by Henry Peach. Asheville, N.C.: Lark Books, 1990. $17.00 paper. The complete manual of how to make a Nantucket basket. Now out of print.

Wood, David. *Catalog: The Lightship Baskets of Nantucket*. Photography by Jack Weinhold. Atglen, Penn.: Schiffer Publishing, 1990. $10.00 paper. This is the catalog of the Nantucket Historical Association exhibition plus two introductory essays and wonderful pictures.

FICTION & AUTOBIOGRAPHY

Benchley, Nathaniel. *The Off-Islanders*. New York: McGraw-Hill, 1961. $8.95 paper. The hilarious book about the accidental invasion of Nantucket by a Russian submarine that became the movie *The Russians are Coming! The Russians are Coming!*

Hallam, Kerry, *Getting to Nantucket: an Artist's Journey*. Illustrated. Mt. Pleasant, S.C.: Corinthian Books, 2000. $24.95. Autobiography of an artist who, with sculptor wife Ruth Hallam, starts the journey in St. Tropez. Full of anecdotes and name-dropping.

Hart, Joseph C. *Miriam Coffin, or the Whale-Fishermen*, Introduction by Nathaniel Philbrick. paper $19.95. Reprint of the 1834 shocker based on the life of Nantucket's Kezia Coffin, the tough businesswoman whose Tory connections kept her personal fleet afloat during the Revolutionary War.

Hilderbrand, Elin, *The Beach Club*. New York: St. Martin's, 2000. $23.95 A page-turner that had everyone trying to guess the identities of the characters who just might be disguised Islanders. Events and encounters of the Island kind that make perfect summer reading on a beach that is true to its billing.

Hynd, Noel. *Ghosts, a Supernatural Thriller*. New York: Zebra Books, 1993. $4.99 paper. Spooky fiction set on the Island to read while munching popcorn on a foggy night.

Keller, Alice, *An Unknown Woman: A Journey to Self-Discovery*, New York: Holt, Rinehart & Winston, 1981. It's 1968 and winter in Sconset, with time for self-analysis and the care of a German shepherd puppy named Logos. This autobiography came early in the women's movement and was read three times in its entirety over National Public Radio.

Langton, Jane. *Dark Nantucket Noon*. New York: Harper & Row, 1975. $5.95 paper. The first Homer Kelly mystery in a wonderful New England series. This one begins with murder at the foot of the Great Point lighthouse during a solar eclipse.

Maness, Larry. *Nantucket Revenge*. Novato, Calif.: Presidio Press, 1995. $19.95. Jake Easton, detective, must save not only his arrogant client but also all Nantucket Town.

Mathews, Francine, *Death in a Cold, Hard Light*. New York: Bantam 1998. $23.95, paper $5.99. Police Detective Merry Folger is at it again, sleuthing about Nantucket this time tying up scalloping, marine biology and heroin. This is Matthews's fourth book in the series and a good vacation read. Her *Death in the Off-Season* (1994) and *Death in Rough Waters* (1995) — both William Morrow, $5.99 paper — are the first two books starring Nantucket police detective Merry Folger. *Death in a Mood Indigo* (New York: Bantam Books, 1997, $22.95), paper $5.99 continues the series.

Rich, Virginia. *Nantucket Diet Murders*. New York: Delacorte, 1985. $5.99 paper. When Mrs. Potter returns to the Island to visit old friends and familiar places, she finds deadly deeds. This one may scare you off your diet.

Thayer, Nancy. *Belonging*. New York: St. Martin's, 1995. $6.98 paper. Rehabbing an old house and a broken heart on Nantucket.

FOLKLORE

Balliett, Blue. *Drawings by George Murphy. Ghosts of Nantucket* and *Nantucket Hauntings*. Camden, Me.: Down East Books, 1990. Each $9.95 paper. Accounts from Nantucketers who stand behind the strange sights they have seen.

Mooney, Robert and Andre Sigourney. *Nantucket Way*. New York: Doubleday, 1980. $12.95 paper. The way of history passed on by true or almost-true tales.

Mooney, Robert F. *Tales of Nantucket*. Nantucket: Wesco Publishing, 1990. $12.95 paper. Stories the author insists are true but you don't have to believe to enjoy.

Miles, Mary, *Nantucket Gam*. Nantucket: Faraway Publishing, 1993. $13.95 paper. Ships and seas and Island talk told the way you'd hear it from an old friend who just happened to be a Nantucketer.

HISTORY

Booker, Margaret Moore, *The Admiral's Academy: Nantucket Island's Historic Coffin School*. Illustrated. 1998. Paper $14.95. Admiral Sir Isaac Coffin, born in Boston, was proud of his Nantucket heritage (a fifth-generation descendent of first purchaser Tristram Coffin) and childless. In 1827 his decision to establish a coeducational free school for Coffin descendents (which amounted to nearly all the children on the Island) was far-reaching. The school on Winter Street is now headquarters of the Egan Institute and an ever more suitable memorial.

Butler, Karen. *Nantucket Lights, An Illustrated History of the Island's Legendary Beacons*. Nantucket: Mill Hill Press, 1996. $44.95. Just the thing for the coffee table of a lighthouse lover.

The Inquirer and Mirror. *Nantucket Argument Settlers: Island History at a Glance 1602–1993*. Nantucket: The Inquirer and Mirror, 1994. $12.95 paper. From 1821 on, Nantucket's newspaper files are scanned; before that, history is agreed upon. This has gone through many editions and is a good browse as well as a last-word reference. You'll find a copy in every inn library, usually quite worn as if no good argument should go unsettled.

Jehle, Michael. From *Brant Point to the Boca Tigris: Nantucket & the China Trade.* Nantucket: Nantucket Historical Association, 1999. $12 paper. A special exhibit of the NHA grows into a book about a time when Nantucket went beyond whales to the mysterious Far East.

Junger, Sebastian. *The Perfect Storm.* New York: W. W. Norton, 1997. $23.95. The Halloween Storm of 1991 had seventy-eight-mph winds, carved forty feet out of Sankaty Bluff, and made islands out of Great Point and Smith Point. Here is the sea around us in all its terrible might.

Lancaster, Clay. *Nantucket in the Nineteenth Century.* $11.95 paper. The heyday, transition, and after.

Leach, Robert J., and Peter Gow. *Quaker Nantucket, The Religious Community behind the Whaling Empire.* Nantucket: Mill Hill Press, 1997. $29.95. The discovery of the complete Quaker meeting records as far back as 1708 was the catalyst for this epic look at both a period and a people. Vignettes help make it personal and immediate.

Philbrick, Nathaniel, *Abram's Eyes: The Native American Legacy of Nantucket Island.* Nantucket: Mill Hill Press, 1998. $35.00. Island historian Philbrick looks at Nantucket through the legends of Native Americans.

―――. Nathaniel. *Away Off Shore, Nantucket Island and Its People, 1602–1890.* Nantucket: Mill Hill Press, 1994. $19.95 paper. A very readable history told in biographies by the director of the Egan Institute of Maritime Studies at the Coffin School, Nantucket.

―――. Nathaniel. *Second Wind: A Sailor's Odyssey.* Masston's Mills, Mass.: Parnassus Imprints, 1998. $24.95 cloth. Historian Philbrick is also a sailor who sharpens his skills on the ponds of Nantucket.

Ulrich, Laurel Thatcher. *A Midwife's Tale: The Life of Martha Ballard.* New York: Random House, 1991. $14.00 paper. The Nantucket Historical Association archives were the beginning of the research that went into this fascinating biography of a Nantucket woman (1785–1812) based on her own diaries.

Whipple, A.B.C. *Vintage Nantucket.* New York: Dodd, Mead., 1978. $14.95 paper. The 1997 reissue of this out-of-print book of Island history and lively lore.

NATURAL HISTORY

Brown, Lauren. *Wildflowers and Winter Weeds.* Written and illustrated by Lauren Brown. New York: W.W. Norton, 1997. $12.95 paper. More than 135 of the most common species of wildflowers and weeds found in the northeast, specifically how to identify them in the winter months.

Griscom, L., and E. V. Folger. *Birds of Massachusetts.* Cambridge: Harvard University Press, 1948. The birders' short bible.

Ludlum, David. *Nantucket Weather Book.* $17.95 paper. For those who want to go beyond the philosophy of: "If you don't like the weather, wait a minute."

The whys and wherefores of the infinite variety of weather on Nantucket.

Newcomb, Lawrence. Illustrated by Gordon Morrison, *Newcomb's Wildflower Guide*. Boston: Little, Brown, 1989. $24.95 hardcover, $16.95 paper. Easy-to-follow reference guide to wildflowers tells all.

Roosevelt, Kim and Corinne. *Exploring Nature on Nantucket.* $15 paper with comb binding. Designed for families to take with them as they investigate the natural bounty of Nantucket.

Schneider, Paul, *The Enduring Shore: A History of Cape Cod, Martha's Vineyard, and Nantucket,* Illustrated, New York: Henry Holt, 2000. $27.50. Social history as well as natural history and topography round out this book about how this very particular region of Massachusetts came to be. Nantucket began as a terminal moraine in the Ice Age. The author predicts Nantucket will be totally built out by 2037, perhaps giving the most pessimistic Islanders a few more years than they expected.

Veit, Richard R., and Wayne R. Petersen. *Birds of Massachusetts.* Lincoln, Mass.: Massachusetts Audubon Society, 1993. $39.95. The birders' unexpurgated bible.

See also the habitat brochures *Heathlands; Bogs; Ponds* produced by the Maria Mitchell Science Center and available there or in Town bookstores; $3.00 for all three.

PHOTOGRAPHIC STUDIES

Aside from the following books, don't overlook the wonderful calendars issued every year using the works of Island photographers.

Dunwiddie, Peter W. *Changing Landscapes.* $6.95 paper. Before-and-after photos of the same place showing how landscapes have changed in time.

Gambee, Robert. *Nantucket.* New York: W.W. Norton, 1993. $29.95 paper. More than 525 color photographs of the architecture, gardens, and art of the Island. No coffee table is complete without it.

Grossfield, Stan. *Nantucket: The Other Season.* Old Saybrook, Conn.: Globe Pequot Press, 1982. $12.95 paper. The Island and its people captured in black and white after the summer people and the tourists have gone home.

Hazelgrove, Cary. Introduction by David Halberstam. *Nantucket: Seasons on the Island.* $29.95. Images and impressions.

Heard, Virginia, and Taylor Lewis. *Nantucket Gardens and Houses.* $50.00. Color photographs of noteworthy houses from all around the Island.

Morris, Paul C. *Maritime Nantucket: A Pictorial History.* $40. Whaling wasn't the only seagoing activity to catch this photographer's eye.

RECREATION

Mullen, Edwin, and Jane Griffith. *Short Bike Rides on Cape Cod, Nantucket & the Vineyard.* Old Saybrook, Conn.: Globe Pequot, 1997. $12.95. Nantucket doesn't have any really long bike rides, but no matter. You can also take your bike to the Cape or Vineyard and end up seeing all three of these wonderful places up close.

Sadlier, Hugh, and Heather Sadlier. *Short Nature Walks on Cape Cod, Nantucket & the Vineyard*. Hyannis, Mass.: Parnassus Imprints, 1996. $14.95. This is for those who would "squantum," not "rantom scoot" — that is, follow interesting and defined trails rather than your nose about Cape Cod and the Islands.

Books You Can Borrow

The Nantucket Public Library (the Atheneum), Nantucket Historical Association Research Center & Edouard A. Stackpole Library, and Maria Mitchell Science Library have complete and comprehensive collections and helpful librarians. They also have original and unpublished material available on site to qualified researchers. The following books are available off-Island and may be obtained through your local library's interlibrary loan system.

Crosby, Everett U. *"95% Perfect." The Older Residences at Nantucket*. Nantucket: Inquirer and Mirror Press, 1944. Dwelling-house architecture analyzed with the hope that it will help further restorations on Nantucket and elsewhere.

Drake, Samuel Adams. *Nooks and Corners of the New England Coast*. Illustrated. New York: Harper & Brothers, 1876. See chapters XX and XXI for Nantucket. A fresh on-site view of the New England coast, with references to the literature of the day.

Lancaster, Clay. *The Architecture of Historic Nantucket*. New York: McGraw-Hill, 1972. In this book, considered the definitive study, the author takes Nantucket architecture street by street, building by building.

Starbuck, Alexander. *The History of Nantucket, County, Island and Town Including Genealogy of the First Settlers*. Rutland, Vt.: Charles E. Tuttle, 1969 (reprint); first published Boston: Goodspeed, 1924. Primary sources with the old spelling reveal what a crafty and crotchety bunch those first settlers were. Small print, too, but their own words give a picture not generally seen in the overviews of later historians.

Audio CDs and Cassettes

Nantucket Sleighride; Mountain; Audio CD; $12.98.

The Narrative of Arthur Gordon Pym of Nantucket; Edgar Allan Poe; Audio Cassette; $39.95 (abbreviated version $16.95).

VHS Tapes

Eyes of the Amaryllis; Ruth Ford; $14.99.

Nantucket; Nantucket Island Chamber of Commerce (508-228-1700); $24.95 plus $4.00 postage; postage free when ordered with a guidebook.

Nantucket: Rock of Ages, 1999, $14.95 VHS NTSC format ASIN 6305374767, Black history of Nantucket, including the school conflict and integration; archival photos and interviews. Recorded March 5, NPR.

Rob Benchley

Sconset during a rare snowstorm.

CLIMATE, WEATHER, AND WHAT TO WEAR

Think fog and be pleasantly surprised by clear. That nickname "The Grey Lady" isn't just on behalf of weathered shingles. Officially, Nantucketers credit the Gulf Stream with temperatures warmer in the winter and cooler in the summer than on the mainland, but the ocean breezes both moderate the sun's rays and keep weather predictors guessing. The weather can change a dozen times in a single day. But wait: Without a smattering of clouds, would you have those fabulous sunsets?

For a five-day weather forecast: www.nantucketchamber.org

Average temperatures on Nantucket Island:

	JAN	MAY	AUG	OCT
Low	20°F	45.7°F	62.2°F	47.7°F
High	38.1°F	60°F	75.3°F	61.5°F
Precipitation	3.73"	3.48"	3.09"	3.64"

Nantucket winters are cold and damp, even though killing frosts are uncommon. Snow, when it falls, is decorative rather than limiting. Summer temperatures rarely reach above eighty degrees, and the nights are invariably cool. Spring is dicey, but autumn is golden in the tradition of all New England. October is considered the month most likely to have perfect weather.

Affordable Nantucket (Not an Oxymoron)

When you hear a cottage sold for $19.6 million; that membership in the new golf club is $250,000; that Nantucket's tiny airport is the second busiest in the state due to the number of private planes using it, you conclude the Island may be a tad pricey.

Furthermore, it's said the cottage had less than 2000 square feet and there's a waiting list for golf club memberships almost as long as the one for yacht moorings. An ad for personal airplanes running in the Wall Street Journal reads "Work in Manhattan; live on Nantucket." What's next, you cry, gold cobblestones?

While the Island's cachet is astronomical its profile both real and figurative is low-lying. Even during the Film Festival no autograph seekers and paparazzi lurk outside the old Dreamland movie theater or hang out around The Summer House dining room. How many of the nation's top screenwriters or Fortune 500 CEOs would you recognize on sight anyway?

So what's all the fuss about? Sure, Nantucket Town is caught in a time warp of the mid 1800s with more than 800 antebellum houses. The Island may have super seafood, 80 miles of unspoiled beaches and be the only place in the hemisphere where Scottish heather is completely naturalized, but affordable?

The secret words are "Out-of-Season."

Before and after the designated High Season — June 15–September 15 — the only things that change are the number of day-trippers and the prices. Most major events actually occur in spring and fall: Daffodil weekend in April; Wine Festival mid-May; Arts Festival and Cranberry Harvest, both in October. While high season makes a brief reappearance the first weekend in December for the "Christmas Stroll," the rest of the month is Nantucket Noel, just as festive and a whole lot cheaper.

Although bikes are the accepted way to get around the Island, neat public shuttle buses run from mid-May to October (50 cents to $1.00 each way; free for those over 65 and under 6). If you travel light and don't mind a short walk, you can even take one from the airport. Taxis, complimentary hotel jitneys and rental cars including 4-wheel drives with beach permits, are also available. Bikes and mopeds may be rented close to the dock, but for $5.00 you can bring your own on the ferry.

The 90-minute sightseeing tours of the Island by air-conditioned vans complete with gossipy driver-guides are only $10–12. The Nantucket Historical Association (508/228-1894) has a walking tour for $5 for adults and $3 for children. You can guide yourself to antebellum downtown or Black Heritage sites using free brochures.

Lodging prices start sliding after Labor Day and positively spiral after mid-October. In vintage houses-cum-B&Bs, the $215 double drops to $65; the $400 cottage goes down to $150. You can book a room a few days in advance or even arrive without a reservation confident the well-organized **Visitor Services & Information Bureau** (508-228-0925, 25 Federal St.) will tell you where there's a vacancy. Ask for a bargain and they will find one. Any time of year you save major money by taking a room with a shared bath.

Complementaries that add up include breakfast, afternoon tea, cocktail snacks before dinner and free local phone calls. If off-street parking is available (not always so) there's no charge; some guesthouses have free bikes. Even the combined state and local room tax of 9.7% is lower than most comparable areas.

Off-season packages of three days or more may include free air or ferry transportation from the mainland, dinner at a local café, or tickets to special Island events. In the mid-season you can get off-season rates by coming midweek.

The deluxe Wauwinet closes for the winter but the rates drop by a third midweek during the shoulder May-mid-June and mid-September through October. The "Taste of the Nantucket" packages cover not only full breakfasts, afternoon wine and cheese, use of tennis courts, bicycles and free shuttle transfers to town, but shellfishing expeditions. Also included are botanical tours and field trips by jeep to Great Point lighthouse (800-426-8718).

Dining around downtown you will find a bowl of quahog (clam) chowder with a basket of puffy crackers for $4.00 the perfect mid-day break whether you are visiting the Whaling Museum, touring the realm of the Historical Society (a $10 museum pass covers 20 houses, museums and individual properties) or shopping.

While it's true that Lightship Baskets can cost as much as $1000 and E-com millionaires snap up $100 golf shirts by the dozen, few places exceed Nantucket in end-of-season bargains. Then the golf shirts drop to $20; the pullovers with discreet "Nantucket" logos are $10 not $50. Cashmeres are half-price and less. Thrift shop volunteers are so anxious to clear the donated merchandise you name your price. Massachusetts has no sales tax on clothing priced below $175.

The casual Friday night auctions at the Point Breeze Hotel (508-228-0313) and the monthly estate auctions (508-228-3942 and 508-332-5852) are full of treasures. In the approximately two dozen antique shops, the urge to negotiate is apparently irresistible once the summer people leave.

From dinner piano in the restaurants, folk and rock in the pubs and nightspots to chamber music evenings, band concerts and even an "organ crawl" sponsored by the churches during the October Arts Festival, live music is reasonably priced or free. The Arts Alliance (508-228-4922) concert series brings international performers October–December and March–May. Tickets are generally $10 for adults and $5 for students.

Live theater at $15 a seat will break no banks. The Actors Theatre (508/228-6325) is a professional company with shows from Memorial Day through Columbus Day. It's had some smashing one-person shows and stand-up comedy routines with Broadway actors trying out their ideas on a sophisticated audience. There are occasional surprise visits by superstars who have houses here, visit friends here, or just like the sound of "live from Nantucket."

At the Atheneum (508/228-1110) you will hear notable contemporary speakers as well as those with books on the New York Times Best Seller list. The cost? $5 to free. At the Egan Institute of Maritime Studies (508-228-2505) the world's foremost specialists in the sea and all its aspects lecture free or nearly so.

Art galleries running from the fine to the quirky welcome browsers and have gala and free opening nights for new shows. The Island's Artists Association (508-228-0722) has year-round exhibits by its more than 200 members, and everyone is welcome at the "Wet Paint Auction" in early October

The beaches are free, and there are tidal pools at the jetties full of marine life. Watching the boats and boat people come and go is never boring. Sunsets are extravagant. Moonlight swims at Steps Beach are made all the more enchanting by the phosphorescent plankton.

Continued on next page

At one point Nantucket had to decide its direction: commercial or natural. It chose natural. So you won't find a McDonald's or a chain hotel or a phalanx of slot machines. You spend nothing but time on the paths through conservation lands. Guided birdwalks and observatory sky-watches among the many offerings of the Maria Mitchell Association at $10 or less (508/228-9198).

While Nantucket has few of the spectacular colors that have made New England autumns famous, the ambers, garnets and purples of the moors are rich and varied. The cranberry bogs are crimson seas, and the elms along Upper Main Street turn the lawns of the ship owners' mansions into gold.

Maybe gold is where you find it. Maybe the best things in life — and on Nantucket — are free.

Packing for a Nantucket holiday is easy. Whoever invented the term "smart casual" must have had places like the Island in mind, and anything you would wear on a golf course or yacht is appropriate. Comfortable shoes with thick soles are necessary to walk on cobblestones. Walking in the bush requires long pants and socks to protect against ticks and poison ivy. Bare feet and bathing suits are not acceptable downtown.

Men will more often than not wear jackets to dinner in the top restaurants. In summer, include a wrap or sweater, especially if you plan to take a night ferry. Umbrellas and rain-resistant cover-ups are likely to come in handy any time of year. Winter requires warm jackets, scarves, knit hats, and gloves. It may be ten degrees warmer than Boston, but this is still New England.

Pack light, and divide your gear instead of using one heavy suitcase. Chances are you'll end up hauling it "a block or so" from the pier to your lodging. As for luggage wheels over cobblestone streets and brick sidewalks — think about it. You may end up carrying as much as pulling.

GUIDED TOURS

Tours of the Island in small vans are casual as well as informative. They last less than two hours and help you choose the places you want to return to at your leisure. Driver-guides will stop so that you can take pictures and cheerfully adapt the itinerary to the wishes of the passengers. Walking tours in Town are considered part of the local entertainment, full of stories and gossip as well as facts. Advance reservations are needed, and the tours are generally given from May to October. Most of the tours also operate Daffodil Weekend in late April, Cranberry Harvest in late October, and the Nantucket Noel in December. And if you can fill a van with friends or family, you'll most likely find that the tour will be provided any time of year. (See Chapter Two, *Transportation*, for a list of tour operators.)

HANDICAPPED ACCESS

Nantucket's cobbled streets and centuries-old structures are not easy for the handicapped. However, the new NRTA shuttle buses are accessible, and many public buildings have ramps and elevators. In Chapter Three, *Lodging*, you'll find those hostelries with partial to good access grouped at the end of the chapter, but you should confirm this when making arrangements to be sure the access is adequate to need. In Chapter Five, *Restaurants*, accessibility is noted for each restaurant. Still, it is prudent to call first if you need help beyond getting a wheelchair through the door. Massachusetts Architectural Access Board regulations need be met only after significant renovation, so many of the well-meant adaptations of older facilities may not be what you have come to expect elsewhere.

Observation, 1876

I have no wish to depreciate the value of real estate upon Nantucket, but by the year 3000, according to our present calendar, I doubt if there will be more than a grease-spot remaining to mark the habitation of a race of vikings whose javelins were harpoons.

— Samuel Adams Drake, *Nooks and Corners of the New England Coast*, 1876

Temporary handicap parking permits are issued by the Police Department (508-228-1212; 20 S. Water St., Nantucket, MA 02554) If you can show you need your car for getting around the Island (HP plates, wheelchair lift, etc.) you may get special treatment on the ferry. However, you will still need to make a reservation far in advance (midweek is far preferable than weekends). None of the taxis are equipped with wheelchair lifts. In addition to the accessible NRTA summer shuttles, the municipal **Elder Services Program** has a door-to-door "Handi-Ride" van service available at twenty-four-hour notice.

The Atheneum has reading machines, and the newly renovated library is entirely accessible. The handicap entrance is on the right-hand side of the main building. The only accessible museums are the Whaling Museum on Broad Street and the Maria Mitchell Association on Vestal Street.

Public restrooms at the Visitor's Center on Federal Street and on Straight Wharf at the All Serve General Store building on the south side are handicap accessible.

Call ahead or write for the booklet *Nantucket Island Guide for Visitors with Special Needs*, provided by the **Nantucket Commission on Disability**: 508-228-2044; Town & County Building, 16 Broad St., Nantucket MA 02554. Also: Nantucket Visitor Services, 508-228-0925; 12 Federal St., Nantucket MA 02554.

TTD/TTY (Telecommunication Device for the Deaf/Tele-typewriter)
   Emergency (direct relay) 911
   Emergency 1-800-249-9949

HOSPITALS AND PHARMACIES

Nantucket has one hospital, a full-service acute-care provider with twenty-four-hour emergency services and intensive care, dialysis, chemotherapy, CAT scan, counseling, and so forth. The hospital has nineteen beds and five full-time physicians on staff; thirty specialists serve in a consulting capacity or schedule regular visits to the Island. Helicopter transfers to the world-famous medical facilities of Boston are arranged as necessary.

Nantucket Cottage Hospital (508-228-1200; 57 Prospect St., Nantucket MA 02554)
Congdon's Pharmacy (508-228-0020; 47 Main St., Nantucket, MA 02554)
Island Pharmacy (508-228-6400; 31 Sparks Ave., Nantucket, MA 02554)
Nantucket Pharmacy (508-228-0180; 45 Main St., Nantucket, MA 02554)

LATE-NIGHT FOOD AND FUEL

Nantucket doesn't exactly sizzle after midnight. Gas stations and cafés shut down early by mainland standards. However, **Brotherhood of Thieves** (no listed phone, no credit cards; 23 Broad St., Nantucket, MA 02554) closes at 12:30am, and you can get at least the bar menu until 11pm at **Kendrick's at the Quaker House** (508-228-9136; 5 Chestnut St., corner of Centre) and upstairs at **Vincent's** (508-228-0189; 21 Water St., Nantucket, MA 02554). **The Atlantic Café** (508-228-0570; 15 S. Water St, Nantucket, MA 02554) serves until 11:30pm. Nantucket's out-Island night spots, **The Box**, (508-228-9717; 6 Dave St., Nantucket, MA 02554) and **The Muse** (508-228-6873; 44 Surfside Rd., Nantucket, MA 02554) stay open past midnight; and in Town **The Rose & Crown** (508-228-2595; 23 S. Water St., Nantucket, MA 02554) goes to 1am.

LAUNDRY AND CLEANING

Coin-operated laundromats and professional cleaners:
Holdgate's Island Laundry (508-228-0750; 4 Vesper Ln., Nantucket, MA 02554) Not only lets you wash your clothes but will clean your blankets, quilts, and sleeping bags.

Nantucket Wash & Dry Clean (508-228-3009; 17-1/2 Old South Rd., Nantucket, MA 02554) Does just what its name implies.

MEDIA

Nantucket gets Boston radio, TV, cable TV, and newspapers, but residents and part-time residents read the local weeklies for Island news. Off-Islanders who want to keep in touch with the Island can receive these by mail.

Magazines

Cape Cod Life Including Martha's Vineyard & Nantucket (800-698-1717, 508-564-4460, fax 508-564-4466; capecodlife.com; PO Box 1385, Pocasset, MA 02559) Always includes a story or two about Nantucket. $3.95.

Home & Garden Nantucket (508-228-3866; Anderson Publishing, 29 Main St., PO Box 1018, Nantucket, MA 02554) Targeted at Island architects, landscapers and interior designers, it's a twice-a-year pleasure to browse. Free.

Island Weddings (508-228-3866; Anderson Publishing, 29 Main St., PO Box 1018, Nantucket, MA 02554) All about getting married on the Island. Free.

Nantucket Magazine (508-228-8700; nanmaga@nantucket.net; 67 Milestone Rd., Nantucket, MA 02554) Stories and pictures about the Island and its residents, published quarterly. $3.95.

Savor Nantucket (508-228-3866; Anderson Publishing Co., 29 Main St., PO Box 1018, Nantucket, MA 02554) Menus and recipes from the Island's restaurants and food purveyors. Readable and free.

Times of the Islands (508-287-1965; shk001@juno.com; www.toti.com; 69 Goldfinch Dr., Nantucket MA 02554; Feature stories about Nantucket in a new publication to be distributed in 40 states, Canada, and parts of Europe. $3.50.

Newspapers

The Inquirer and Mirror (508-228-0001; newsroom@ack.net; www.ack.net; 1 Old South Rd., PO Box 1198, Nantucket, MA 02554) The major weekly newspaper since 1821 wins prizes for its photography and coverage of local events. Published every Thursday, it's available by subscription on and off-Island. Islanders call it "The Inky Mirror." Also publishes *Nantucket Holiday*, a monthly vacation guide.

Nantucket Map & Legend (508-228-6161; PO Box 2233, Nantucket, MA02584) Free weekly arts and events newspaper published in summer and available everywhere.

Yesterday's Island (508-228-9165; yi@nantucket.net; www.yesterdaysisland.com; PO Box 626, Nantucket MA 02554) A free weekly paper full of interesting tidbits.

For a wider look at the world, you can also buy the **Boston Globe, New York Times,** and **Wall Street Journal** at newsstands. Your lodging may have these delivered by 8am, so you can browse over your morning coffee just as you do at home.

TV & Radio

Nantucket's local television channels are Channel 17 (508-228-2903) and Channel 22 (508-228-8001). You should be able to pick up Boston and Providence channels, and your lodging is almost sure to have cable. NAN 91.1 FM (508-548-9600; www.cian.org) is Nantucket's National Public Radio Station. Sunday's **Boston Globe** has a weekly TV and radio guide.

Is Nantucket Haunted?
(You Better Believe It!)

Doubtless there are logical explanations for rattling windows and dimming lights; doors that open and shut untouched by human hands. But when the Atlantic fog is wrapping Nantucket like a shroud and a fog horn lows, few Islanders would deny the possibility that disembodied spirits are at work.

And why not? Weren't cemeteries and houses built willy-nilly over Native American burial grounds? Aren't the Shoals a graveyard for sailors from lost fishing boats to the *Andrea Doria*? Isn't it logical that with over 800 antebellum houses in Nantucket Town more than a few would have sheltered rebellious or at least persistent spirits? Was the nickname "Gray Lady" applied to the Island for reasons more sinister than its weathered houses?

The Atlantic Silk Company at the head of Gay Street closed in 1844 and has become the Sherburne Inn, but vaporous images are reported from time to time. Even before it was transformed into a B&B, a translucent woman was seen bustling about the empty factory rooms.

Kids misbehaving in Old South Church (Unitarian Universalist) on Orange Street may find themselves scolded by "Seth," that is Seth Swift, the minister from 1810 to 1834.

An early miller named Barnabas Bunker said to have been a notable tippler, died on one of the mill arms and is blamed for any malfunctions of the machinery today.

Nantucket's Great Bank Robbery of 1795 left an angry ghost. William Coffin, wig-maker, was a suspect in the $20,000 heist. It was 21 years before someone else confessed, and he grew increasingly morose as whispers followed him about. He vented posthumous fury by vehement movement in an apparently empty rocking chair.

Capt. George Pollard whose journey on the ill-fated whaler *Essex* became the catalyst for Herman Melville's epic "Moby Dick" lived at 46 Centre Street. Shunned by many townspeople for his admitted cannibalism and reduced to being a town night watchman, he is said to have made post-mortem visits to his old home even after it was turned into a gift shop.

With the exception of the infamous Capt. Pollard and a wraith described as looking suspiciously like Kesia Folger Coffin, the 18th- century Tory millionaire who tried to foreclose the town, Nantucket ghosts seem to be the specters of ordinary people inexplicably living beyond their past lives. Nevertheless, they have their own agendas.

More than one departed housewife with a passion for neatness is challenged by the inadequacies of later residents so tears down offending curtains and keeps putting things back in place. A Quaker house where music was forbidden occasionally tinkles with tunes popular at the turn of the 18th century played on an invisible harpsichord.

The Old Mill (it creaks now and probably did when it was built in 1746); the graveyards (especially when mists rise from the ground); the old houses (sounds of settling or of spirits settling in?); any structure (the rustle of birds under the roof and mice in the walls?) have sounds inevitably subject to interpretation. Cemeteries are said to be the province of "setstills," as in apparitions who "set still on headstones and fences."

Tales have been told, retold in articles and collected in books. Never mind that some of them are classics given a Nantucket setting ("The Telltale Heart" by Edgar Allan Poe (1809-1849) becomes a ceramic gewgaw that beats) or are the descendents of "gams," those tall tales exchanged by whalers met at sea. Poe's classic horror story "Narrative of Arthur Gordon Pym of Nantucket" (1838) utilizes all the fearful images of the 19th century sailor.

First person experiences with ghosts have been collected in *Nantucket Hauntings* and *The Ghosts of Nantucket* by Islander Blue Balliett (Down East Books). The spirits are remarkable for the very ordinariness of their nonbeing. On occasion they are recognized as a long departed member of the family or as a longago resident with particular characteristics such as a schoolteacher who played the piano or a friendly child persistently putting off bedtime. The scent of roses is reported but not brimstone.

While off-Islanders tend to flee, exorcism by year-round residents has usually been a matter of giving the bothersome spook a good talking to. That, after all, is "the Nantucket way."

No one has to take spectral visitors lying down (so to speak). If you are the owner or renter of an old house, you can research your ghost at the Nantucket Historical Society (508-228-1894). If your interest is more general, the Atheneum library has a large collection of Nantucket ghost writings.

The Maria Mitchell Association (508-228-9198) does a summer evening tour to the sites of friendly ghosts, and Murray's Camp (508-325-4600) ends its juvenile S'conset Ghost Walk with ice cream for all.

Bill Jamieson conducts a "Nantucket Ghost Walk"(graveyard included) three or four nights a week from Daffodil Weekend to early December and including Halloween.No reservations necessary. Those who are brave enough meet in front of the Atheneum at 7 p.m. for tales and tour lasting approximately one hour and 45 minutes. Adults $10, 6–12 year olds $5 (508-325-8855).

For all its possibilities, Halloween on-Island is celebrated the old fashioned (mainland) way with costumed trick-or-treaters going door to door; a 4:30 p.m. parade on Main Street sponsored by the Inquirer & Mirror and parties, notably the Fire Department's "Halloween Happening" for teenagers regularly held at the high school (508-228-2324).

PETS

A pooch waits his turn at the animal hospital.

Rob Benchley

The Island has stringent rules about pets. Dogs may not run free, for example. If you've been meaning to get yours to an obedience school, this may be the time and place (See Chapter Six, *Recreation*, "Dog Obedience Schools"). The Commonwealth of Massachusetts requires rabies virus vaccination for cats and dogs, resident or visiting. If your pet needs medical care, Massachusetts Society for the Prevention of Cruelty to Animals (MSPCA) has a hospital and shelter (508-228-1491; mspca@nantucket.net; 21 Crooked Ln., Nantucket, MA 02554).

REAL ESTATE

Nantucket has been experiencing the highest rate of growth of any county in Massachusetts, and Islanders hate it. Prices for existing homes are extremely high, while both cost and stringent environmental rules have kept new building somewhat under control. Still, the weekly newspapers have extensive listings, turnover appears to be relatively rapid, and you'll find brokers galore in the telephone book. Apparently it is not an impossible market if you have pools of money. Most realtors also handle rentals and are quick to suggest renting before buying. Look in the telephone book under "Property Managers" both for short- and long-term leases. Off-season rentals are reasonable, since people who only come in summer prefer not to leave their valuable houses empty. These are usually snapped up by locals, but if you are a soon-to-be-famous writer or someone similar, you may be able to talk your way into one.

A classic Sconset cottage with grapy shingles and roses growing up the trellises.

Frederick G. S. Clow

RELIGIOUS SERVICES AND ORGANIZATIONS

Thursday's newspaper lists the religious services and times for the weekend.

Baha'i Faith (508-228-1861; 120 Madaket Rd., Nantucket, MA 02554)

Christian Science Society (508-228-0452; 2 Madaket Rd., Nantucket, MA 02554)

Church of Jesus Christ of Latter Day Saints (508-325-7118; 1 Pleasant St., Nantucket, MA 02554)

Congregation Shirat HaYam (508-228-6588; PO Box 1145, Nantucket, MA 02554)

First Baptist Church (508-228-4930; 1 Summer St., Nantucket, MA 02554)

First Congregational Church (508-228-0950; 62 Centre St., PO Box 866, Nantucket, MA 02554)

Kingdom Hall of Jehovah's Witnesses (508-228-0816; 43 Milk St., Nantucket, MA 02554)

Nantucket Worship Center (508-228-5616; 10 Surfside Rd., PO Box 1379, Nantucket, MA 02554)

Sconset Union Chapel (508-257-6616; 18 New St., PO Box 201, Siasconset, MA 02564) Summer only: Catholic 8:45am and Protestant 10:30am services.

Society of Friends Quaker Meeting House (508-325-4045; 7 Fair St.; Mail: 121 Main St., Nantucket, MA 02554)

St. Mary's Catholic Church – Our Lady of the Isle (508-228-0100; Federal St., PO Box 1168, Nantucket, MA 02554)

St. Paul's Episcopal Church (508-228-0916; www.stpaulsnantucket.org; 20 Fair St., PO Box 278, Nantucket, MA 02554)

Unitarian Universalist Church (508-228-5466; 11 Orange St., PO Box 1023, Nantucket, MA 02554)

United Methodist Church (508-228-1882; 2 Centre St., PO Box 264, Nantucket, MA 02554; at Main St.)

In addition to the celebration of holy days, there are special events through the year. The second Sunday in July is "Rose Sunday" at the First Congregational Church, when the church is festooned with roses. Church fairs include St. Mary's (July), First Congregational (August), and St. Paul's (August). Pageants and house and garden tours are frequent in summer.

If you wish to be married in an Island church, be aware that it will require a good deal of advance planning. Send for a copy of the free brochure *Romance, Nantucket Style* from the Nantucket Chamber of Commerce (508-228-1700; 48 Main St., Nantucket, MA 02554). You should also get a copy of the magazine *Island Weddings* from the Anderson Publishing Company (508-228-3866; PO Box 1018, Nantucket 02554). The magazine is free, but off-Island you'll need to add $6 for shipping and handling.

ROAD SERVICE

Towing and automotive services are **Harry's Towing & Road Service** (508-228-3390, 508-325-3390; 49 Hummock Pond Rd., Nantucket, MA 02554) for twenty-four-hour towing, including beach towing; **Holdgate's Towing** (508-228-0951; 82 Hummock Pond Rd., Nantucket, MA 02554); **J&M Towing Service** (508-228-1306; 13A Surfside Dr., Nantucket, MA 02554) twenty-four-hour service; **AAA-Nantucket Auto Body** (508-228-4659; 36 Sparks Ave., Nantucket, MA 02554), and **All Point Beach Towing** (508-325-3390; 49 Hummock Pond Rd., Nantucket, MA 02554).

SEASONAL EVENTS

The Nantucket calendar of chamber of commerce–sponsored and co-sponsored events begins the last weekend in April and runs through October, plus the Christmas Stroll in the month-long Christmas holiday. Other fairs, festivities, galas, and happenings — both annual and spontaneous — go on just about every week. See Chapter Six, *Recreation*, for boat and other outdoor competitions. See Chapter Four, *Culture*, for more information on festivals.

APRIL

Daffodil Festival (508-228-1700) Includes the Antique Car Parade and coincides with the Garden Club's Daffodil Flower Show.

The annual Waiter/Waitress Race runs over the cobblestones of Main Street every July 14, in celebration of Bastille Day.

Rob Benchley

MAY

Nantucket Wine Festival (508-228-1128) Brings wineries from all over the country to show and taste. Nantucket foods and restaurants are also emphasized.

JUNE

Nantucket Film Festival (212-642-6339) Screenwriters bring their craft to the Island.

JULY

4th of July (508-228-7213, 508-228-0925) Main Street festivities from 10 to noon; games, races, and band concert at Jetties Beach in the afternoon; fireworks at dusk.

On The Internet

Many of the inns and merchants of Nantucket are on the Internet — the restaurants even post their menus — but you will be able to access most of them using the all-purpose http://www.nantucket.net or at the **Nantucket Chamber of Commerce** website, http://www.nantucketchamber.org.

InterNet Café (508-228-6777; info@nantucket.net; 2 Union St., PO Box 626, Nantucket, MA 02554) charges $10 per hour for computer use.

Other helpful sources of current information are online editions of:

Yesterday's Island (www.yesterdays island.com)
Nantucket Map & Legend (www.nantucketinfo.com)
The Inquirer and Mirror (www.ack.net).

Fourth of July festivities include fireworks, a fire department water fight on Main Street, and a kids' (and pets') bike parade in Sconset.

Rob Benchley

AUGUST

Sandcastle & Sculpture Day (508-228-1700) Annual competition on Jetties Beach, with ribbon prizes for all.

SEPTEMBER

Nantucket County Fair (508-228-4748) Not a chamber of commerce spectacular but a down-home family event on Tom Nevers Field.

OCTOBER

The Nantucket Arts Festival (508-228-4922) All the arts and venues celebrated. Free or discounted admissions when you buy an Arts Festival button.

NOVEMBER–DECEMBER

Nantucket Noel (508-228-1700) A month of Christmas that begins the day after Thanksgiving and includes the famous Christmas Stroll on the first Saturday

Santa waves to the crowd during his arrival at the annual Christmas Stroll

Rob Benchley

of December. The Christmas Stroll is so popular that lodgings fill up early. Confirm yours as far in advance as possible. The three-day weekend commands the top rate in hotels, but the rest of the month is off-season, with plenty of room and remarkably affordable lodgings. Many restaurants and shops stay open through Christmas Stroll, then shut down until spring.

TOURIST INFORMATION

A s you might expect on an Island long focused on tourism, Nantucket has exceptionally well-organized and helpful service facilities.

Nantucket Visitor Services & Information Bureau (508-228-0925; 25 Federal St., Nantucket, MA 02554) Large, central, and staffed with kind people. Call and describe your needs and desires. When you arrive, this should be your first stop for information and to load up on the giveaway tabloids and brochures. If you arrive without a lodging reservation, you will be assisted;

Permits are required for driving on beach paths (508-228-2884, 508-228-0006) and beaches (508-228-1212) and for taking noncommercial shellfish (508-228-7620). Hunting permits for waterfowl, game birds, rabbit, and deer in season are at the town clerk's office, (508-228-7216, fax 508-325-5313; twnclerk@nantucket.net; 16 Broad St., Nantucket, MA 02554). Massachusetts licenses are valid on Nantucket. Fire permits are necessary for cooking outdoors, including your own yard (508-228-2324).

The Visitor Information Service on Federal Street supplies maps and finds rooms as well as providing a place to rest.

Rob Benchley

they keep a daily list of cancellations and last-minute openings. After hours a list of guesthouses with available space is posted outside the door.

Nantucket Chamber of Commerce (508-228-1700, fax 508-325-4925; www. nantucketchamber.org; 48 Main St., Nantucket MA 02554) The office is upstairs. Ask questions, pick up brochures, and request their excellent annual free *Official Guide*. The guide is also available by mail, with a handling fee.

Public Restrooms:
Visitor Services & Information Bureau, 25 Federal St.; enter from side of building.
Straight Wharf (where the Hy-Line docks) at the General Store.
Nantucket Memorial Airport.
Beaches: Children's, Dionis, Jetties, Madaket, and Surfside.
Sconset: Just off the main square.

IF TIME IS SHORT

Sankaty Head lighthouse, built in 1850, sits atop the bluff in Siasconset.

Rob Benchley

Time is always too short on Nantucket — which is why so many people are return visitors. What you do with your time is subjective. Do you want a beach above all else? Did you bring your bike? Are you there for one of the special events? Or suppose you just want to enjoy a nice weekend, and you've come without any particular agenda in mind.

In that case, the size of the Island makes a good overview feasible, so plan for a one-and-a-half-hour Island tour with Gail (508-228-6557) or Betty (508-228-5786). First, stop at the **Nantucket Visitor Services & Information Bureau** (508-228-0925; 25 Federal St., Nantucket, MA 02554). They can tell you about the tour schedule. If you're without a lodging reservation or need a recommendation for lunch or wonder where to buy a lightship basket that doesn't cost an arm and a leg, they will take care of that, too. Always ask what's going on during the time of your stay. Missing the

Boston Pops playing outdoors on Jetties Beach or a house tour of the old and beautiful would be a shame.

But to begin at the beginning, here are some — a few among many — personal favorites:

GETTING THERE

My first visit was by ferry after a drive to Hyannis on the Cape, but now I regularly take the funky little Cessnas of Cape Air from Boston to Nantucket, not only because I want to get there quickly but also because I love seeing the Island from the air. Once on the ground, I take a taxi to my inn.

STAYING THERE

Accommodations Et Al (508-228-0600, 800-588-0086, 11 India St., Nantucket, MA 02554) The four inns and two cottages under the O'Reilly umbrella give me an option I can't refuse. The locations are in the heart of the historic district; they are open year-round, and the choice of rooms is vast. While the ambiance is circa 1846, I also like the room refrigerators, phones, coffee makers, and the other accoutrements of right now.

Pineapple Inn (508-228-9992; 10 Hussey St., Nantucket, MA 02554; May–December) This small luxury B&B comes as close to perfection as any I know. The renovation, restoration, and refurbishment of an 1838 whaling captain's house in the historic district was completed in 1997. Now every one of the twelve rooms is special as is the gourmet breakfast by the fountain on the brick patio.

The Wauwinet (508-228-0145, 800-426-8718; 120 Wauwinet Rd.; Nantucket, MA 02554; mid-May–mid-October) As a "country inn by the sea," the Wauwinet is Nantucket's high-end resort at the famous haulover neck of the Island. The inn's own jitney takes me to Town and brings me back on the half hour; the inn's own boat sails twice a day ferrying diners to lunch or dinner at the renowned Topper's Restaurant. I like a choice of Atlantic or Harbor beaches outside the door, and the rooms are downright elegant. Frightfully expensive except in shoulder season.

DINING THERE

The Chanticleer (508-257-9756; 9 New St., Siasconset, MA 02564) French cuisine of the highest caliber in a French provincial setting.

The Sea Grille (508-325-5700; 45 Sparks Ave., Nantucket, MA 02554) Seafood in all its guises, including straight-on simple preparations. Mid-Island location.

De Marco (508-228-1836; 9 India St., Nantucket, MA 02554) Northern Italian food in a small romantic restaurant in the historic district.

Arno's at 41 Main St. (508-228-7001; 41 Main St., Nantucket, MA 02554) Good, fast service and good food nearly any time of day or evening and very conveniently located.

FOOD PURVEYORS

Bartlett's Ocean View Farm (508-228-9403; 33 Bartlett Farm Rd., Nantucket, MA 02554) Whether you want fresh, fresh, fresh produce or a ready-made main course, Bartlett's has it all. On the road to Cisco Beach.

L'Ile de France (508-228-3686; 18 Federal St., Nantucket, MA 02554) If I can't get to Paris to shop for my groceries, this is the next best place. Right across the street from the Visitor Services Center.

Sweet Inspirations (508-228-5814; 26 Centre St., Nantucket, MA 02554) My first stop when I settle in and my major indulgence. I often skip dessert in a restaurant and opt for a chocolate-cranberry truffle in my room instead.

CULTURAL ATTRACTIONS

The Whaling Museum (508-228-1736; 15 Broad St., Nantucket, MA 02554) The primary theme of Nantucket; and I always combine it with a stop at the **Peter Foulger Museum** next door to see the current special exhibit. It closes in the winter but is open weekends midseason as well as daily in summer.

Nantucket Atheneum (508-228-1110; 1 India St., Nantucket, MA 02554) The Golden Age of contemporary literary lectures continues at the Atheneum. No matter how short my time is on the Island, if an author is speaking, I get there early.

Artists' Association Little Gallery (508-228-0294; 19 Washington St., Nantucket, MA 02554) My regular quick peek before I start on the galleries down South Wharf or along Centre Street.

RECREATION

Bicycle from Town to Sconset on the Milestone Road bike path (one hour); after oohing and aahing at the rose-trellised cottages, return via the Polpis Road bike path (one hour plus). Next day take the Madaket bike path to the end and back.

Beaches: It's Jetties for activities, Dionis for dunes, Cisco for surf, Madaket for sunsets.

Whale and Seal Watching: Nantucket Whale Watch (508-283-0313, 800-332-0013; in the summer; Harbor Cruises (508-228-1444; slip #1012

Straight Wharf, Nantucket, MA 02554) for seal watches aboard the *Anna W II* in winter.

SHOPPING

Think of the downtown as one maxi-boutique. Go up one side of Main Street and down the other; do the same to Centre and Federal Streets. Don't forget Straight Wharf and South Wharf; the lanes and side streets. Then there's the Museum Shop next to the Whaling Museum. . . . I can keep this up indefinitely. Are you an antiques freak, too? Try the auction houses for fun as well as bargains. If you think you can't take it with you, think again — Nantucket ships.

Index

LODGING BY PRICE CODE

RESTAURANTS BY PRICE CODE

RESTAURANTS BY CUISINE

About the Author

When Betty Lowry moved to New England from California, she added travel writing to her shelter magazine essays and little-magazine poetry. She began with family travel in the *New York Times*; her stories have appeared in more than one hundred newspapers and magazines in the United States and Canada. These include the Sunday travel sections of the *Boston Globe, Los Angeles Times, Newsday, Asbury Park Press, Arkansas Democrat-Gazette, BuffaloNews, New York Post, Bergen Record, Chicago Tribune, Cleveland Plain Dealer, Miami Herald, Denver Post, Dallas News, San Antonio Express News, St. Petersburg Times, Chicago Herald, Boston Herald, The Norwalk Hour, Quincy Patriot-Ledger, San Jose Mercury, Providence Journal, Toronto Globe & Mail, Toronto Star*, and *The National Post*. She has also contributed sections and chapters to eight guidebooks, four national newsletters, and writes a regular column on ecotravel on the Internet (www.goodmoney.com/ecotravl.htm) as well as appearing online in hundreds of archives. She is a member of the Society of American Travel Writers, The Boston Authors Club, Working Writers, and the New England Poetry Club. Although her travel writing crosses every continent and sea, Nantucket has been a recurring and favorite topic since her first visit to the Island.

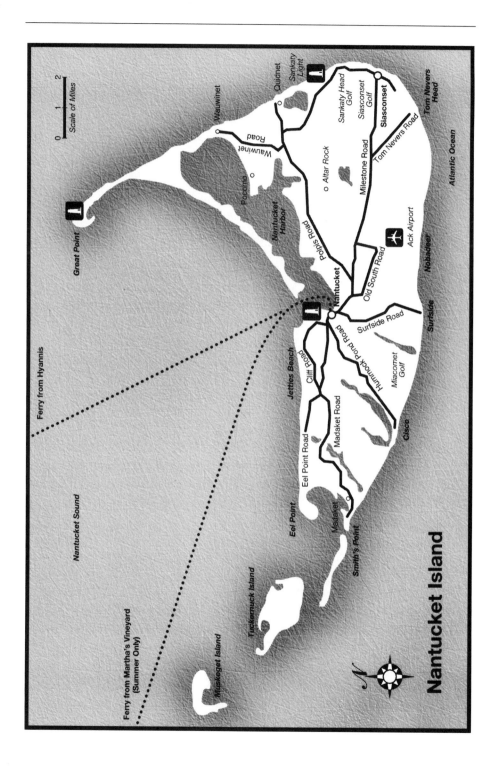

Nantucket Island

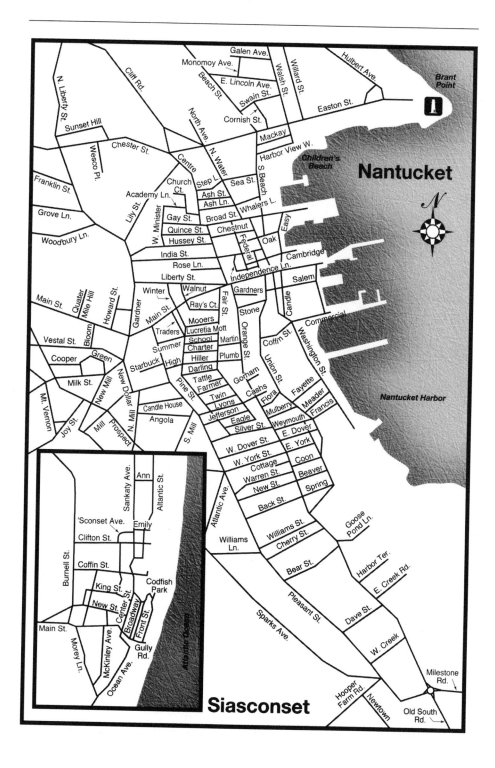

Nantucket

Nantucket Harbor

Siasconset